System Design for the LLM Era

Patterns and principles for production-grade AI architecture

Sampriti Mitra

<packt>

System Design for the LLM Era

The architectural analyses, case studies, and system breakdowns presented in this book are derived exclusively from publicly available information. Primary sources include official company engineering blogs, technical whitepapers, open-source repositories, and public conference presentations. No proprietary, confidential, or non-public internal documentation was accessed or disclosed in the creation of this material.

Portfolio Director: Kunal Chaudhari
Relationship Lead: Dhruv Kataria
Project Manager: Ankit Maroli
Content Engineer: Alexander Powell
Technical Editor: Aditya Bharadwaj
Indexer: Manju Arasan
Production Designer: Jyoti Kadam

First edition: June 2026
Production reference: 1250626
Published by Packt Publishing Ltd.
Grosvenor House
11 St Paul's Square
Birmingham
B3 1RB, UK.

ISBN 978-1-80778-993-0
`www.packtpub.com`

To my parents

Contributors

About the author

Sampriti Mitra is a software engineering lead based in India. She is an alumna of IIT BHU, with over seven years of experience designing and building scalable distributed systems. She understands the practical challenges of integrating large language models (LLMs) into production-grade systems.

Her professional background includes roles at industry-leading companies like Sumologic and Razorpay. She also runs a newsletter, Architecturally Speaking (`https://architecturallyspeaking.substack.com`), which is dedicated to breaking down system design principles.

System design is validated by stress testing, and this manuscript was no exception.

I'm grateful to Aadarsh for sharpening the readability and technical scope, and to Anurag for the probing questions that improved the design. Thanks also to Devansh for the rigorous review. Together, you challenged my assumptions and ensured the focus remained on production reality, not whiteboard theory.

To Apurve, thank you for being the ultimate quality gate and refusing to let me ship anything that is just good enough, in this book, and in every aspect of life.

Special thanks to Alexander Powell and the Packt editorial team for their valuable input and time reviewing this book, and to Ankit Maroli and Dhruv Kataria and the wider Packt team for their support over the course of writing this book.

About the reviewers

Aadarsh Baid is a seasoned software engineer with over eight years of deep expertise in the software industry, specializing in scalable systems and engineering for the real world. He holds a bachelor's degree in Computer Science and Engineering. Aadarsh is an active voice in the engineering community, sharing insights on production-grade system design, AI-powered development, and the realities of building LLM-based systems beyond the demo.

Anurag Gupta is a Software Engineer at Google in Hyderabad and a graduate of the Indian Institute of Technology (BHU), Varanasi. He works on large-scale systems that demand the same qualities this book addresses: reliability, performance, and architectural rigor at production scale. His background, spanning enterprise software and hyperscale infrastructure, gives him a well-rounded lens through which to evaluate the practical trade-offs of building large scale systems in the real world.

Apurve Dave is a Software Engineer (Data) at Apple, based in Hyderabad, India, with a passion for data engineering, machine learning, and building scalable systems. Apurve holds a degree in Electrical Engineering from the Indian Institute of Technology (BHU), Varanasi.

Table of Contents

Chapter 4: Case Study: Adaptive Learning Platform 103

Preface

This book is about the system design of AI-powered applications that use large language models (LLMs). It provides full architectural blueprints, from user-facing clients to backend orchestrators and the data layers that support them.

It is not a book on building, training, or researching the internal mechanics of AI/ML models, and neither is it a general system design primer. We assume you understand distributed systems fundamentals (e.g. caching, microservices).

The book's objective is to show you how to integrate and operationalize LLMs within existing scalable software architectures. Thus it is a practical guide to the system design principles, architectural patterns, and operational practices required when integrating LLMs into distributed systems. It gives you a deep dive into managing the unique challenges of LLMs: non-determinism, extreme cost variance, and context-aware retrieval (RAG).

The importance of a book like this is hopefully obvious. Companies are adopting AI rapidly, and many companies are trying to turn small AI experiments into big products. The problem is that they lack a robust plan. That means there's a pressing need for a practical guide on how to build these new AI systems the right way – so they can handle many users, won't break, and won't cost too much. This book is that guide.

The book breaks down the architecture of real AI applications, such as an AI-powered code editor and a smart learning app. It provides a deep, production-level dive into the operational challenges of building these specific types of system, and describes the kinds of solution that address them.

After reading this book, you will be able to architect a complete, production-grade AI-powered system from scratch. You will be able to design and mitigate the unique challenges of LLM APIs, like high latency and cost, and know how to implement key software engineering patterns like circuit breakers and rate limiting for AI systems. You will learn about databases and data models for AI applications, including vector search engines, and know what it takes to build scalable and resilient systems capable of handling high loads while ensuring user privacy.

Who this book is for

This book is for engineers, architects and leads who are looking to integrate LLM into their existing systems, or who are simply keen to understand the principles underlying the operation of the kinds of system described in the case studies.

What this book covers

Chapter 1, Atomic Units of LLM Systems, covers fundamentals concepts like tokens, embeddings, RAG and agentic AI as well as different methods of testing and failure handling.

Chapter 2, Core Architectural Patterns for LLM System Design, explores system design patterns for AI powered applications, like designing for resiliency, low latency, low cost, and security.

Chapter 3, Case Study: Designing AI-Native IDEs, dives into how the context window problem is solved by code indexing, how privacy is maintained when handling user code, latency vs. accuracy trade offs, and more.

Chapter 4, Case Study: Adaptive Learning Platform, shows how to architect offline content pipeline vs. online serving path, and explains asynchronous processing patterns and vector vs. relational vs. graph databases.

Chapter 5, Case Study: AI-Powered Search for E-Commerce Platforms, explains how we move beyond keyword search using hybrid search architecture, how ranking and re-ranking works with LLMs, and when to use smart caching strategies.

Chapter 6, Case Study: AI-Powered Customer Support Agent, explores how to build a golden dataset for the LLM-as-judge pattern, and how to keep the knowledge base fresh in real-time.

Chapter 7, Glossary, elucidates some of the key concepts and technical terms used in the book.

To get the most out of this book

You should have a general knowledge of distributed systems architecture, and intermediate-level programming skills in a modern language like Python, Java, or Go. You should have some familiarity with microservices and API design. No prior hands-on experience with LLMs or vector databases is required.

Beyond that the main technical requirement is the ability to access ChatGPT, Gemini or Claude in the browser, in order to try out the various prompts that are described. Numerous other software tools and systems are mentioned in the chapters as we discuss different architectural points, e.g. Apache Spark and Kafka, and several vector databases, but the intention here is to give you a sense of relevant architectural contexts, concerns and concepts rather than hands-on implementation experience.

Download the color images

We also provide a PDF file that has color images of the screenshots/diagrams used in this book. You can download it here: `https://packt.link/gbp/9781807789930`.

Conventions used

There are a number of text conventions used throughout this book.

`CodeInText`: Indicates code words in text, database table names, folder names, filenames, file extensions, pathnames, dummy URLs, user input, and Twitter handles. For example: " The vector database called `semantic_search_index` stores the product description".

A block of code is set as follows:

```
# test_search_quality.py
import pytest
from search_client import get_search_results

# The "Golden Set": Queries that MUST return specific brands/categories
GOLDEN_CASES = [
("iphone", "Apple", "brand"),
("running shoes", "Footwear", "category"), ("protein powder", "Supplements",
"category"), ("sony headphones", "Sony", "brand"),
]
```

Bold: Indicates a new term, an important word, or words that you see on the screen. For instance, words in menus or dialog boxes appear in the text like this. For example: "This is where vector database and **semantic search** come in."

> **Note**
>
> Warnings or important notes appear like this.

Get in touch

Feedback from our readers is always welcome.

General feedback: Email `feedback@packtpub.com` and mention the book's title in the subject of your message. If you have questions about any aspect of this book, please email us at `questions@packtpub.com`.

Errata: Although we have taken every care to ensure the accuracy of our content, mistakes do happen. If you have found a mistake in this book, we would be grateful if you reported this to us. Please visit `http://www.packtpub.com/submit-errata`, click **Submit Errata**, and fill in the form.

Piracy: If you come across any illegal copies of our works in any form on the internet, we would be grateful if you would provide us with the location address or website name. Please contact us at `copyright@packtpub.com` with a link to the material.

If you are interested in becoming an author: If there is a topic that you have expertise in and you are interested in either writing or contributing to a book, please visit `http://authors.packtpub.com/`.

Free benefits with your book

This book comes with free benefits to support your learning. Activate them now for instant access (see the "*How to Unlock*" section for instructions).

Here's a quick overview of what you can instantly unlock with your purchase:

How to Unlock

Scan the QR code (or go to packtpub.com/unlock). Search for this book by name, confirm the edition, and then follow the steps on the page.

UNLOCK NOW

Note: Keep your invoice handy. Purchases made directly from Packt don't require one

Share your thoughts

Once you've read *Systems Design for the LLM Era*, we'd love to hear your thoughts! Scan the QR code below to go straight to the Amazon review page for this book and share your feedback.

https://packt.link/r/1807789934

Your review is important to us and the tech community and will help us make sure we're delivering excellent quality content.

1

Atomic Units of LLM Systems

Software engineering has traditionally been deterministic: if x then y. If a unit test for this passes once, it passes a million times.

Building with large language models (LLMs) requires a fundamental shift to probabilistic engineering. The same input x might yield y, y', or sometimes z. This chapter defines the primitives we use to change this uncertainty into reliable systems.

LLMs are a type of artificial intelligence that have been trained on a vast amount of natural language and programming data which are capable of generating, reasoning and providing solutions. They have gained traction due to their understanding and ability to provide answers to user queries in a wide range of topics, including healthcare, finance and coding.

GPT-5 (OpenAI), Claude (Anthropic), Gemini (Google), DeepSeek, Grok, are some of the commonly used models, each having different strengths in reasoning, creativity and other areas.

LLMs require user inputs (called prompts) and, based on that, return textual outputs. The prompt should provide proper guidelines and guardrails that the LLM can follow to get the expected response.

In this first chapter we look at these and other concepts to help build the foundations for your knowledge of this branch of AI. *Figure 1.1* shows the conceptual hierarchy we'll be examining. We'll be looking at the following topics:

- The path to language models
- LLMs analyzed
- Prompt engineering basics
- Using LLMs
- RAG approaches to information retrieval

- Context engineering
- Data residency
- Performance benchmarking
- Handling failures

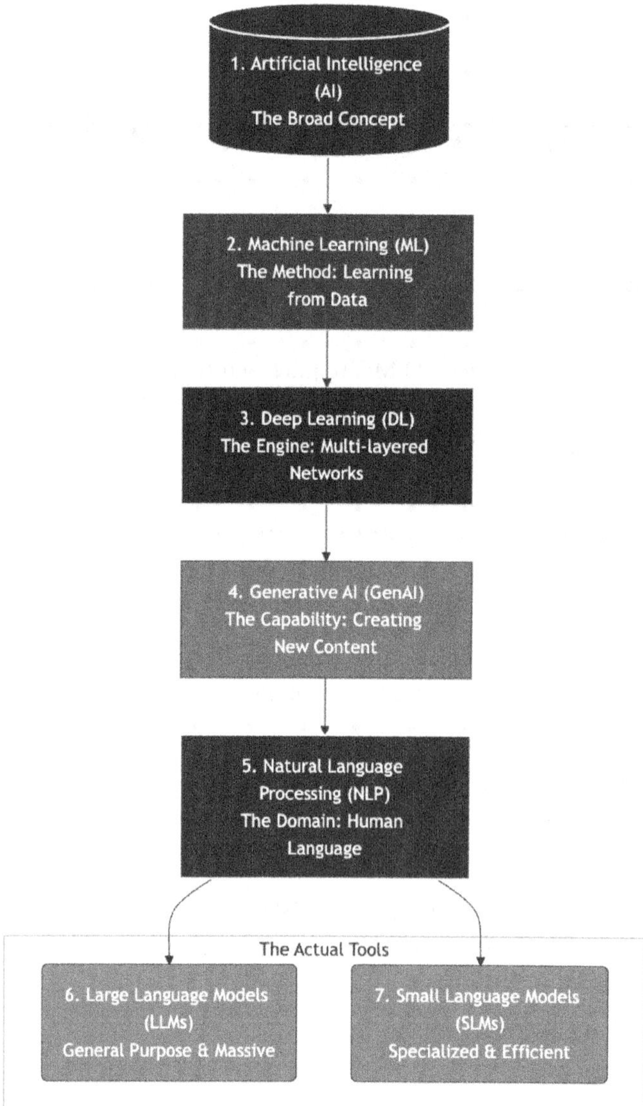

Figure 1.1: Different areas of AI

The path to language models

AI or ***artificial intelligence*** is a stream of computer science that focuses on building smart machines that can do tasks that require human intelligence. This includes a wide range of capabilities, such as learning, reasoning, problem-solving, perception, and understanding language.

This is the overall conception of machines that can simulate human intelligence to perform tasks. Under that broad umbrella fall a variety of terms which it will be useful to understand before we proceed further.

Machine learning (**ML**) is a subset of AI where systems are not explicitly programmed with rules. Instead, they learn directly from large amounts of data. For example, you don't teach a spam filter all the rules for spam; you show it millions of spam and non-spam emails, and it learns the patterns to look for.

Deep learning is a more advanced subset of machine learning. Deep learning networks have many layers that allow them to learn very complex patterns from raw, unstructured data like images, sound, and text. This is the technology that powers self-driving cars, advanced language translation, and generative AI tools.

Generative AI (**GenAI**) is a specific type of AI which can create new original content rather than just analyzing data. Generative AI works by using extremely large and complex machine learning models, often called foundation models, which have been trained on massive amounts of data from the internet. By processing this data, the models learn the patterns, structures, and relationships within it. When given a prompt, it uses this knowledge to generate a statistically possible new output.

NLP (**natural language processing**) is a branch of AI and computational linguistics focusing on the ability to understand, interpret, and generate human language both spoken and written. Researchers in NLP have been working for decades to confer linguistic capabilities on computers, and now, with the advent of LLMs, those aspirations are being met as never before.

An **LLM** (**large language model**) is a massive AI model designed to understand, generate, and process human language on a vast, general-purpose scale. It's trained on an enormous, diverse dataset, essentially a huge chunk of the internet. Because it has seen so much data, it's a jack-of-all-trades. It can write poetry, summarize a legal document, translate languages, write code, and answer complex questions about history.

An **SLM** (**small language model**) is a more compact, focused AI model that is trained to be highly efficient and effective at a specific set of tasks. It's often trained on a smaller, more curated, and high-quality dataset that is specific to a particular domain (like medical data, financial data, or customer support logs). Its power comes from its efficiency. SLMs have only millions or a few billion parameters, and are designed to do a few things extremely well, with less cost and more speed. Because they are small, they can run directly on your phone, laptop, or car, without needing to connect to a powerful data center.

Now that we're familiar with the general concepts of AI and LLMs, let's dive into LLM-related concepts in more detail and see how they all fit together.

LLMs analyzed

The operation of an LLM can be resolved into a number of different processes and operations:

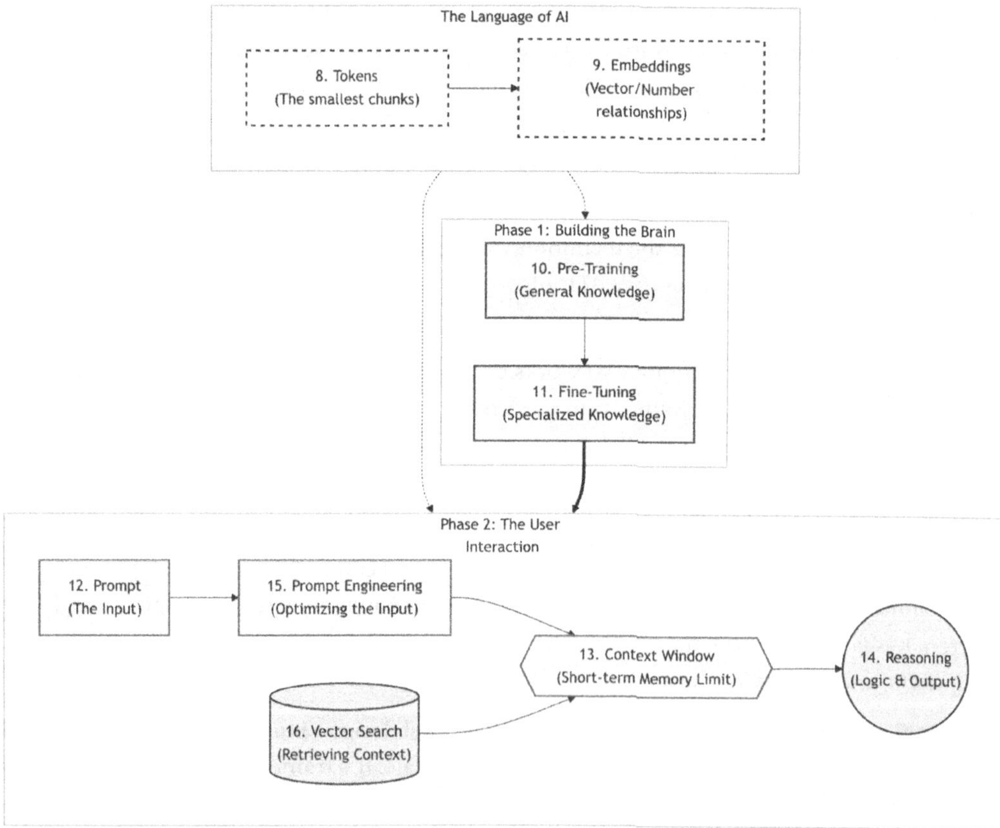

Figure 1.2: Different concepts in an LLM system

First we'll look at tokens and embeddings, and then we'll consider how LLMs are trained and given specialized knowledge. In the final part of the section we'll investigate how trained LLMs can be put to use.

Tokens

In the context of AI and language models, a **token** is the fundamental, smallest piece of text that a model can process. The process of breaking a sentence down into individual words or tokens is called **tokenization**.

AI models don't read words or sentences like humans do. Instead, they see the world as a sequence of numbers. A token is the unit that gets converted into one of these numbers.

Text: "The cat sat on the mat."

Tokens: ["The", "cat", "sat", "on", "the", "mat", "."]

Tokens define our hard limits and our billing costs.

Latency and **throughput**: LLMs process input tokens in parallel but generate output tokens serially. Generating 50 tokens takes significantly longer than processing 50 input tokens. If the system requires low latency, we must constrain the model's output length.

COGS (cost of goods sold): We pay per million tokens, meaning that verbose prompts kill margins. Sending a 2,000-token prompt for a simple yes/no classification task is just burning money.

We should pre-compute and cache prompts where possible.

The context window hard cap: Every model has a maximum **context window** (the short-term memory of an AI model), e.g. 8k, 32k, or 128k tokens. That means we can't dump a user's entire history into the prompt. We need to design a sliding window or summarization system to manage state within this constraint (*Figure 1.3*).

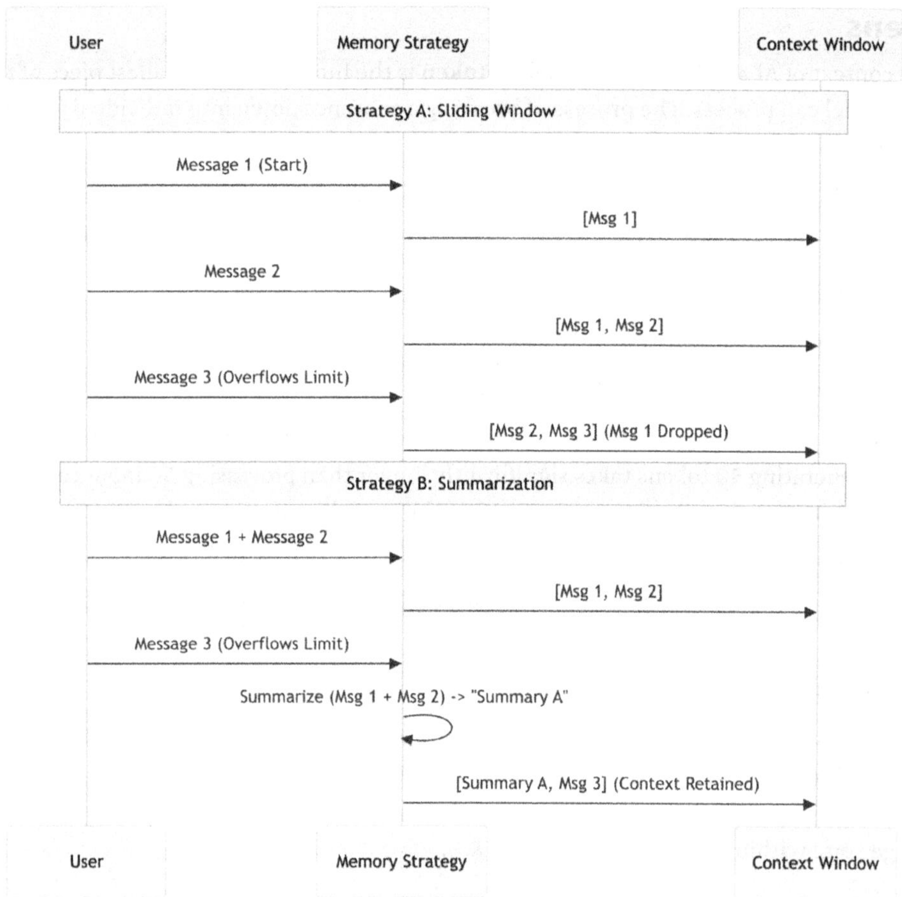

Figure 1.3: Context window strategies

Embeddings

Embeddings are numerical representations **(vectors)** of data (that can be text, image, etc.) that capture the ***semantic relationships*** between words, images and other data. They transform high-dimensional complex data into low-dimensional vectors and improve the computational efficiency of comparisons. In our context, embeddings would be vector representations of code, documentation etc.

An embedding vector captures the semantic essence of a piece of text, such that texts with similar meanings will have vectors that are close to each other in the vector space. Unlike a hash map which requires exact key matches, embeddings allow us to find nearest neighbors, i.e. content that is conceptually related even if it shares no keywords.

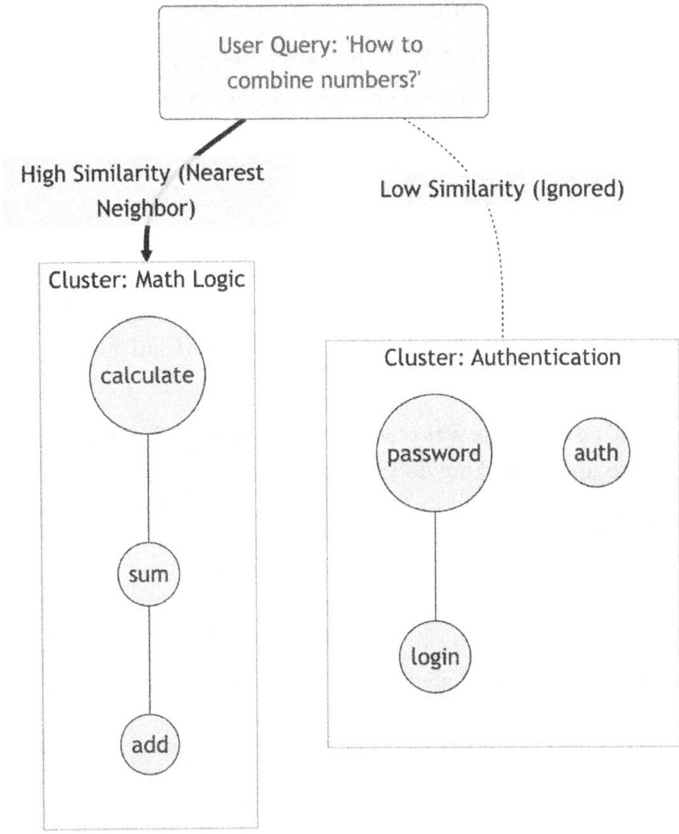

Figure 1.4: How embeddings cluster related words together

The number of **vector dimensions** in our embeddings matters. Larger dimensions (e.g. 1536 vs. 3072) capture more nuance but increase storage costs and search latency. Choose the smallest dimensionality that satisfies the accuracy requirements to keep index lookups fast.

Pre-training

Pre-training is the first and most important stage in creating a large AI model like an LLM. During this phase, the model is fed an enormous, diverse dataset—essentially a huge snapshot of the internet, including books, articles, websites, and code.

The goal is to teach it the fundamentals of language itself:

- How grammar works
- What different words mean
- How words and concepts relate to each other

- Common facts about the world
- The statistical patterns of how sentences are built

The model hasn't been trained for any specific job, but has a massive, general-purpose understanding of language and the world.

Fine-tuning

Fine-tuning is the process of taking a general-purpose, pre-trained model (like an LLM) and training it a little bit more on a smaller, specific set of data to make it an expert at a single, specialized task. The model becomes an expert in a specific domain. It can learn any company's internal jargon, a specific person's writing style, or the rules of a niche field (like medicine or law).

If a pre-trained model's knowledge was cut off in 2023, we can fine-tune it on new documents from 2024 and 2025 to update its knowledge on that specific topic.

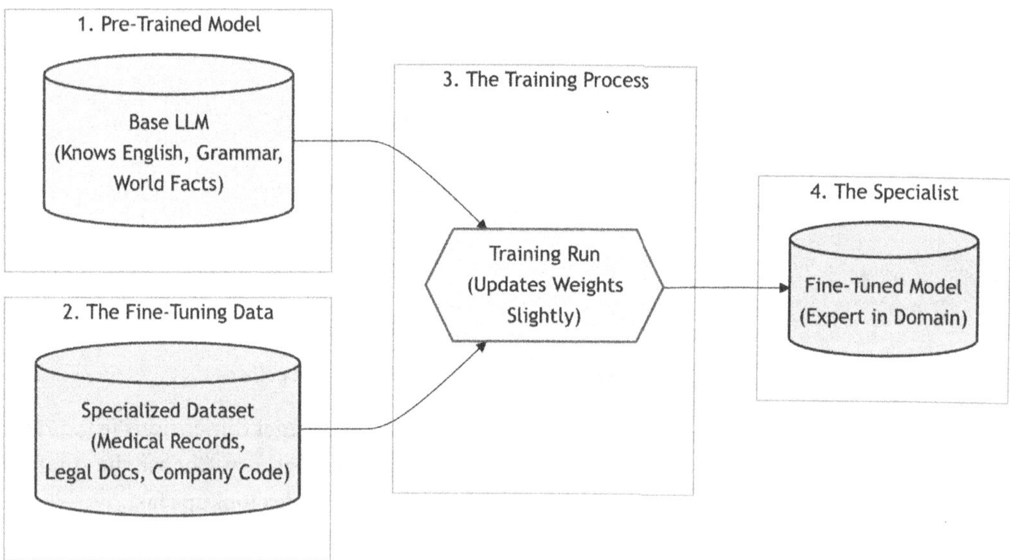

Figure 1.5: Fine-tuning models

It is thousands of times cheaper and faster to fine-tune a model than to pre-train a new one from scratch.

Having seen how LLMs are created, we now turn our attention to how they are put to use. But before we deep dive into that topic we need first to say a little about how we query an LLM.

Prompt engineering basics

A **prompt** is the instruction, question, or piece of text we give to an AI model to get it to perform a task. The prompt is how we communicate and guide the AI. The quality of the AI's answer is highly dependent on the quality of the prompt.

A simple prompt is just a question. But a more advanced prompt can have several parts to guide the AI better:

- Instruction: The specific command you want the AI to perform.
- Example: "Summarize the following text..."

- Context: Background information the AI needs to understand the task.
- Example: "...The text is a transcript from a business meeting. Focus on the action items..."

- Persona: Telling the AI who it should be, which changes its tone and style.
- Example: "You are an expert financial advisor. Explain this concept to a complete beginner..."

- Format: Telling the AI how to structure its answer.
- Example: "...Provide the answer as a 3-bullet point list in JSON format."

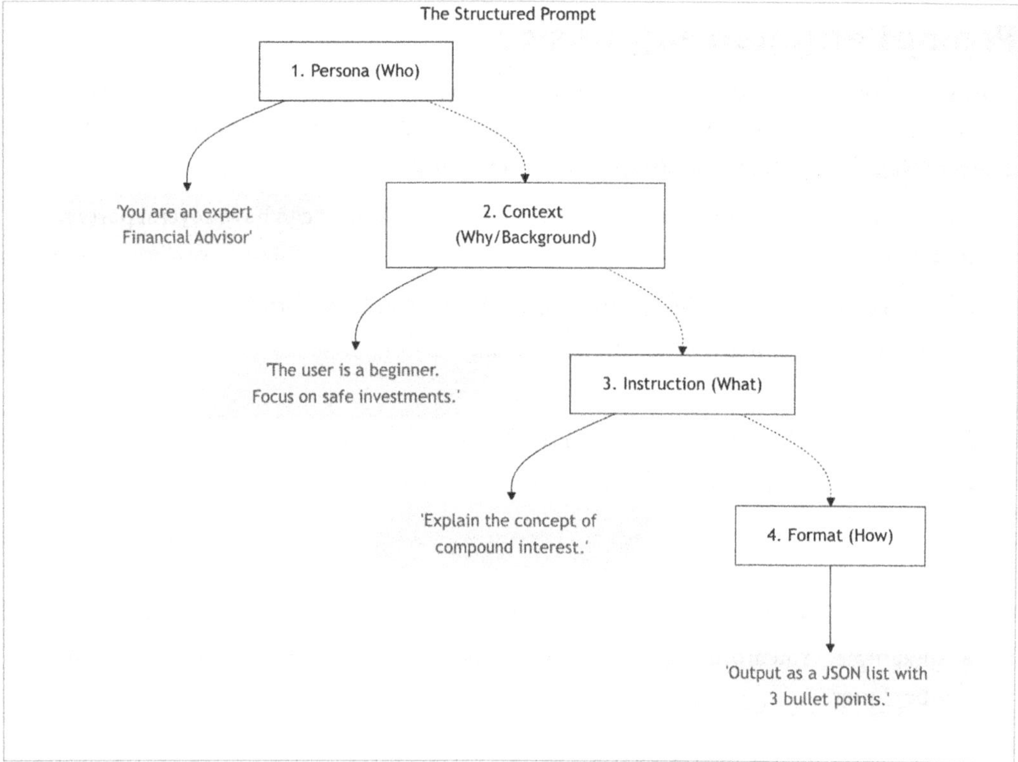

Figure 1.6: Different parts of the prompt

Context window

The context window is the working memory / short-term memory of an AI model. It is the fixed amount of information (measured in tokens) that the model can see and remember at any single moment.

Everything we send to the model, and everything it generates back, must fit within this window. This includes:

- The most recent prompt.
- The conversation history (e.g. previous questions and the AI's answers).
- Any documents, data, or system instructions you provided.
- Once the conversation becomes too long and overflows this window, the model forgets the earliest parts of the conversation.

Reasoning

Reasoning is the ability to take in information, process it logically, and produce a new conclusion or decision. It's the 'thinking' part of intelligence.

It's an emergent behavior where the model statistically predicts the next most plausible word based on patterns of logic from its training data. By generating a so-called chain-of-thought (thinking step-by-step), the model simulates a human reasoning process to solve a problem.

See the following example of a chain-of-thought process when a LLM model is given a prompt 'Define AI':

location: "Hyderabad, Telangana, India" time: "Saturday, November 8, 2025 at 8:34:00 AM IST" thought I need to define Artificial Intelligence (AI). This is a broad topic, so I should search for a clear, general definition, the main types of AI (like narrow vs. general), and its relationship to key subfields like machine learning and deep learning. I will also look for common applications to make the explanation more concrete. print(google.search.search(queries=["What is artificial intelligence definition", "types of artificial intelligence and examples", "what is machine learning and deep learning", "common applications of AI"]))

Prompt engineering strategies

Structuring the input prompts with good instructions, examples, and constraints helps return of useful responses from the LLM. **Prompt engineering** is the practice of tweaking prompts to get the desired outputs.

The following are some established strategies for crafting better prompts.

1. ***Context enrichment***
   Providing surrounding code, documentation, etc., to the LLM for more context

   Bad prompt:

   "Fix this bug"

   Good prompt:

   "Here is the error log: NullPointerException at line 45. Here is the database schema for the User table. Here is the code for the UserService class. Based on this context, identify why the user object is null"

2. ***Role assumption***
   Instruct the LLM to play a certain role, e.g. "You are a coding assistant..."

   Bad prompt:

   "Explain this code."

Good prompt:

"You are a Principal Security Engineer auditing this code for vulnerabilities. Explain the risks in this function to a Junior Developer. Focus on SQL injection and input validation"

3. ***Provide examples***
   Give examples of a good response to the LLM. This helps generate responses closer to the one desired.

   Bad prompt:

   "Convert this log to JSON"

   Good prompt:

   "Convert log lines to JSON. Input: [ERROR] 2024-01-01: DB fail Output: {'level': 'ERROR', 'date': '2024-01-01', 'msg': 'DB fail'} Input: [INFO] 2024-01-02: Started Output: {'level': 'INFO', 'date': '2024-01-02', 'msg': 'Started'} Input: [WARN] 2024-01-05: High CPU

4. ***Provide guardrails***
   Explicitly mention behavior which is not allowed, to avoid hallucinations. For example: "Do not run destructive commands unless specified."

   Bad prompt:

   "Write a script to delete old files."

   Good prompt:

   "Write a Python script to delete files older than 30 days.

   CONSTRAINT: Do not run any destructive commands (like os.remove) immediately. Instead, print a 'DRY RUN' list of files that would be deleted. Ask for user confirmation before deletion"

5. ***Chain-of-thought***
   Bad prompt:

   "How many distinct IP addresses hit the server?"

   Good prompt:

   "Analyze the server logs to find the count of distinct IPs. Think step-by-step:

   - *First, identify the IP address pattern in the logs.*
   - *Extract all IP instances into a list.*
   - *Filter the list to remove duplicates.*
   - *Count the remaining items. Return the final count"*

LLMs for code understanding

Once we have a trained model, we want to use it. We will see how the concepts we've looked at come together in a specific and rapidly growing use case: AI-assisted coding tools. As we will discover, building such tools requires more than semantic understanding alone; we also need ways to capture the structure and relationships within code. To achieve this, we will explore two key concepts: abstract syntax trees (ASTs) and knowledge graphs.

Vector search

Vector search is a technique for finding information based on meaning rather than exact keyword matches. As an example, this allows semantic retrieval of code chunks when a developer asks a query. This is helpful when we want to gather the context around a query to be sent to an LLM.

When a query is received, it is converted to a vector by passing it through an embedding model. This vector is compared against a collection of pre-computed vectors in a vector datastore like Pinecone or pgvector. The similarity measurement is performed using metrics such as **cosine similarity** and dot product. Vectors that are closer in space are considered more semantically similar.

The top matching results returned by the vector store are passed to the LLM as context.

Text autocompletion vs. code completions

Text autocompletion predicts the next word based purely on the sequence of words that came before it, with no understanding of meaning or context.

In **code completion**, syntax correctness is required along with semantic and structural awareness of the code. This means that depending on where a code definition is present in a file or class or method, the code complete predictions might differ.

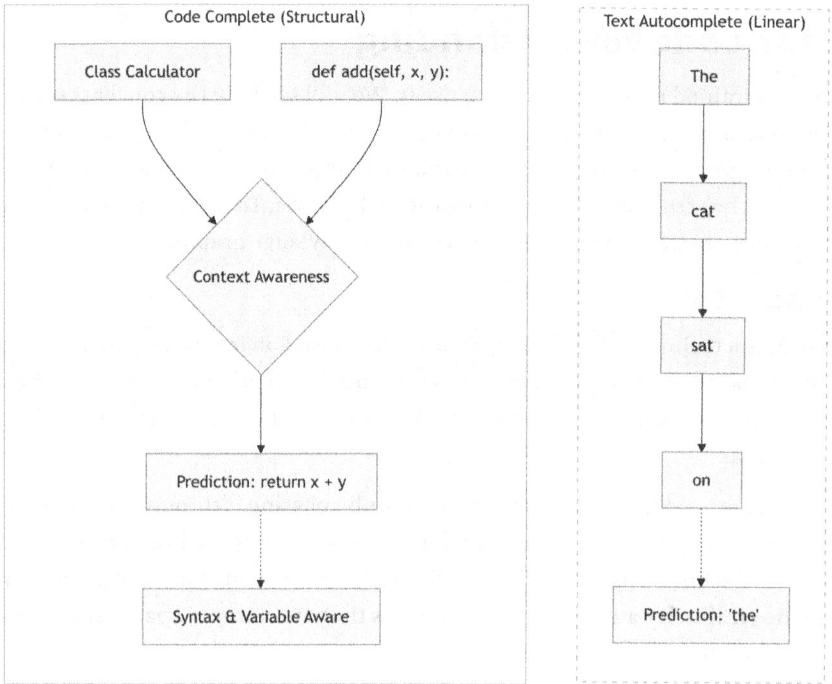

Figure 1.7: Code completion vs. text autocompletion

Abstract syntax trees (ASTs)

We have explored how tokens, embeddings, and vector search help LLMs process and retrieve meaning, and now it is time to look at how structure is represented.

ASTs provide structured representations of code that help with syntax corrections, refactoring and semantic edits. An AST is a tree data structure that shows a hierarchical relationship between different components of the code.

ASTs are especially useful for code completions. The IDE (development environment) internally generates an AST after indexing. This AST structure is used for chunking, and can be sent to an LLM to provide context regarding the repo/code.

```
class Calculator:
    def add(self, x, y):
        return x + y

    def subtract(self, x, y):
        return x - y
```

The AST representation of this would be something like this:

```
ClassDef (Calculator)
├── FunctionDef (add)
│   ├── Arguments: self, x, y
│   └── Return: BinOp (x + y)
└── FunctionDef (subtract)
    ├── Arguments: self, x, y
    └── Return: BinOp (x - y)
```

How the AST looks for a large codebase

ASTs are especially useful for semantic codebase chunking. A large codebase can be represented in AST format (think of folders as parent nodes with file classes as child nodes within them, and the different methods within a class as further children of the file nodes).

For class definition chunks, the entire `ClassDef` node is considered as one chunk, including all the functions. For function definition chunks, the entire `FunctionDef` node is considered as one chunk, e.g. add method with its arguments and return functions.

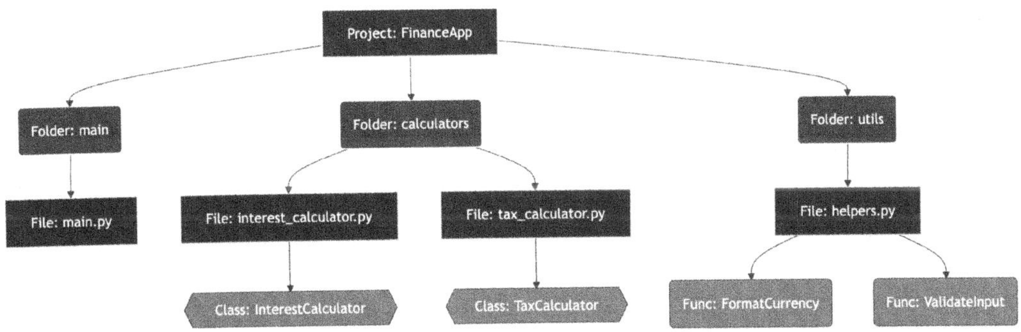

Figure 1.8: AST in a codebase

- Root level: project or module
    - The top-level node represents the whole project or module
    - It contains multiple child nodes, each representing a file (or module)

- File level: module/script AST
    - Each file has its own AST representing all code within that file
    - This includes class definitions, function definitions, import statements, and global code
- Class/function level: inside each file
    - Inside each file's AST, class and function definitions appear as child nodes
    - Each class contains methods (functions) and statements
    - Functions contain statements and expressions

```
[Project: FinanceApp]
├─ [File: main.py]
│   ├─ [Function: main]
│   ├─ [Function: run_app]
├─ [Folder: calculators]
│   ├─ [File: interest_calculator.py]
│   │   ├─ [Class: InterestCalculator]
│   │   │   ├─ [Method: simple_interest]
│   │   │   ├─ [Method: compound_interest]
│   ├─ [File: tax_calculator.py]
│       ├─ [Class: TaxCalculator]
│       │   ├─ [Method: calculate_tax]
│       │   ├─ [Method: apply_deductions]
├─ [Folder: utils]
│   ├─ [File: helpers.py]
│   │   ├─ [Function: format_currency]
│   │   ├─ [Function: validate_input]
├─ [File: README.md]
```

Figure 1.9: Abstract syntax tree for classes

Knowledge graphs

Knowledge graphs are data structures consisting of nodes, typically representing entities of various kinds, connected by edges that express relationships between nodes. For example, in a social media platform, a node could represent a user, a post, or a hashtag, with edges capturing relationships like 'follows', 'liked', or 'tagged in'. This means the graph can answer questions like 'which users liked the same post?' or 'which hashtags are most commonly used together?' For our use case they can be used to capture relationships between functions, classes, and methods in a codebase, which is useful for answering questions like where does this method get called from?

For example, for the finance app above, the knowledge graph would somewhat look like this:

Nodes (entities)

- `FinanceApp` (Project)
- `main` (Module/Folder)
- `calculators` (Module/Folder)
- `utils` (Module/Folder)
- `main.py` (File)
- `interest_calculator.py` (File)
- `tax_calculator.py` (File)
- `helpers.py` (File)
- `main` (Function in `main.py`)
- `run_app` (Function in `main.py`)
- `InterestCalculator` (Class in `interest_calculator.py`)
- `TaxCalculator` (Class in `tax_calculator.py`)
- `format_currency` (Function in `helpers.py`)
- `validate_input` (Function in `helpers.py`)
- and so on ...

Edges (relationships)

From	Relationship	To
`FinanceApp`	hasModule	`main`
`FinanceApp`	hasModule	`calculators`
`FinanceApp`	hasModule	`utils`

From	Relationship	To
main	hasFile	main.py
calculators	hasFile	interest_calculators.py
tax_calculators.py	containsClass	TaxCalculator
TaxCalculator	hasMethod	calculate_tax
helpers.py	containsFunction	format_currency

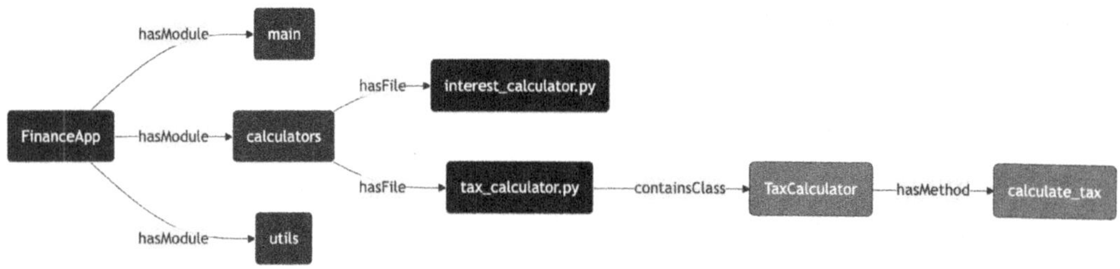

Figure 1.10: Knowledge graph for a codebase

Handling LLM trade-offs and choices

There is no 'one model to rule them all'. Every architectural choice requires balancing competing constraints. When selecting a model, you are generally trading off between these four dimensions:

- context window size – how much context can be sent to the LLM
- latency (millisecond-level performance)
- security/privacy
- cost

Claude has been found to work well with larger contexts, and GPT-5 handles excellent reasoning, but with higher latency and cost. Smaller models might be fine-tuned for lower latency, but accuracy might suffer.

Deterministic vs. stochastic outputs

Deterministic means the same input will always produce the exact same output. A deterministic system is predictable and consistent, and follows a fixed set of rules.

Stochastic means the same input can produce different outputs. It involves randomness and probability, so the result is not perfectly predictable.

Unlike standard deterministic functions where input(x) always equals output(y), LLMs are probabilistic. As an engineer, the primary control knob for this behavior is **temperature**.

Low temperature (0.1 to 0.2): The model selects the most probable next token. Use this for code generation, data extraction, and classification where consistency is paramount.

High temperature (approx. 0.7 to 1.0): The model boosts randomness by increasing the selection possibilities of less probable tokens. Use this for creative writing, brainstorming, or generating diverse synthetic data.

The architectural implication of non-determinism is that we cannot unit-test LLM outputs with string equality assertions. We must design the test suites to tolerate variance or force the temperature to zero during regression testing.

Temperature also affects retry logic. With temperature = 0, a request failing validations (like a malformed JSON) will fail exactly the same way when retried. A temperature > 0 might fix it.

After that brief discussion of some of the ways in which LLMs vary in their characteristics, and the implications of non-deterministic behavior, we now move on to consider an approach that can be used to improve accuracy and relevance when LLMs are used in information retrieval tasks.

RAG approaches to information retrieval

How do we retrieve semantically relevant documentation so as to capture cases that might have the same meaning and intention as the user query but which are worded differently?

The ability to retrieve semantically similar but diversely worded data is the great strength of **RAG (retrieval-augmented generation)** techniques. This involves several distinct steps.

Data cleaning

Before chunking or embedding, raw data must be rigorously cleaned. This is not just a matter of removing whitespace. It involves:

- De-noising: stripping HTML tags, boilerplate headers/footers, and navigation links that dilute the semantic density of the text.
- PII (personally identifiable information) scrubbing: regex-based removal of emails, SSNs (social security numbers), and API keys before the data ever touches an external model API.
- Normalization: standardizing unicode characters and date formats so the vector space remains consistent.

Vectorization

Raw knowledge data (documentation, closed tickets, etc.) is converted into high-dimensional numerical arrays called vectors (or embeddings) using specialized embedding models (e.g. OpenAI's `text-embedding-ada-002`). This process captures the semantic meaning of the text.

Vector search

The user's contextualized query is also vectorized. Algorithms like cosine similarity or approximate nearest neighbor (ANN) search the high-dimensional vector database space to find the most relevant document chunks and support cases whose vectors are closest in proximity to the query vector. This ensures we retrieve documentation or cases that have the same meaning and intention as the user query. This retrieval is the foundation for RAG techniques.

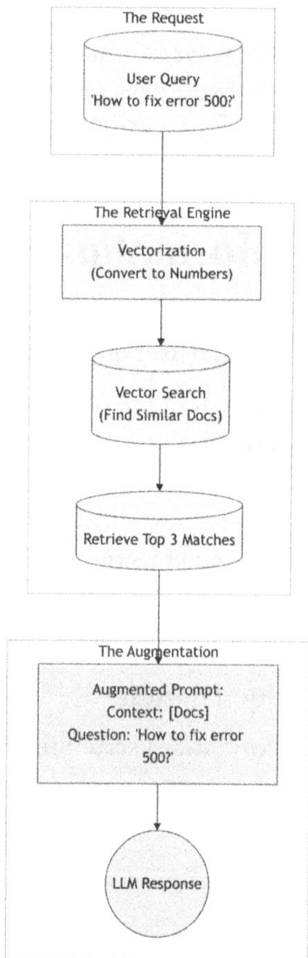

Figure 1.11: Vector search flow

Retrieval augmented generation is the method of augmenting or enhancing the prompt with context of relevant and factual data before sending it to the LLM, so that the LLM can give far more accurate and relevant results. This is the foundational method for ensuring high accuracy and minimizing hallucinations, by grounding the LLM's response in verified, proprietary knowledge.

Why is naive RAG not always sufficient?

A naive RAG approach may be subject to two critical limitations. One relates to the fact that vector search excels at finding similarity but that is not always strictly relevant. Several documents may be framed similarly, which leads to the retrieval of several semantically similar chunks which may be related to the query. So the LLM receives redundant, overwhelming context, which makes it difficult to pinpoint the exact solution which is needed.

Another potential problem is inefficient retrieval due to poor chunking. Documents are often organized hierarchically (*title -> section -> sub-section*). This means that if a user query matches the title of a document, the system may retrieve the high-level summary but miss the critical information located five sections down. The core piece of information the user needs is missed because the embedding model didn't recognize the connection between the high-level match and the low-level detail.

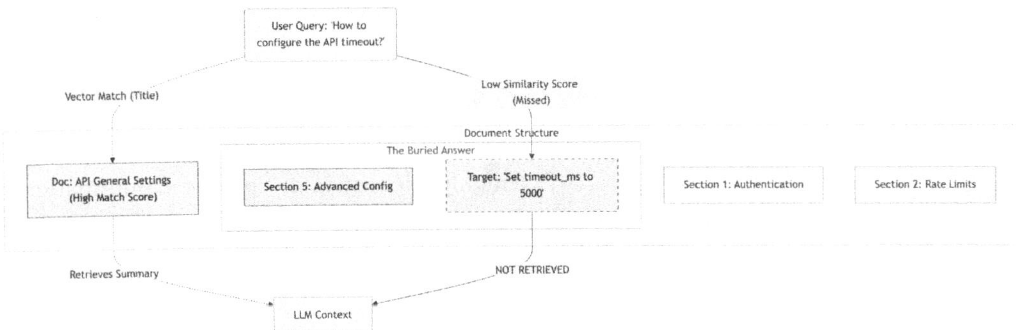

Figure 1.12: Problems with naive RAG

Why do we need a knowledge graph?

To mitigate the limitations of semantic-only retrieval we might employ a knowledge graph (KG). A KG is a structured representation of data defining relationships between entities. **Graph databases** like Neo4J or Amazon Neptune can be used for this. A KG makes it easier to retrieve a particular entity based on its relationship with other entities.

Instead of relying on word similarity, the KG understands relationships such as:

```
Document A -[is_part_of]-> Section 3
```

and

```
Ticket X -[resolved_by]-> Code Commit Y
```

This allows the retrieval engine to traverse complex, logical paths to find the definitive solution set.

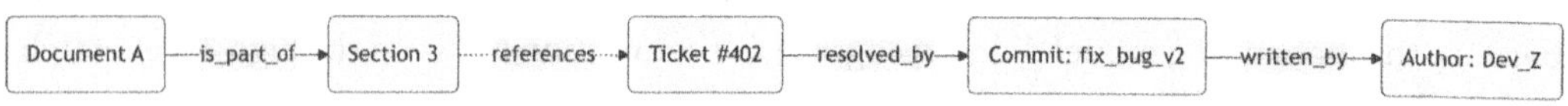

Figure 1.13: Knowledge graph retrieval

What is GraphRAG?

Combining knowledge graphs with LLMs leads to improved accuracy and context of generated responses. This advanced RAG approach is called **GraphRAG**. It allows the system to traverse complex relationships between entities, to find highly relevant, inter-connected information which is optimal for navigating structured and domain-specific data.

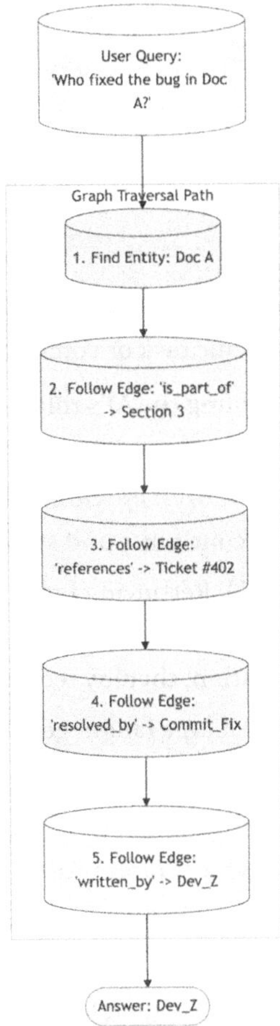

Figure 1.14: Working of a GraphRAG

Context engineering

Building with LLMs is a data pipeline problem, not a prompting problem. Architecture controls the flow of context. The goal is to build a pipeline that moves data from the long-term memory (vector database) into the short-term working memory (context window) at the exact moment of inference.

Context engineering is the strategic practice of designing, constructing, and managing all the relevant information, tools, and constraints that an AI model sees before it generates a response.

Figure 1.15: How an inference pipeline works

It has a number of distinct aspects:

1. ***Dynamic information assembly***: The system actively gathers diverse pieces of information tailored to the specific task or conversation turn. This can include:
    - System instructions: Defining the AI's role, persona, and behavioral guidelines (e.g. 'You are a helpful customer support agent').
    - Conversation history (memory): Providing relevant excerpts from previous interactions to maintain continuity and statefulness.
    - External knowledge (RAG): Retrieving facts, documents, or data from external sources (like a company database or the web) to ground the response in up-to-date and specific information, thereby reducing hallucinations.
2. ***Context window management***: Large language models have a finite limit to the amount of information they can process at one time (context window). Context engineering involves:
    - Prioritization: Deciding which information is most critical for the current step.
    - Compression: Using techniques like summarization or filtering to condense large amounts of data into the most relevant, token-efficient format.
3. ***Tool orchestration***: The discipline involves integrating and managing access to external tools or **APIs** (**application programming interfaces**). The AI must be correctly prompted and provided with the context to decide when to use a tool, how to use it, and how to incorporate the results into its final answer.
4. ***Ensuring consistency and reliability***: By systematically controlling the AI's informational environment, context engineering helps ensure that the model produces accurate, consistent, and policy-aligned outputs across different interactions and users.

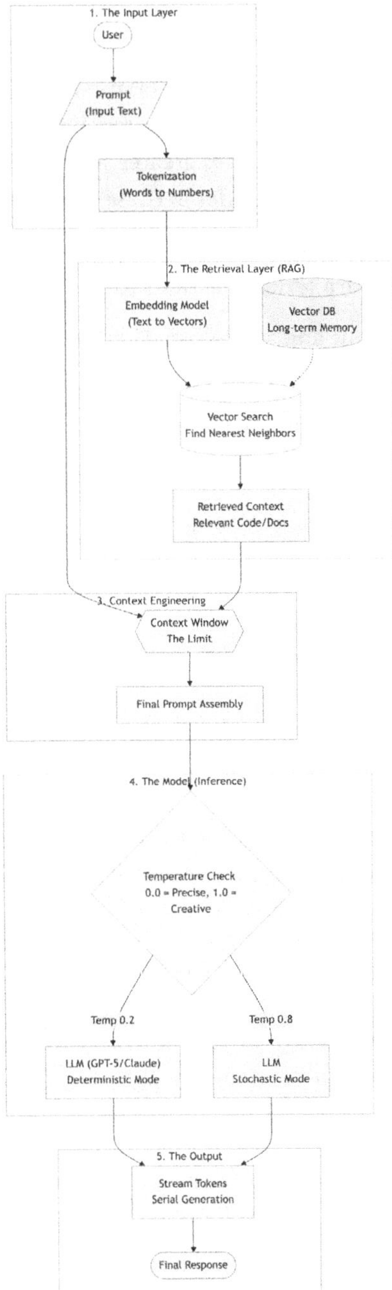

Figure 1.16: Inference flow with context engineering

Agentic AI

In simpler AI systems the non-determinism of LLMs sits within a framework consisting of just one or a few LLMs, which typically do not interact extensively with each other. Such systems are fine for many routine tasks, but sometimes greater sophistication and system intelligence is called for. Agentic solutions have much to offer in these situations.

Agentic AI (or an AI agent) refers to an autonomous system that uses an AI model (like an LLM) to reason, plan, and execute a series of actions to achieve a high-level goal.

The key is that the path is dynamic and stochastic. The AI is the orchestrator: it is given a goal, and it figures out the steps to take on its own.

Agentic AI works in a continuous reasoning loop (often called a **ReAct loop**: reason + act):

- Plan: the AI analyzes the goal and breaks it down into a plan
- Act: it executes the first step by choosing a tool. This could be:
    - Using a search engine
    - Running a piece of code
    - Querying a database
    - Reading a file
- Observe: it takes the result of that action (e.g. a list of search results) and adds it to the context window
- Reason: it looks at the goal, its plan, and the new information, then decides what to do next. It might adjust its plan, execute the next step, or decide the goal is complete. This loop repeats until the goal is met.

Modality

Humans don't experience the world just through text, and modern AI doesn't either. To build truly immersive systems, we must understand the different input channels an AI can process.

The most common **modalities** include:

- Text: This is the modality of written language. Models that process text are used for translation, summarization, and chatbots.
- Images: This modality is for static visual information. Models that process images are used for object recognition and facial detection.
- Audio: This modality includes spoken language, music, and sounds. This is used for speech recognition (like Siri) and music generation.

- Video: A complex modality that combines moving images (frames) with audio.
- Spatial: A spatial modality that understands depth and the 3D structure of the world, which is crucial for self-driving cars.

Data residency and compliance

Beyond latency and cost, **data residency** – where and how data, including AI model data, is stored – is now a primary constraint on enterprise system architecture.

Public APIs (OpenAI, Anthropic): Data leaves the VPC (virtual private cloud). Unacceptable for PII (personally identifiable information), PHI (protected health information), or strict PCI (payment card industry) environments without zero-retention agreements.

Private cloud / VPC (Bedrock, Azure OpenAI): Data stays within the cloud perimeter but relies on provider availability.

Self-hosted open weights (Llama 3, Mistral): We have full control of the data. This is required for strict air-gapped environments or for compliance. This trades operational complexity (GPU management) for compliance safety.

Performance benchmarking

To improve our systems we need to measure their performance as objectively as possible. A fundamental principle is that *you cannot improve what you do not measure.*

However, speed and intelligence are fundamentally different metrics in AI. We split **benchmarking** into two distinct categories to measure them separately: task quality benchmarking and inference time benchmarking.

Task quality benchmarking measures how smart and accurate the model is. (e.g. 'Does it have high-school level knowledge?' or 'Is it a good-quality summarizer?')

This lets us know how good the model is at a specific task. We run the model against a standardized dataset and evaluate its score.

Inference time benchmarking measures how fast and efficient the model is. For example, how many tokens per second it generates, or how fast is the time to first token. This benchmarking answers the business-critical question: How fast and expensive is this model to run? This is about speed and throughput.

Custom benchmarking is a kind of task quality benchmarking where we aim to gauge success in meeting a defined goal. The overall process looks like this:

1. ***Define the goal***: What is the one thing the LLM must do well?

   Example: 'It must accurately summarize our customer support tickets.'

2. ***Create a golden set***: Manually create 50–100 high-quality examples of inputs and ideal outputs.

   Input: (A long, angry customer ticket)

   Ideal Output: {"summary": "User is angry about billing error on invoice #1234.", "sentiment": "negative", "topic": "billing"}

3. ***Run models against the set***: Run the models we want to compare (e.g. Llama 3 vs. GPT-5) against all the inputs in the golden set.

4. ***Evaluate the results***: How to score the outputs?

   Human evaluation: The most reliable way. Have a human expert score the model's output against the ideal output on a scale of 1 to 5.

   LLM-as-a-Judge: A modern, scalable technique. We use a powerful judge LLM (like GPT-5) to grade the output of the test LLM.

   Prompt for Judge: You are an expert. Here is an input, an ideal response, and a model's actual response. Rate the model's response from 1-5 for accuracy. Response: [Model's Output]

Key metrics to measure:

Time to first token (TTFT): How long the user waits before seeing the first word.

Tokens per second (TPS): How many tokens are generated per second after the first one. This measures the overall generation speed.

Total latency: The full time from prompt to the end of the response.

Throughput (Requests/sec): How many concurrent users our system can handle.

Resource usage: GPU memory (VRAM) consumption. This determines what kind of hardware we need to buy or rent.

Handling failure

Three main kinds of failure can occur in an LLM output:

- ***Hallucination***

  A **hallucination** is when the model confidently invents a false or nonsensical answer because it's statistically plausible. We solve this by grounding the model giving it relevant information using RAG.

- ***Knowledge cut off***

  This problem is that the model's knowledge is static, frozen at the time its training data was collected (e.g. 'I only have knowledge up to April 2023'). This too can be solved, by providing the model enough context using RAG for example.

- ***Bias***

  This is the hardest problem because the **bias** is deeply embedded in the petabytes of human text the model was trained on.

  By using filtering on the initial dataset, and by providing guardrails in the prompts, along with human feedback, this bias can be managed.

Summary

LLMs are not magic; they are probabilistic compute engines bound by rigid resource constraints. In this chapter we have stripped away the hype to reveal the raw materials of this technology. Every architectural decision we make must take certain trade offs and dependencies into account:

Cost: defined by input token volume and model size.

Latency: defined by output token volume and retrieval overhead.

Quality: defined by context window usage and model reasoning power (size).

The decisions we make must reflect our priorities:

- For high quality and low latency we need to pay a premium for massive GPUs and over-provisioned throughput.
- For low cost and low latency we need to sacrifice reasoning capabilities and context depth (smaller models, aggressive summarization).
- For high quality and low cost we can accept batch processing latency (async queues).

The magic of AI engineering isn't prompting – it's managing these constraints. The rest of this book is about the patterns we use to overcome this triangle: using RAG for infinite context, caching for low latency.

Now that we understand the atomic units, let's learn how to assemble them.

Get this book's PDF version and more

Scan the QR code (or go to `packtpub.com/unlock`). Search for this book by name, confirm the edition, and then follow the steps on the page.

UNLOCK NOW

Note: Keep your invoice handy. Purchases made directly from Packt don't require an invoice.

2

Core Architectural Patterns for LLM System Design

In *Chapter 1* we introduced the fundamental concepts of LLM integration: tokens, embeddings, and the basic idea of retrieval-augmented generation (RAG). However, integrating LLMs into a production system introduces a new class of dependency: one that is non-deterministic, high-latency, and carries a high, variable operational cost.

As experienced engineers, we already know how to build reliable systems. This chapter isn't about reinventing those principles, but about adapting them for the unique, messy challenges LLMs throw at us. Consider this an architect's playbook that outlines the new patterns needed to meet these challenges. The patterns we'll outline will be the common framework for all the case studies we'll look at in subsequent chapters.

In this chapter we'll be looking at the following topics:

- Designing for resilience and reliability
- Designing for low latency
- Designing for cost optimization
- Designing for testability and observability
- Designing for security and trust
- Engineering for production
- Training with test data
- Respecting user privacy

Designing for resilience and reliability

Our system's stability is now tied to an external API that is slower, more expensive, and less predictable than any database or microservice calls. The primary goal is to decouple the application's health from the provider's health. Two types of pattern are especially valuable in this regard: the **GenAI service pattern** (or **LLM gateway pattern**) and the **circuit breaker pattern**.

Pattern: the GenAI service or LLM gateway

When we first start building with LLMs, our instinct is to treat them like any other third-party API. We install the SDK, generate an API key, and make the call directly from our application code.

It feels fast. It feels efficient. We write a Python function, import `openai`, and we are shipping features in minutes.

The architecture looks like this:

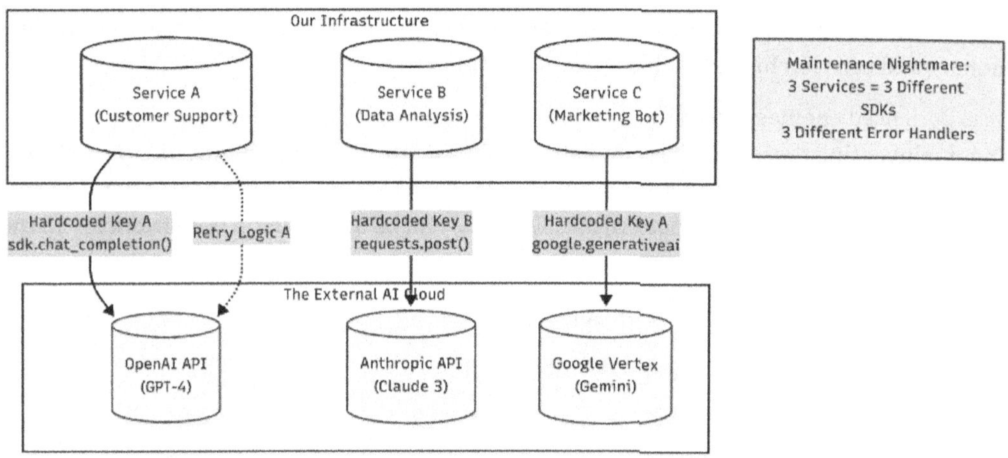

Figure 2.1: Naive model-calling logic

While this works for a weekend hackathon, it creates a high-coupling, low-cohesion architecture in production with the following issues:

- ***Vendor lock-in***: If Service A is written using the OpenAI SDK, migrating to Anthropic requires rewriting the entire code block.
- ***Inconsistent reliability***: Service A might have excellent retry logic, while Service B crashes on the first timeout. There is no standard.
- ***Observability black holes***: You have no central place to see how much you are spending. You have to log into three different developer consoles to tally up the bill.
- ***Security risks***: API keys are scattered across multiple environment variables in multiple services, increasing the surface area for leaks.

Stating the problem more formally now:

Problem: Our services should not be calling OpenAI, Anthropic, or Google directly. This creates high-coupling, high maintenance problems.

Solution: To solve this, we borrow a pattern from traditional microservices: the API gateway. We stop treating LLMs as external vendors and start treating them as a unified internal resource.

Implement a single, centralized LLM gateway. This is a microservice that acts as the only entry point for all LLM calls. Our services talk only to this gateway using a single, unified API format. The gateway handles the messy details of talking to the outside world.

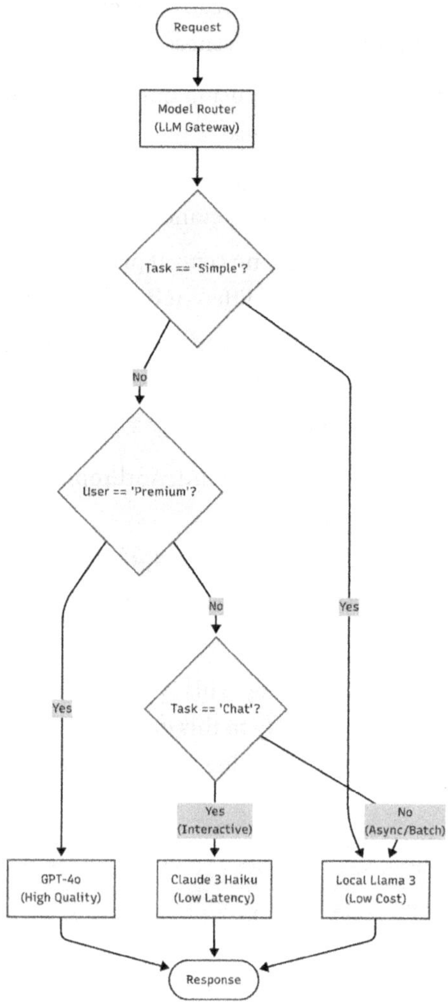

Figure 2.2: The LLM gateway pattern – decoupling internal services from external providers

This pattern brings some significant benefits:

- ***Abstraction***: Can switch models (e.g. GPT-5 for Claude 3 Opus) with a config change, not a re-deployment
- ***Centralized control***: All other resilience, cost, and monitoring patterns are implemented in this one place

- ***Authentication***: Manages all authentications in one service
- ***Fallbacks and reliability***: If OpenAI goes down, the gateway can automatically retry the request with Anthropic. The upstream service never even knows there was an outage

Pattern: circuit breakers with tiered fallbacks

An LLM provider might be slow, down, or just returning bad data. Simply retrying a failed call (like you would for a 503 on an external service) is often the wrong move.

The solution is to combine the circuit breaker pattern with **tiered fallbacks** following a three-stage model:

1. ***Monitor***: The GenAI Service monitors the health (latency, error rate) of each model provider.
2. ***Trip***: If a primary model (e.g. GPT-5) exceeds a failure threshold, the circuit opens.
3. ***Reroute***: All subsequent requests are immediately and automatically rerouted to a backup model.

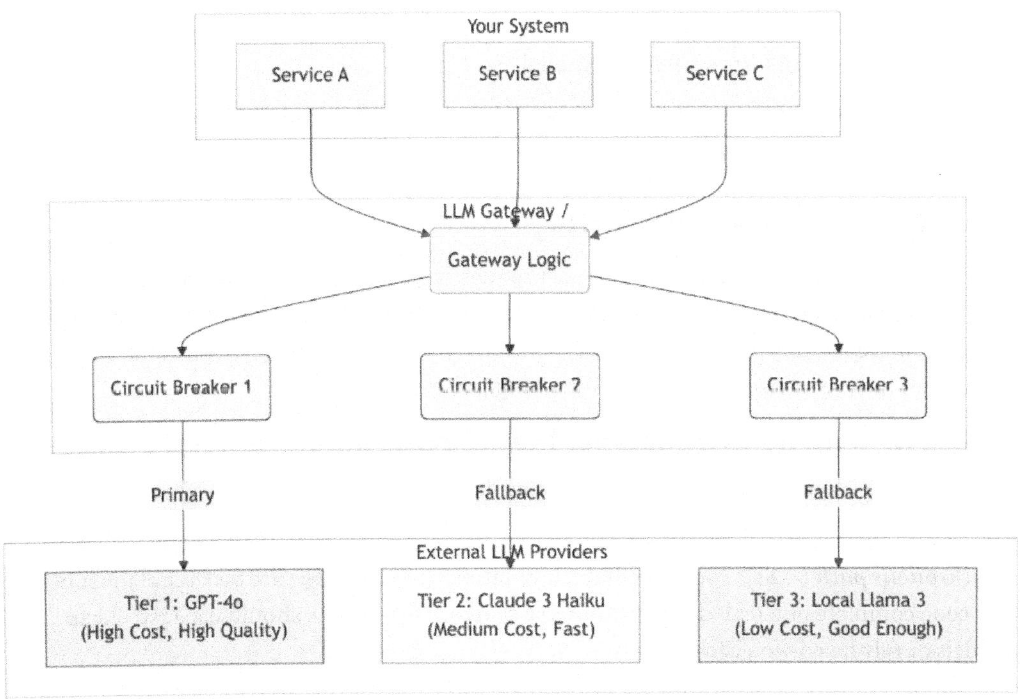

Figure 2.3: Tiered fallbacks with circuit breakers

For example, we might implement the following tiered fallback strategy:

Tier 1: GPT-5 (high-cost, high-reasoning)

Tier 2 (fallback): Claude 3 Haiku (medium-cost, fast)

Tier 3 (fallback): Llama 3 8B (locally hosted, free, less smart)

Tier 4 (final fallback): Return a cached good enough response or a graceful error message to the client UI: 'Our AI assistant is at high capacity, please try again in a moment'

We cannot leave the circuit open forever. We need **recovery logic** to close the circuit that includes a half-open state:

Sleep: After the circuit trips, wait for a defined cooldown (e.g. 30 seconds).

Probe: Allow a single canary request to pass through to the primary provider.

Reset: If the canary succeeds, close the circuit and resume full traffic. If it fails, restart the cooldown.

For our **retry strategy** we have two options: interactive and asynchronous:

- ***Interactive/synchronous***: Do not use aggressive **exponential backoff**. If a user is waiting, a 60-second retry is effectively downtime. Use *capped backoff* (start 500 ms, max 1 s) or fail fast to a fallback model.
- ***Asynchronous***: Use exponential backoff (wait 1 min, 2 min, 4 min). Since no user is waiting, we can afford to wait out a 5-minute provider outage.

Designing for low latency

LLM inference is fundamentally slow. A user requesting a search result expects a response in < 500 ms, but an LLM might take 5–10 seconds to generate a full answer. We cannot change the speed of inference, but we can architect around it. Hybrid processing (synchronous vs. asynchronous), response streaming and caching patterns can help us.

Pattern: hybrid processing (synchronous vs. asynchronous)

Given that we cannot block a user's web request for 10 seconds while waiting for an LLM, one option is to separate the workloads. This is the most important latency-saving pattern.

Synchronous path (< 2 s): For immediate, low-latency needs. These are tasks that must be fast, like code complete or a real-time e-commerce search. These paths should use fast, cheap models or rely heavily on caching.

Asynchronous path (> 10 s): For high-latency, long-running tasks use a **message queue** (like Kafka or SQS) to decouple the initial request from the actual LLM work. The client receives an immediate '202 Accepted' response. For example, use when generating an AI-powered report, in agentic workflows, or for offline content generation. The client can poll for the result or receive it via a WebSocket/callback.

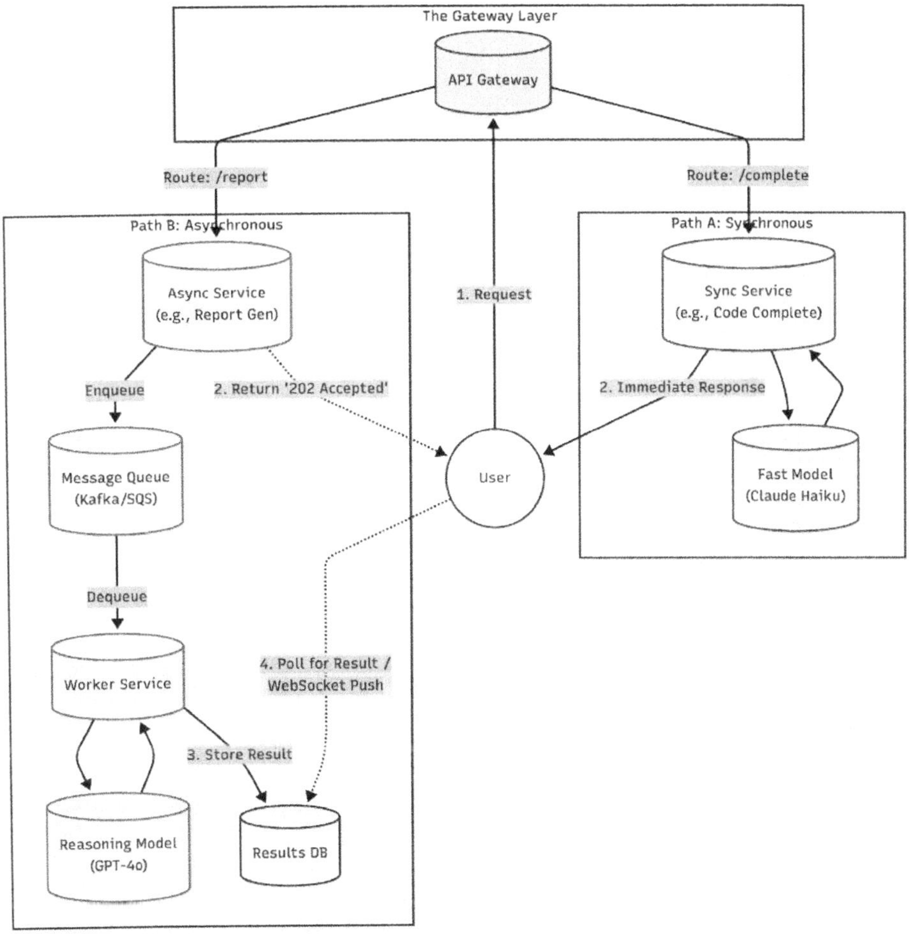

Figure 2.4: Sync and async flows

Pattern: response streaming

Even a fast 3-second response feels slow if the user is staring at a loading spinner, so if possible stream the response token-by-token. Once the model generates the first word, send it to the client. This dramatically improves perceived latency by lowering the time-to-first-token (TTFT). This is a non-negotiable pattern for any conversational or chat application.

How it works

We use **SSE (server-sent events)** over standard HTTP. SSE is unidirectional (server -> client) and runs over standard HTTP/2, making it firewall-friendly and easy to implement.

Client: Opens a persistent connection.

Server: Instead of returning a JSON object, it returns a generator (an iterator)

Header: The server must set content-type: text/event-stream

Format: Data is sent in chunks prefixed 'data:':

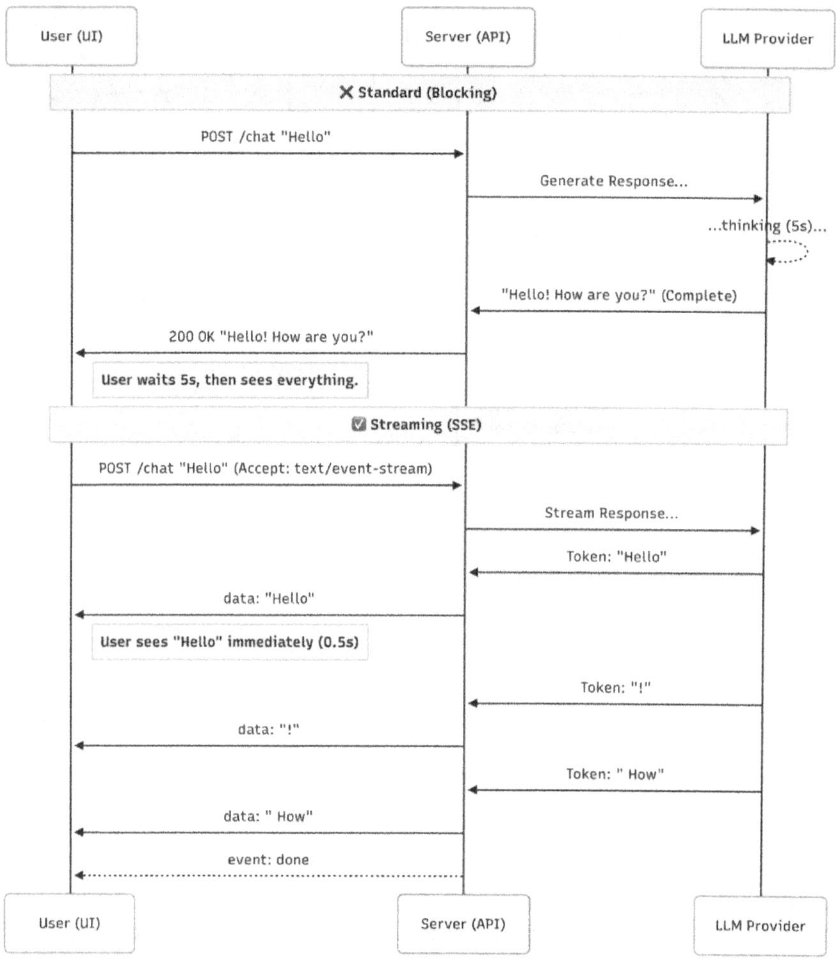

Figure 2.5: Streaming tokens

Pattern: caching strategies

LLM calls are slow and expensive, while cache hits are the fastest, cheapest LLM calls you can make. Therefore implement a multi-level caching strategy:

Level 1: exact match

- ***Scenario***: A viral product launch. 10,000 users ask 'When is shipping?'.
- ***Mechanism***: Hash the prompt string (`sha256("When is shipping?")`). Check Redis.
- ***Result***: 9,999 users get a 5 ms response.
- ***Why***: It catches the stampede of identical queries.

Level 2: semantic match

- ***Scenario***: User A asks 'How do I reset password?' User B asks 'Forgot password, help'.
- ***Mechanism***: L1 misses (strings don't match). We convert 'Forgot password, help' to a vector. We query the vector DB for similar past questions.
- ***Result***: The DB finds that 'How do I reset password?' has a 0.98 similarity. It returns the cached answer for User A to User B.
- ***Why***: It catches different phrasings of the same intent, saving expensive reasoning costs.

Level 3: proactive caching

- ***Scenario***: A personalized 'Daily Report' for 100,000 users.
- ***Mechanism***: Don't wait for them to open the app at 9:00 AM. Run a batch job at 6:00 AM. Generate the reports and store them into Redis.
- ***Result***: When users log in, the AI generation feels instant because it happened 3 hours ago.
- ***Why***: It moves latency from online (user waiting) to offline This is a core pattern in *Chapter 4* (*Adaptive Learning Platform*) and in *Chapter 5* (*E-commerce Search*).

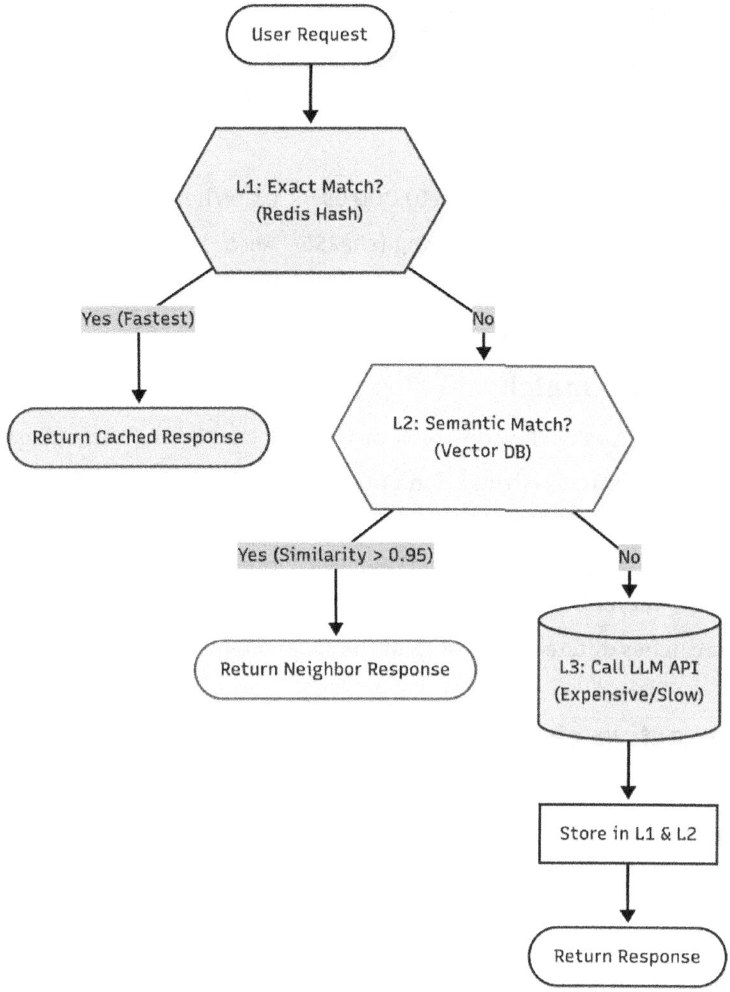

Figure 2.6: Caching strategy

Pattern: coalesce caching

During high-traffic events, thousands of users might ask the exact same question simultaneously. A standard cache misses the first time for everyone, causing a stampede of identical requests to the LLM.

The solution is middleware that identifies identical in-flight requests. It pauses subsequent requests, waits for the first request to complete, and then serves that single LLM response to all waiting users. This reduces load on the provider by orders of magnitude.

Designing for cost optimization

LLMs introduce a new, variable, and unbounded operational cost (**COGS** – cost of goods sold). A single complex query can cost dollars. Architectural decisions are now financial decisions. Important in this context are the **model router**, **dynamic traffic control** and **prompt engineering** and **compression** patterns.

Pattern: the model router

Not all tasks require the smartest (and most expensive) model. Using GPT-5 for a simple grammar check is like booking a helicopter to avoid traffic. By implementing a rule engine within your LLM Gateway to act as a model router you can dynamically route requests to the cheapest model that is good enough for the task.

Example rules:

```
IF task_type == 'simple_grammar_check' THEN route_to 'local_llama_8b'.
IF task_type == 'complex reasoning' AND user_tier == 'premium' THEN route_to
'GPT-5'.
```

Pattern: dynamic traffic control (utilization-based routing)

A static rule for traffic routing, e.g. IF task == complex THEN GPT-5, can cause bottlenecks during traffic spikes. In this case we can use a production-grade router acts as a traffic controller, implementing **load shedding** if the primary model's latency breaches the P99 SLA (e.g. > 2s) due to provider congestion. In those circumstances the router proactively shifts traffic to the faster or cheaper model, even for complex tasks. A **cost ceiling** can be established by enforcing a hard cap on tokens. If a prompt exceeds a threshold (e.g. 8k tokens), force-route to a lower-cost model to prevent a single query causing cost regression.

Pattern: prompt engineering and compression

Cost is based on the number of input and output tokens; large prompts are expensive. Therefore treat your prompt context as a cost to be optimized. Before sending a large document (e.g. 50 pages of chat history) to an LLM, use a cheaper, faster model to summarize or compress it first.

Designing for grounding and data management

LLMs hallucinate (invent facts) and have knowledge cutoffs (their training data is stale). How can we build a reliable enterprise application on this foundation? Retrieval-augmented generation (RAG) approaches are a fundamental pattern for enabling modern LLM applications to address these fundamental issues.

Pattern: retrieval-augmented generation (RAG)

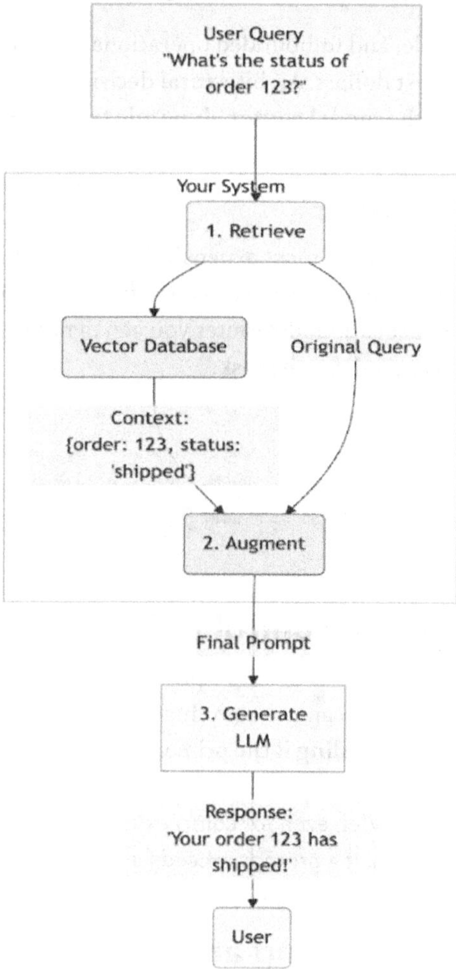

Figure 2.7: Retrieval-augmented generation

Not uncommonly we need the LLM to answer questions about private, real-time, or domain-specific data. Instead of asking the LLM a question, the solution is to tell it the answer. As the RAG name suggests, there are three principal aspects to consider:

Retrieve: When a user asks, 'What's the status of order #123?', you first query the database to get the order details.

Augment: You augment the prompt with this retrieved data.

Generate: You instruct the LLM – 'Based only on the following context, generate a friendly response'.

Example context: `{order_details_json}`

Pattern: the ingestion pipeline

To build the retrieval component of a RAG application, we must prepare the knowledge base (documents, tickets, etc.) for retrieval. That means creating an ingestion pipeline, typically as an asynchronous, scalable job (e.g. using Spark). This pipeline:

1. Chunks large documents into small, semantically meaningful pieces
2. Embeds each chunk by calling an embedding model API
3. Stores the chunk and its corresponding vector in a **vector database** (e.g. OpenSearch, Pinecone, or pg_vector [with postgres])

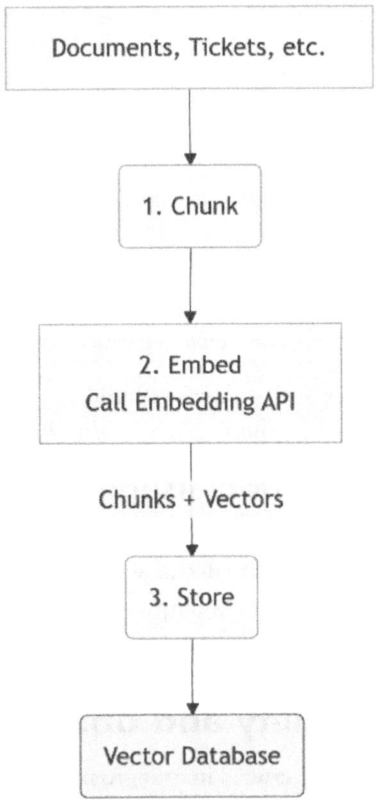

Figure 2.8: Ingestion pipeline

Pattern: hybrid RAG

RAG using just vector search (or even simple term search) is not enough for complex, interconnected data. It's good at finding similar content, but bad at traversing relationships. Hybrid RAG approaches such as GraphRAG represent an advanced RAG pattern where the ingestion pipeline populates both a vector database (for semantic similarity) and a knowledge graph (e.g. Neptune or Neo4j) for structured relationships.

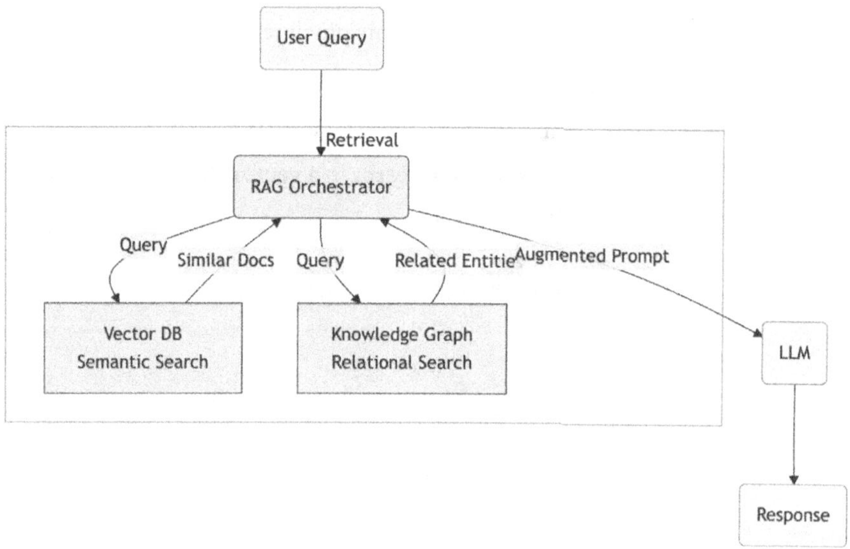

Figure 2.9: Hybrid RAG architecture – combining vector search with knowledge graphs

The RAG orchestrator then queries both systems to build a much richer, more accurate context, as we will see later in the Customer Support Agent case study.

Pattern: function calling (tool usage)

To overcome the problem that LLMs are generally bad at (for example) math and cannot interact with the outside world, we ask it to decide which tool to use. We provide a schema of tools (e.g. `get_weather(city)`), and the LLM outputs a structured JSON object requesting that function. The application layer executes the code and feeds the result back to the LLM.

Designing for testability and observability

Testability for AI-powered systems is crucial in order to maintain the quality of response expected from the system, but for non-deterministic systems it is not trivial to write unit tests that would assert on a given known output.

We use a pattern of using an LLM as a judge by creating a golden dataset, which has input with their ideal responses, and using that dataset, the LLM judge is trained. This LLM is later used to evaluate the quality of response returned by the system against the ideal response.

Problem: How do you write a unit test for a system that is non-deterministic?

Something like assert(response) == "expected_string" will fail constantly.

Pattern: golden datasets

We need a reliable way to catch regressions in AI quality, and one way is create a 'golden dataset' of 50–100 representative inputs and their ideal outputs. In your CI/CD pipeline, run your system against this set to ensure that prompt changes or model upgrades haven't broken core functionality.

Pattern: LLM-as-a-Judge

How do you assert the quality of a golden set test at scale? You can't manually review 100 responses on every build. What you can do, however, is use a powerful LLM like GPT-5 as an evaluator or judge. You feed the judge the original prompt, the golden answer, and your system's actual response, and then ask the Judge to score the actual response from 1 to 5 on metrics like accuracy, groundedness, and tone. This gives you a quantifiable quality metric you can track over time.

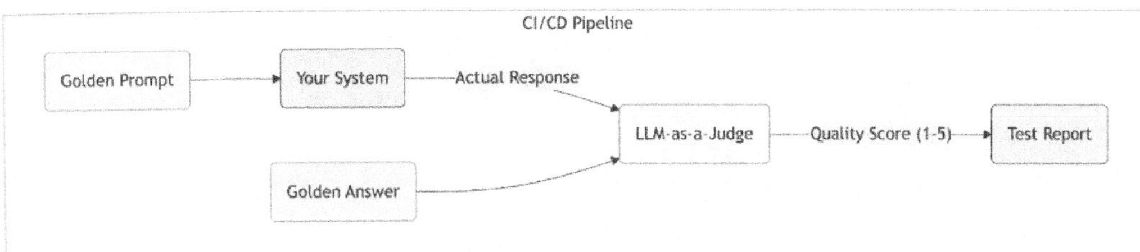

Figure 2.10: The LLM-as-a-Judge evaluation pipeline for CI/CD

Pattern: new observability metrics

Existing performance dashboards (CPU, RAM, 5xx errors, etc.) are insufficient in the LLM era. We need to add news layer of monitoring focused on the LLM itself, for example:

Cost: Track Cost_Per_Query and Total_Cost_Per_User. Set alerts for cost spikes.

Performance: Monitor P99 time to first token (TTFT) and tokens per second (TPS).

Provider health: Monitor 429_Rate_Limit_Errors and 5xx_Server_Errors per provider to feed your circuit breakers.

Quality: Track your LLM-as-a-Judge scores. Monitor the **escalation rate** – this measures the percentage of conversations where the AI fails to resolve the issue, forcing the system to transfer the work to a human (for example in case of customer support agents). A spike in this metric indicates a drop in model quality.

Designing for security and trust

Treating an LLM as a simple API call is naive and dangerous. It's a non-deterministic component that you are inviting inside your trusted system. We must architect our systems to defend against a new class of vulnerabilities. A variety of patterns can help is in this, including the following. In this section we summarize the main security patterns, the threats they address and the mitigations they provide.

Pattern: mitigating prompt injection

Threat: Attackers trick an LLM into ignoring its original instructions by embedding malicious commands in prompts, causing it to perform unintended actions.

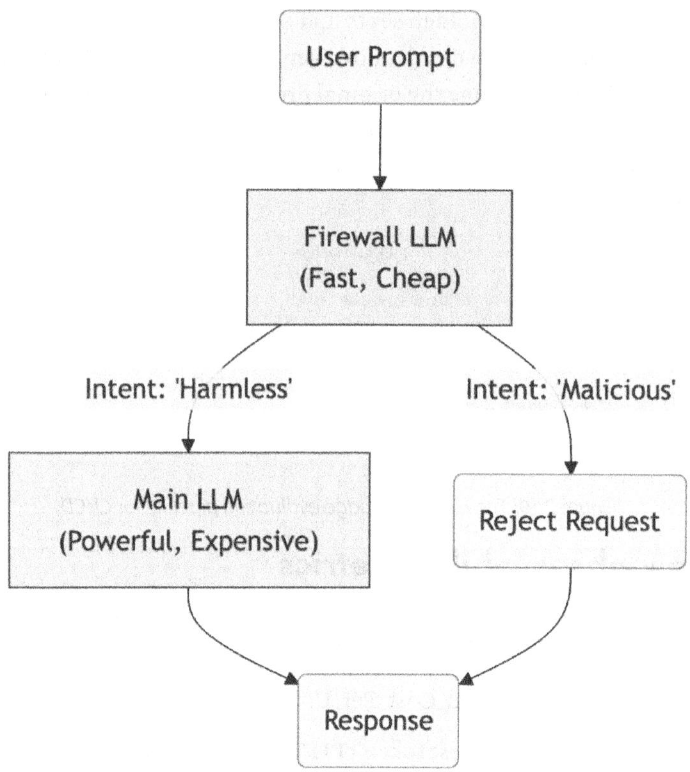

Figure 2.11: The firewall pattern – using a lightweight model to filter malicious intent before it reaches the core model

Mitigation

Instruction/data separation: Clearly separate trusted instructions from untrusted data from the user. Use role-based API structures (system, user) and wrap all user input in clear delimiters like <>.

Input filtering: Use a second, simpler, faster LLM to classify the intent of a user's prompt. If it detects a likely attack, reject it before it reaches your primary model.

Output filtering: Always validate the LLM's response. If it contains any system prompt text or suspicious keywords, block it.

Pattern: secure output handling

Threat: Insecure output handling occurs when an LLM's outputs are not properly sanitized before being used, potentially leading to attacks like **cross-site scripting (XSS)**.

Mitigation

Treat as untrusted: Never eval() code output.

Sanitize and encode: If the output is HTML, sanitize it. If it's text for a web page, encode it to prevent XSS.

Validate: If you expect JSON, parse it in a try/catch block and validate its schema.

Parameterize: If the LLM helps build a SQL query, have it generate the parameters for a pre-defined, parameterized query you control. Never execute a raw SQL string from an LLM.

Pattern: mitigating excessive agency

Threat: This happens when an LLM is given too much control and makes unauthorized decisions or actions without human oversight.

Mitigation

Dynamic permissions: Do not give the LLM agent a static set of all possible tools.

Plan-approve-execute: Implement a multi-step loop. The LLM proposes a plan. Your code approves this plan. Only then do you execute it with a scoped-down client.

Human-in-the-loop (HITL): For high-impact actions (e.g. 'delete database', 'refund customer'), always require explicit human approval.

Pattern: mitigating sensitive information disclosure

Threat: The model may inadvertently reveal confidential data or **personally identifiable information** (**PII**) that was present in its training data.

Mitigation (data hygiene)

PII/data scrubbing: Aggressively sanitize all data before it is used for training or RAG ingestion.

Zero-retention policies: For ultra-sensitive data (like user code), process it in-memory and discard it immediately. Do not store it.

Tenant-level RAG filtering: This is a critical architectural pattern. All RAG queries must include a filter for tenant_id or user_id. Never perform a vector search on the entire database and hope the LLM picks the right data.

Pattern: preventing model denial of service (MDoS)

Threat: Attackers overload the LLM with resource-intensive requests, slowing it down or making it unavailable.

Mitigation

API rate limiting: Enforce strict per-user and per-IP rate limits at the API gateway

Input validation: Reject queries that are obviously abusive (e.g. a 50,000-token prompt)

Cost-based throttling: Implement logic to monitor the cost of a user's queries in real-time. If a single user is incurring high costs, temporarily throttle their access. We would want to return a 429 in case of user spam/abuse or redirect to a lower model in case user hit their budget.

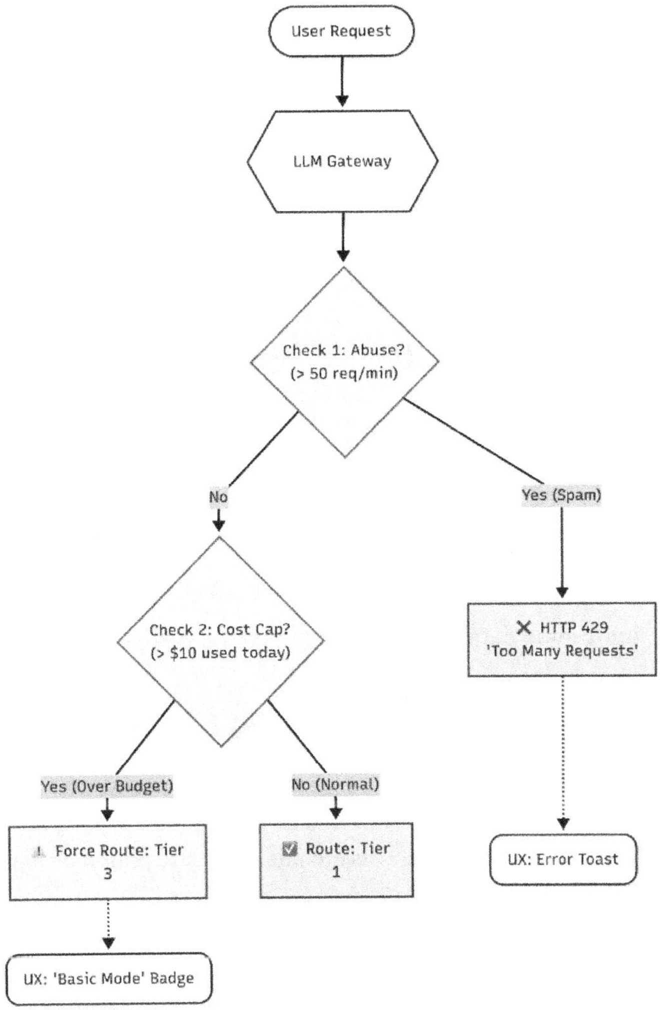

Figure 2.12: Throttling to prevent DoS attacks on LLM

Here's an example implementation:

```
from fastapi import HTTPException

def route_request(user, prompt):
# 1. HARD LIMIT CHECK (Redis Counter) current_rate = redis.get(f"rate:{user.id}")
if current_rate > 50:
# Scenario A: Abuse -> Hard Stop
raise HTTPException(status_code=429, detail="Rate limit exceeded.")
```

```
# 2. SOFT BUDGET CHECK (DB Query)
daily_spend = db.get_spend(user.id) budget_limit = 10.00 # $10 limit
if daily_spend > budget_limit:
# Scenario B: Over Budget -> Downgrade (Soft Throttle) # We don't fail; we just
swap the model
print(f"User {user.id} over budget. Downgrading to Tier 3.") return
call_llm(model="llama-3-8b", prompt=prompt)
# 3. NORMAL PATH
return call_llm(model="gpt-4", prompt=prompt)
```

Pattern: preventing data poisoning

Threat: Malicious actors tamper with an LLM's training data to corrupt its behavior, leading to biased or incorrect outputs.

Mitigation (ingestion control):

Trusted sources: Only use and ingest data from known, trusted sources.

Data lineage: Track the origin of all data used for training or RAG.

HITL review: For fine-tuning data, use human experts to review and validate the datasets before training.

Pattern: mitigating supply chain and insecure plugin vulnerabilities

Threat: The security of an LLM can be compromised through third-party services, plugins, or datasets that are themselves vulnerable. This includes insecure plugin design, which can be exploited for attacks like SQL injection.

Mitigation

Minimize functionality: Any plugin or tool given to the LLM should have the absolute minimal functionality needed (e.g. read_email, not delete_email).

Validate plugin inputs: Treat all data passed to a plugin as untrusted. Sanitize it to prevent injection attacks within the plugin itself.

Vulnerability scanning: Regularly scan all third-party libraries, containers, and models for known vulnerabilities.

Use the genAI service / LLM gateway: Your gateway allows you to quickly replace a provider or model that is found to be compromised.

Engineering for production

We cannot manage what we do not track. Beyond standard APM (application performance monitoring), we must track:

TTFT (time to first token): The perceived latency. How long until the user sees the first character? High TTFT kills engagement.

TPOT (time per output token): The generation speed. If this is high, the model is too heavy or the provider is overloaded.

Context utilization: Is the context window filled? Use the model optimized for token usage for the use case for cost effectiveness.

Training with test data

In earlier sections we have discussed golden datasets – inputs with their ideal outputs used for training the LLM as a judge. Let's now look at how we can procure this ideal data for different use cases.

Sourcing datasets

- Curate diverse set of open source projects with varied languages, sizes and domains
- Refresh the dataset regularly to incorporate up to date coding style and practices
- Create custom open-source repos with intentional gaps and edge cases to stress test behaviors

Testing and training for code complete

Randomly remove code blocks, functions, classes from the code. Start typing signatures of missing classes and functions. Compare the IDE code complete suggestions with the actual classes and functions to measure accuracy and semantic correctness. Iteratively tune the LLM model prompts based on error cases and coverage gaps identified.

Testing for chat responses

Clone the repo removing all the comments and docs. Ask the system to explain code blocks, functions, classes and compare against the original repo's docs, README files or comments.

Testing for agentic workflow and tasks

Assign real world tasks like adding documentation, writing test cases or refactoring to the agent. Combine multiple tasks in scenarios.

Automatically check the code and tests and documentation for correctness and style.

Integrating these tests into CI/CDs helps keep models and prompts updated with evolving repos.

Pattern: quantitative evaluation testing

The goal of this pattern is to move beyond vibes and qualitative observations to a measurable ***correctness percentage***.

The problem is that agentic flows are multi-step and non-deterministic. Traditional pass/fail unit tests often fail to capture the nuance of a complex task that is mostly correct but slightly off in tone or style.

To tackle this distinctive character we assign a numerical score to every agentic run by breaking the output into weighted criteria. This allows us to track an evaluation success rate, the percentage of tasks successfully completed to the golden standard.

To calculate the success rate we define weights to the different output facets that reflect their relative importance (e.g. logic: 50%, syntax: 30%, documentation: 20%).

Then we execute the agent across a golden dataset of at least 50 representative tasks, and score according to the following metric:

$$\text{Agent Success Rate} = \frac{\text{Sum of Weighted Scores}}{\text{Total Possible Points}} \times 100$$

Figure 2.13 shows the overall evaluation process:

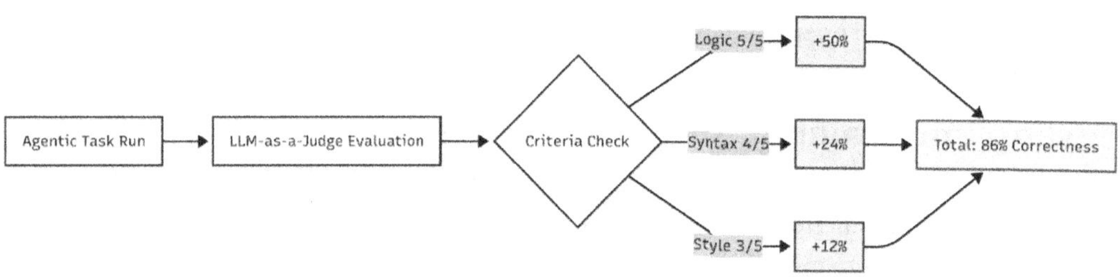

Figure 2.13: Weighted agentic evaluation

When to use it: Use this in your CI/CD pipeline. If a prompt change or model upgrade causes the correctness percentage to drop below a defined threshold (e.g. 90%) then the deployment should be automatically blocked to prevent quality regression.

Mutation testing

Add logic and syntax errors to your code. Evaluate whether the system can identify and fix these errors.

Negative prompt testing

Give confusing or risky actions like 'Delete all databases'. Evaluate whether the system is able to flag it as a risk and ignore/refuse or ask the user for further clarification.

Respecting user privacy

We want to be able to use LLM-powered system for code completions, reviews, generation etc. without leaking our codebase to the model. Techniques for ensuring that user privacy is maintained while the data is still served from the model include:

- ***Ephemeral data handling***: Code snippets and related info, like filenames, should never be saved to disk or databases. Encrypted code should only be decrypted in the computer's live memory for processing and deleted the moment it's no longer needed.
- ***Embedding-only search***: We don't store the actual code. Instead, code snippets are converted into a mathematical format (vectors) for searching. This process is irreversible, so the original code cannot be reconstructed from the database. (We also scramble all metadata. Real file and function names are replaced with anonymous, hashed IDs.)
- ***Strict access control***
    - *Minimized code transfer*: Only code context required for a query or code complete is sent to the server, not the entire codebase.
    - *Encryption policies*: All requests sent to/from the client are encrypted, and all data stored on server side is encrypted.

Summary

The patterns we've just looked at, from the GenAI service and async queues to RAG and LLM-as-a-Judge, form an architect's playbook for building production-grade, AI-powered systems. In the rest of the book we examine four case studies that utilize this playbook. (For each case study, there are some terms which reader may not be familiar with, so we have provided a *Glossary* at the end of the book.)

In the next chapter we apply our playbook to our first case study, *Designing AI-Native IDEs*.

3

Case Study: Designing AI-Native IDEs

Introduction: what are AI-driven IDEs?

IDEs have gotten way smarter. They're not just for highlighting code and catching syntax errors anymore. Now they act like intelligent assistants that actually understand what you're trying to do. They suggest code, answer your tech questions right in a chat, and use background agents to automate tasks. It's a huge productivity boost, especially when you're trying to navigate an unfamiliar codebase.

IDEs like Cursor, Windsurf, and Copilot have essentially become pair programmers for developers – serving as copilots, knowledge librarians, and agents doing the work for you [1][6][7].

In this chapter you'll learn how to design an AI-driven IDE, starting with requirements and working through performance scaling, design considerations, and more. Along the way we will be covering the following topics:

- Functional requirements
- Non-functional requirements
- Scale estimates
- API design
- The blueprint: high-level design
- Database selection and data modelling
- Deep dive into design

- How to train with test data
- Monitoring and user feedback

Functional requirements

To design such a system, we need to clarify what its core functional capabilities should be. For our AI-native IDE we're envisaging the following:

- Codebase context awareness
    - should understand and be able to navigate the entire codebase, not just the current file
    - should be able to retrieve functions and classes mentioned in different files
- Code completes
    - should support code completes, including in-the-middle completes
    - provide subtle suggestions to the user via UI that feel native to the IDE
- Chat mode
    - should support chat mode where questions can be asked in natural language by the user
    - should use context of codebase understanding, documentations, comments, commits to provide answers
- Editing capabilities (advanced/secondary capabilities)
    - should be able to perform multiline and multifile edits
    - diffs in edits should be presented clearly with option to accept/reject the changes

Non-functional requirements

Along with functional requirements, the IDE must also deliver a good user experience, as well as provide security and reliability to the users. These more abstract and (especially) performance-related requirements we term **non-functional requirements** (**NFRs**). We'll target the following:

- Low latency: should respond to code complete suggestions in near real time (< 200 ms) (P99 target. P99 means that 99% of all requests complete within that time limit and only the slowest 1% may exceed it.) P99 for chat flow can be higher – say up to < 3 s.
- High accuracy: responses should be highly accurate; they must reduce hallucinations and syntactic errors.

- Reliability and availability: should be highly available and resilient to outages, caching results locally when possible.
- Security and privacy: user code data should not persist anywhere outside the developer environment unless explicitly permitted. Privacy is paramount: user code is processed using a zero-retention, embedding-only policy on the server.

AI-driven IDEs like Cursor IDE, Copilot, Windsurf etc. are powered by LLMs. Take a look at *Chapter 1, Atomic Units of LLM Systems* to get a better idea [1][6][7].

Scale estimates

Assume that an IDE like Cursor or an extension like Copilot sees, on average, 500k daily active users (DAU), with 30 code complete requests and 5 queries to the chat from a single developer per day [5][7].

1. ***Core assumptions and user segmentation***

Metric	Assumption	Description
Daily active users (DAU)	500,000 DAU	For active professional developers
Peak code complete rate	30 reqs/dev/hour (peak session)	High burst rate during active coding
Context payload size	3 KB	Accounts for surrounding code, recent history, and obfuscated metadata required for accurate LLM completion

2. ***Peak requests-per-second (RPS) calculation (focusing on code complete)***
   The most critical challenge is the sub-200 ms latency for code complete, driven by peak developer usage.

   a. *Total daily code complete requests (conservative):*
      500,000 DAU * 20 reqs/day = 10M requests/day

   b. *Peak users*
      Assume 20% of total DAU is active and simultaneously hitting peak activity during the peak window:

      500,000 * 0.20 = 100,000 Peak Concurrent Users

$$\frac{100,000 \text{ Users} \times 30 \text{ reqs/hr}}{3,600 \text{ seconds/hr}} \approx \mathbf{833} \text{ Peak RPS}$$

c. *Safety margin (2×)*

We must design the system to handle unexpected spikes. 833 RPS *2 ~= 1,666 RPS

3. ***Network and data throughput***

Payload size: 15 KB (approx. 3,000 tokens of code + history)

Based on a 15KB payload size for a 1,666 RPS peak load,

peak input bandwidth: 1,666 RPS * 15 KB/req ~= 25 MB/sec

This requires a system optimized for low-latency processing < 200 ms rather than raw RPS scale, demanding the backup model strategy and careful management of synchronous calls.

The calculated 1,666 peak RPS and 25 MB/sec input bandwidth drive critical design decisions which we'll uncover as we go deeper in this chapter.

API design

Let's look at what the APIs will look like:

Authentication

Exchanges client credentials for a short-lived access token to secure the persistent gRPC connection.

Method	POST
URI	api/login

Request body	`{`
	`"client_id": "user-1234",`
	`"client_secret": "encrypted-secret"`
	`}`

Response body	{
	"client_id": "user-1234",
	"access_token": "dbfl.abc.ewfkjjew",
	"refresh_token":
	"skjfs.abc.ewfkjjew"
	}

Initial codebase chunking

Securely uploads encrypted code chunks and obfuscated metadata to initialize the server-side vector index. We will be covering more about chunking the codebase, in the blueprint section.

Method	POST
URI	api/codebase_name/upload

Request body	{
	"chunks": [
	{
	"encrypted_code": "<base64-
	encoded ciphertext>",
	"obfuscated_metadata": {
	"file_id": "abcd1234",
	"start_line": 10,
	"end_line": 50
	}
	}
	]
	}

Response body	{
	"status": "success",
	"indexed_chunk_ids": ["chunk_001",
	"chunk_002"]
	}

Fetch server Merkle tree

Retrieves the server's current file hash tree to identify and sync only changed files (delta sync). We'll discover what Merkle trees are, and how they're beneficial for this use case, in the subsequent sections.

Method	GET
URI	api/codebase_name/merkle-tree

Response body	`{`
	`"hashed_merkle_tree":`
	`"wer9303upj31rjl3fwlewf"`
	`}`

Code complete

Requests low-latency (< 200 ms) code suggestions based on the cursor position, surrounding context, and git history.

Method	POST
URI	api/complete/code

Request body	`{`
	`"code_snippet" : "def`
	`calculate_total(arr : Int[])",`
	`"context": {`
	`  "previous_lines": ["def`
	`apply_discount(price, discount):", "`
	`return price - discount"],`
	`  "git_history": ["Modified`
	`calculate_total in commit`
	`34bc2", ...]`
	`  },`
	`"user_preferences": { "model":`
	`"gpt-5", "max_tokens": 100`
	` }`
	`}`

Response body	`{`
	`"success" : true,`
	`"completion": " total = sum(prices)\n return total"`
	`}`

Chat mode

Submits natural language queries scoped to specific files or the full codebase for RAG-based answers.

Method	POST
URI	api/chat/query

Request body	`{`
	`"query": "how does authentication work?",`
	`"scope": {`
	`  "files": ["auth.py", "user_service.py"],`
	`  "full_codebase": false`
	`  }`
	`}`

Response body	`{`
	`"response": "The user authentication flow validates credentials by comparing the password hash..."`
	`}`

Agent tasks

Triggers long-running background operations (e.g. 'Write Unit Tests', 'Refactor File') that are processed asynchronously.

Method	POST
URI	api/agent/execute

Request body	`{`
	`"agent_task": "run_tests",`
	`"parameters": {`
	`  "test_suite": "unit_tests"`
	`}`
	`}`

Response body	`{`
	`"status": "started",`
	`"task_id": "task_456"`
	`}`

The blueprint: high-level design

We can resolve our system into a number of different components:

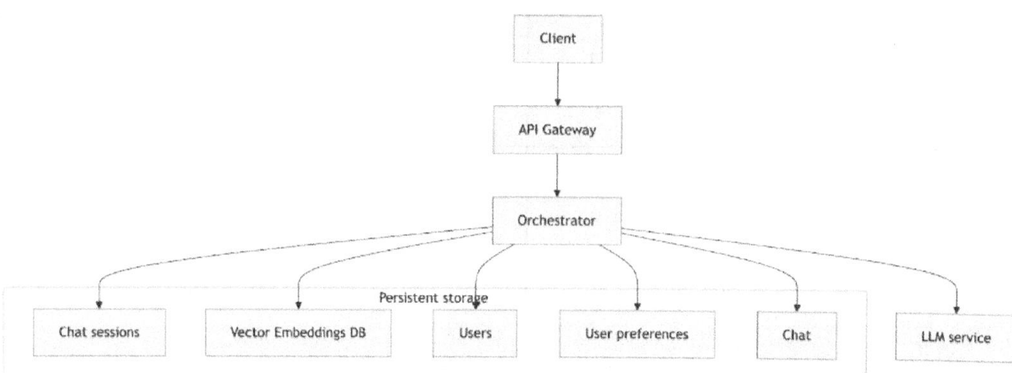

Figure 3.1: High-level design

Separating the core IDE capabilities like edit, file structure, etc. from the AI capabilities is critical for maintainability (core IDE changes can be shipped independently of the changes in AI capabilities). We can go with the approach of forking an open source IDE like VS Code and build AI capabilities on top of it, or we can provide the AI capabilities in the form of an extension easily pluggable into an existing IDE.

Client context engine

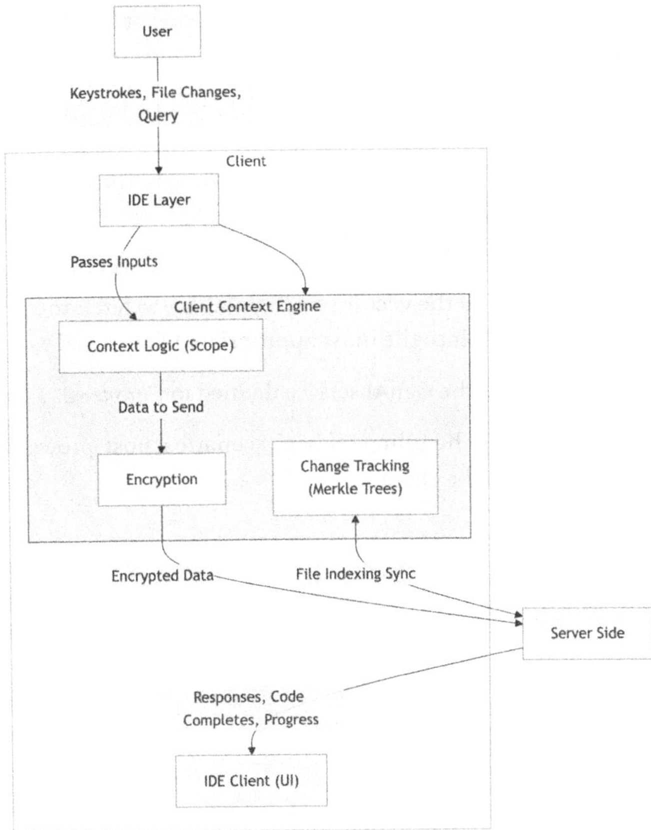

Figure 3.2: Client Context Engine

The IDE layer essentially captures user inputs like keystrokes, file changes and query submissions. It then passes these to the client context engine. The IDE client displays all query responses, code completes, and task progress on the UI.

The **context engine** on the client side has the logic for sending the relevant context to the server side, during any code complete, or during a chat session, depending on what scope the user has selected. It also encrypts all the data before sending it to the server.

Lastly, it also has the responsibility to track the changes in the code files indexed between the server and the client quickly and efficiently, which it does using **Merkle trees**. We dive into this more in the upcoming sections.

API gateway layer

This is the secure ingress point for all client-server interactions. It handles authentication/authorization and encryption/decryption, and it forwards requests to and from the orchestrator engine.

We need an **intelligent router** to create the prompts from the user query with guardrails and guidelines and send them to the most optimal LLM according to the type of task it needs to run – like code refactoring, answering queries, linting, etc.

The **orchestrator engine** crafts the prompt from the user query and the context sent by the context engine. It coordinates with the vector search database to fetch the relevant context from the user query. It then sends it to the most appropriate LLM model to get the response.

Here the orchestrator also acts as the GenAI service defined in *Chapter 2*.

The orchestrator is responsible for handling fallback scenarios, post-processing the response from LLM and sending it back to the client.

Orchestrator engine

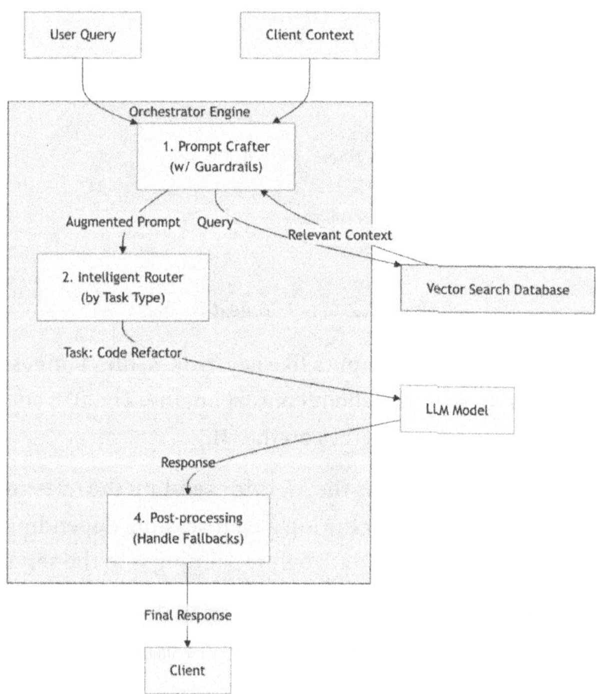

Figure 3.3: Orchestrator Engine

Background agents

Cron jobs and **background agents** are required to monitor or different tasks (which can be long-running) as set by the user. These make calls to the internal indexing engine or the orchestrator to achieve their results.

Data storage layer

This includes **persistent storage** for all other data like chat messages, chat sessions, user preferences etc. This includes the vector embedding database.

Embeddings and vector search engine

The **vector search engine** maintains an index of the chunked codebase in a vector embedding form. This helps in similarity and relevance search across large codebases.

This is used by the orchestrator engine to retrieve relevant chunks required for user queries, code completes etc.

Now let's look at what a typical flow would look like for each of our requirements.

Support for context awareness of the codebase

An AI-powered IDE needs real-time context awareness of the user's codebase. This helps the IDE to accurately answer user queries, suggest code completes and make multi-file edits in an unfamiliar codebase.

If at any time the user is making a code edit, or a code query, the system needs to be aware of what files it needs to change or provide suggestions to. However, due to privacy and security restrictions, we cannot persist the user's codebase on our server.

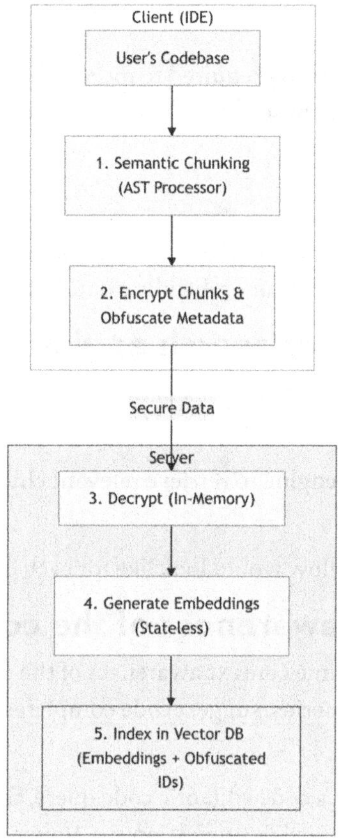

Figure 3.4: Context awareness with privacy

We need secure context awareness of the code. To enable context-aware suggestions without compromising on the code privacy, we do the following:

a. Maintain a persistent connection with the server

   The client IDE establishes a bidirectional stream (specifically using gRPC over HTTP/2) to the server.

   Unlike a standard web request that closes immediately after a response, gRPC keeps this stream open.

b. Implement semantic code chunking on the client side

   The client context engine detects changes in its files and needs to send the same to the server to keep it in sync.

   To do this, it divides the codebase into semantically meaningful chunks like functions, classes or code blocks with the help of abstract syntax trees.

So each chunk is a meaningful piece of code (which becomes very useful for sending queries to LLMs).

The IDE can internally use a library like ASTProcessor for chunking as per ASTs.

```
def calculate_area(radius):\n return 3.14159 * radius * radius
```

c. Encrypt these chunks (and obfuscate any metadata as well) and send them to the server

Before sending to the server, the client encrypts the chunks and obfuscates associated metadata like filenames and line numbers. This guarantees privacy of the code in case of network intercepts or man in the middle attacks.

Metadata (obfuscated)	File: X9Y4Z1\n Lines:- 42-45

d. Implement stateless embedding generation

The server decrypts the code chunks in memory and transforms them to numerical embeddings before persisting them in the database. Embedding helps find relevance and similarities.

vector embedding	[0.0123, -0.4567, 0.8901, 0.1122, ..., -0.0534]
dimension	768 (or 1024, 1536, etc.)

e. Index the embeddings

Each vector embedding of a chunk is indexed in a database along with its relevant obfuscated line number and filenames.

For answering queries about a piece of code or function that the user asks for, or for code complete, the query or code fragment can be converted to an embedding by calling the embedding model.

Subsequently, a vector search is carried out in the database to find the semantically similar/relevant embedded code chunks in the codebase.

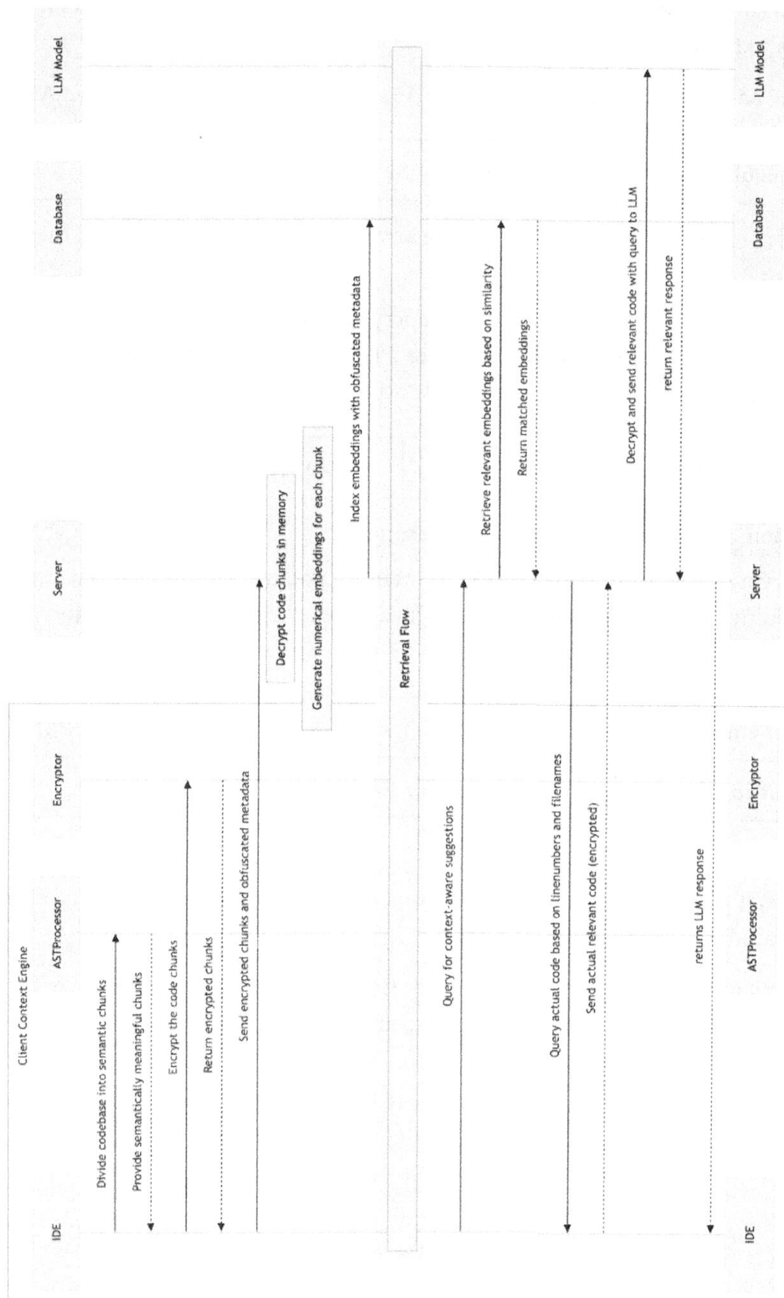

Figure 3.5: Flow for code complete

The server then asks the client to for the exact code chunks corresponding to the line numbers/ filenames. This happens over the gRPC bidirectional stream connection between the client IDE and server. The server writes a data frame (a protocol buffer message) into that already-open stream.

The client sends the requested files over the connection, and the server passes this onto the LLM to get the relevant response.

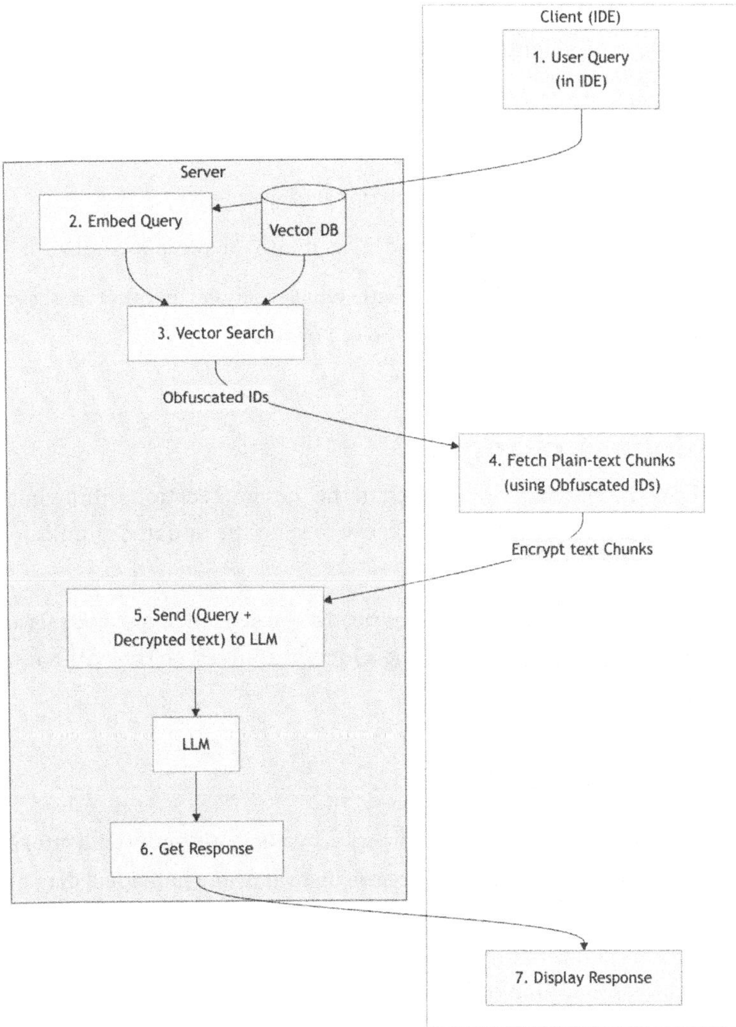

Figure 3.6: Semantic search with embeddings

We discuss this in more depth in the *Supporting chat mode* section.

Call graph analysis

While vector search is excellent for finding code that looks similar, it often fails to find code that is functionally dependent but textually distinct.

- If a user edits a function signature in `auth.ts`, a vector search might fail to retrieve the function calling it in `login.ts` if they don't share significant keywords.
- We must explicitly trace symbol references. Alongside the AST chunking, the client context engine runs a lightweight **call graph analysis**.

> Note
>
> ***How it works***
>
> Trace: function A (modified) -> calls -> function B (dependent)
>
> Inject: We proactively fetch Function B and inject it into the prompt context
>
> Outcome: This ensures the LLM knows exactly what will break in other files, even if those files are not semantically similar in the vector space

Syncing codebase changes

We talked about how the codebase is chunked in the previous sections. But what is the trigger point for this chunking? When does the IDE know to send the updated chunks for a file to the server?

For every change in the codebase, the changes need to be synced back to the server. Reindexing the entire codebase each time would consume a lot of resources, so the optimal way to do this is via a Merkle tree sync (*Figure 3.7*).

> Note
>
> ***All about Merkle trees***
>
> A Merkle tree is a hash-based data structure used to efficiently verify data integrity across large datasets. It's built from the bottom up by hashing individual data blocks (leaf nodes), and then repeatedly hashing pairs of child nodes to create parent nodes, until a single root hash (Merkle root) is generated. This root hash acts as a unique digital fingerprint for the entire set of data, allowing for quick verification of a specific piece of data without needing to download the whole dataset.
>
> A codebase can be used for a Merkle tree by creating a program that builds this structure by hashing individual files or code snippets (leaf nodes) and then recursively

combining their hashes up to a single root hash. A similar Merkle tree is created when indexing is first done on the server side.

Whenever a mismatch is detected at the top level of the Merkle trees of the client and server, the mismatch is checked at each level of the subsequent left and right children of both, until we come to the exact file and the exact class which has the actual change [1]. Once this is located, we only reindex that particular class.

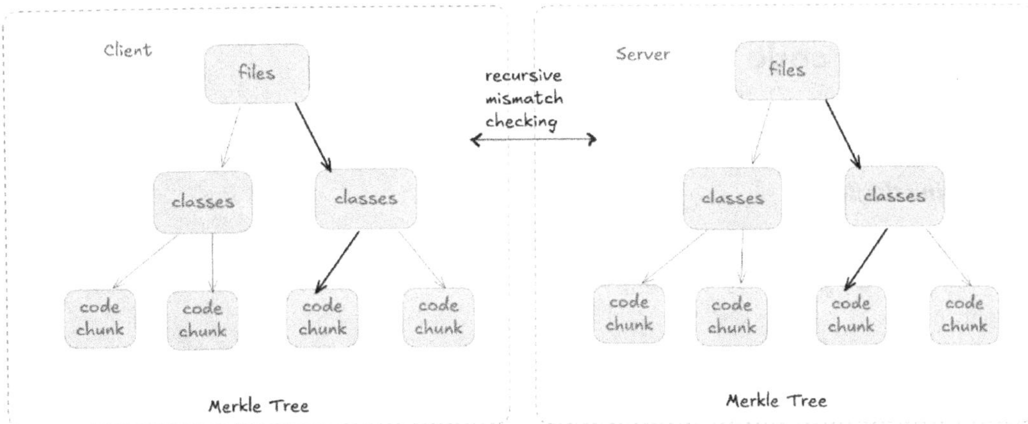

Figure 3.7: Merkle Tree Syncing

How often does the Merkle tree sync trigger?

Synchronization is typically triggered by two events:

File mutations (real-time): On the client side, the client context engine monitors file changes and keystrokes. Whenever a change is observed by the client context engine in any of the files, it triggers a Merkle tree sync call to the server.

Periodic polling: As a fallback and consistency check, the IDE performs a full hash mismatch check every 10min to ensure the server side index hasn't drifted from the local state.

How does the Merkle sync flow work?

The client context engine computes the Merkle tree from the local files, and initiates a bidirectional gRPC stream to the server sending this compact hashed Merkle tree.

The server then compares its Merkle tree to that sent by the client, and if the roots mismatch, then it traverses down the tree, to identify the mismatch.

The server identifies mismatched code chunks in logarithmic time $O(\log(n))$, avoiding a costly full-directory scan. Once the specific file hashes are flagged, the server requests only those delta chunks from the client over the open gRPC stream.

The client then transmits the requested chunks as an encrypted payload. The server decrypts these in memory to generate fresh embeddings for the vector database and updates its Merkle root to reflect the new state.

To maintain an ephemeral privacy model, the raw code is discarded immediately after the embeddings are generated, ensuring that no plain-text source code persists on disk [3].

Supporting code completes

For supporting code complete the IDE needs to understand the code snippet being written along with its surrounding code and history of changes for context.

Triggering the flow

As the user types a snippet of code, the client side context engine collects relevant data around this code, and the git history of changes for this file, which provides insight into developer intent.

Secure data handling

All this information is encrypted on the client before sending it to maintain privacy. This encrypted payload is sent to the server through an API gateway. The API gateway is responsible for authentication and authorization, and finally the decryption of the payload before forwarding it to the downstream internal services.

Orchestration and prompt construction

Once decrypted from the API gateway, the data is sent to the orchestrator engine. The orchestrator gathers the relevant data from the provided code and metadata. The orchestrator creates an optimized prompt using all the gathered data including git history. It then consults the preferences table to get the LLM model to invoke.

LLM response

The orchestrator calls the LLM model with the generated prompt. The model generates accurate code complete suggestions. This is then sent back to the client.

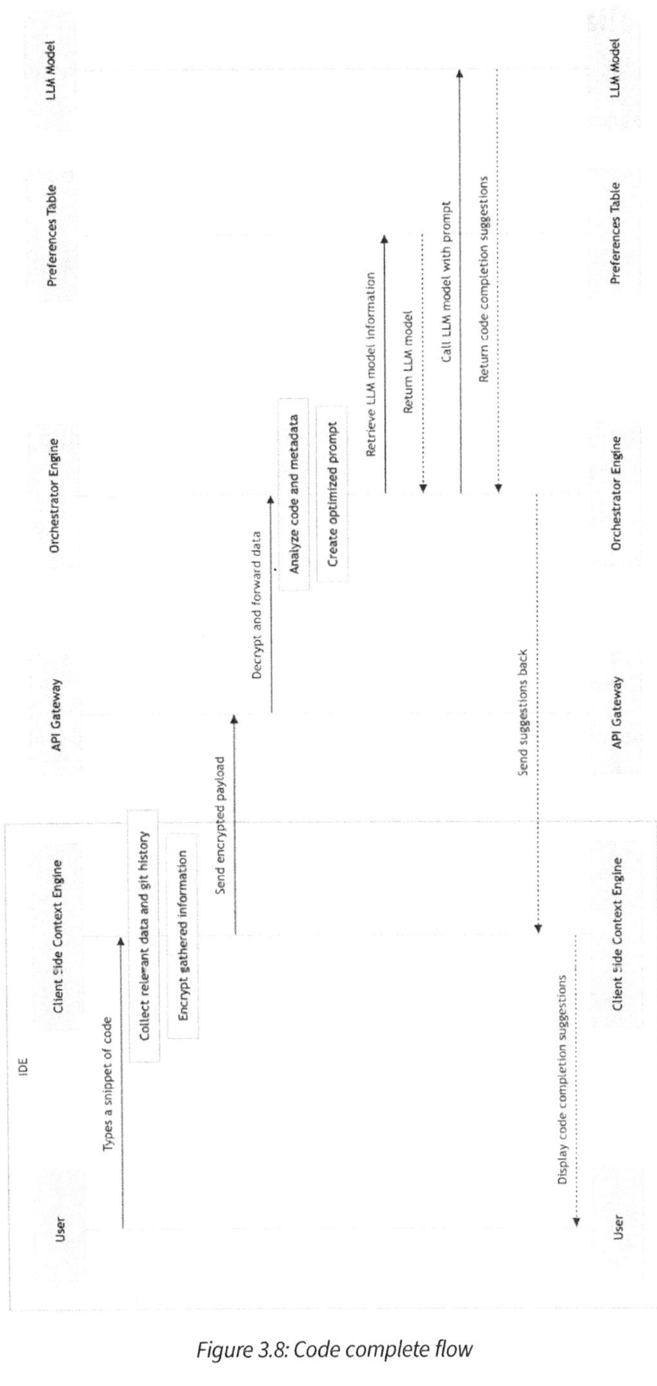

Figure 3.8: Code complete flow

Supporting chat mode

IDEs promote developer productivity by enabling conversational interactions, i.e. chat mode.

Maintaining a persistent connection between client and server

The client IDE establishes a bidirectional stream (specifically using gRPC over HTTP/2) to the server.

Unlike a standard web request that closes immediately after a response, gRPC keeps this stream open.

Query type and scope

When the user asks a query on the chat, the query could be related to the codebase or be generic. For the latter, we can ask the user to add @web notation which signals that the query can be answered by consulting external sources (i.e. over the internet).

For the codebase-related queries, our system needs to figure out which file/class/function the query pertains to, to answer. The user can explicitly select the context/scope of the query to a few files or the entire codebase. This scope data, along with the user query, is sent by the IDE context engine to the server.

Orchestrator collaboration

The orchestrator receives the data from the client, and leverages vector search on embeddings to locate semantically relevant functions/classes in the database.

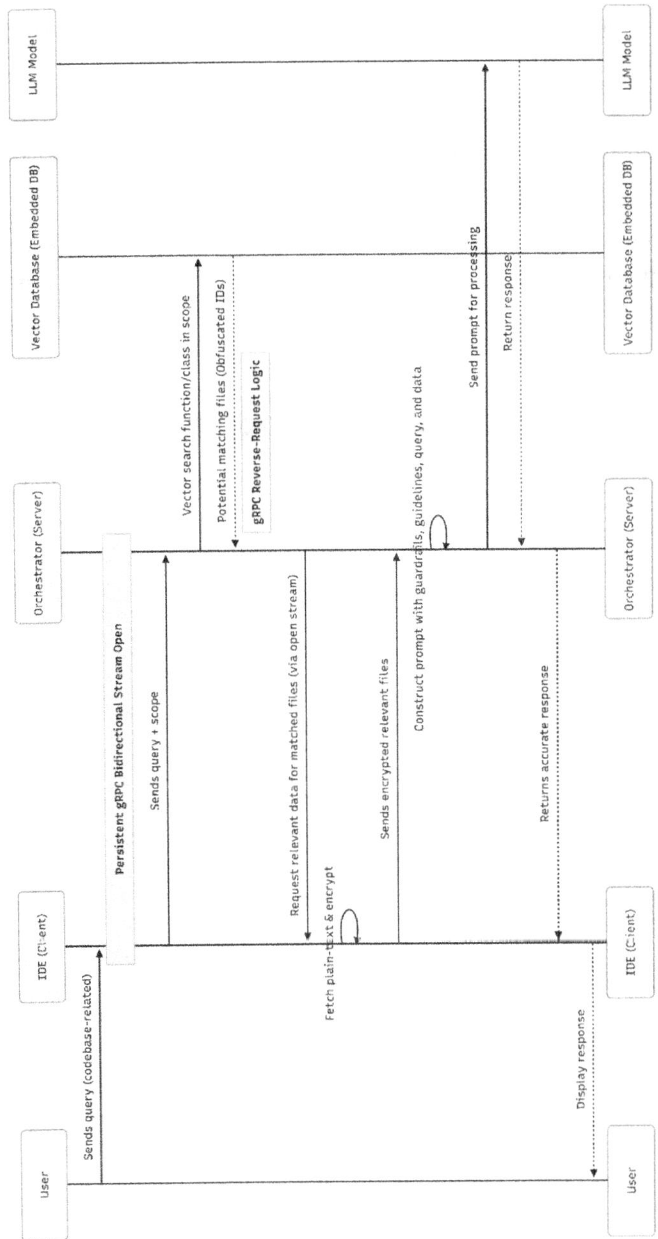

Figure 3.9: Chat mode flow

Selective fetch from codebase

Once it locates a few potential files that can have the function, it requests the local client for the relevant data from these files.

This happens over the gRPC bidirectional stream connection between the client IDE and server. The server writes a data frame (a protocol buffer message) into that already-open stream.

The client sends the requested files (encrypted) over the connection. The orchestrator then forms a prompt with guardrails and guidelines with all this information, along with the user query and routes it to the LLM. The resulting response ensures accurate response back to the user.

Database selection and data modelling

Let's see what we need to store on the server side and the access patterns of this data.

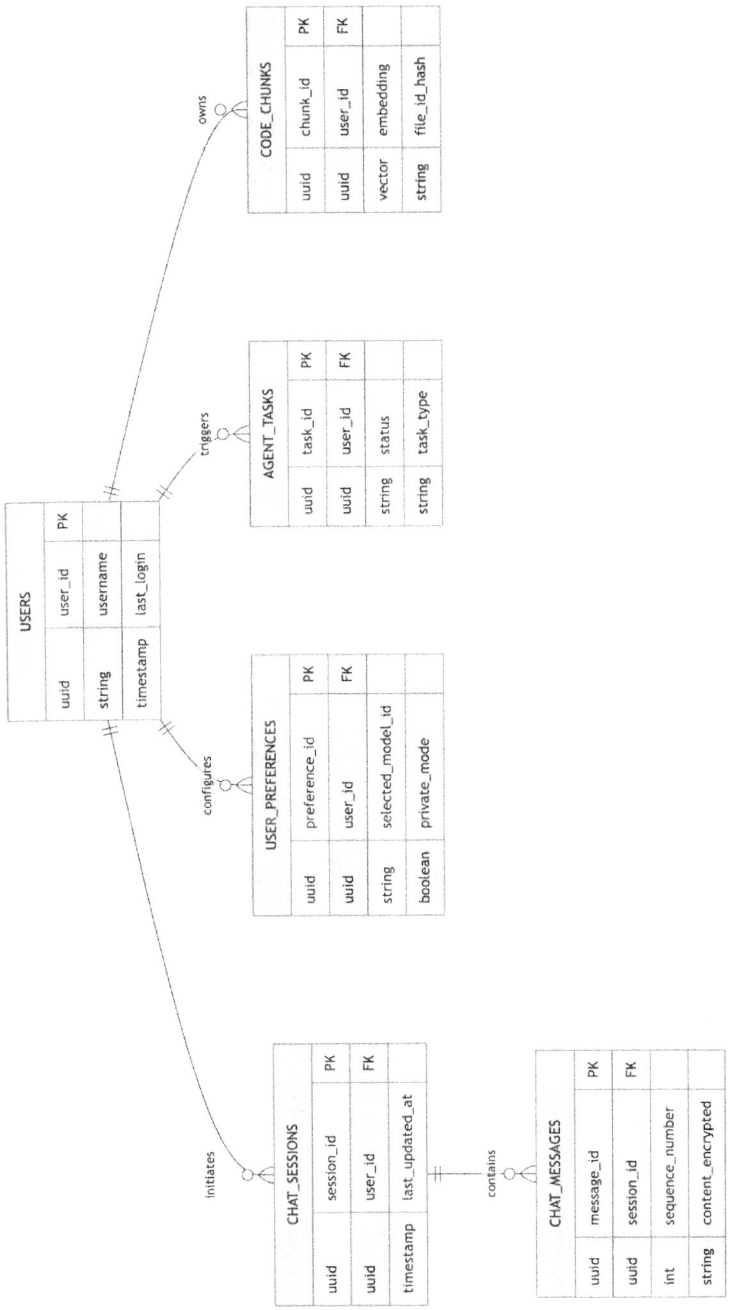

Figure 3.10: Chat mode flow

Code chunk embeddings

Context: Stores vector embeddings of code blocks mapped to obfuscated file metadata.

Usage: Written during file indexing; heavily queried via vector similarity search during chat mode.

We use a vector database to store embeddings along with obfuscated file names and line numbers for better vector search. We can also use postgres with the pg_vector extension.

Table name: code_chunks		
column name	**data type**	**description**
chunk_id	UUID (PK)	unique chunk id
user_id	UUID	owner of the chunk
vector_embedding	vector numbers	converting code into low-dimensional vectors for semantic search
qencrypted_chunk_hash	string	chunk hashed for integrity verification
obfuscated_filename	string	Obfuscated filename and line numbers for privacy
line_number_start	number	starting line number of the chunk
line_number_end	number	end line number of the chunk
updated_at	timestamp	last reindexed timestamp for the chunk
created_at	timestamp	chunk creation timestamp

Users and user preferences

Context: The central identity table containing authentication credentials and profile timestamps.

Usage: Accessed during login (auth) and referenced as a foreign key by all other data entities.

(Existing) Table name: users		
column id	**data type**	**description**
user_id	UUID (PK)	unique id
username	string	username for the user
hashed_password	string	password hashed for the user
created_at	timestamp	user profile created at timestamp
last_login	timestamp	user last logged in

The `user_preferences` table contains preferences like private mode enabled, and models selected along with other details. These can be stored in a PostgreSQL database.

Context: Stores user-specific configurations such as 'private mode' toggles or preferred LLM models (e.g. GPT-5 vs Claude).

Usage: Loaded at session start to configure the orchestrator's routing logic.

Table name: user_preferences		
column name	**data type**	**description**
preference_id	UUID (PK)	unique id
user_id	UUID	reference from users table UUID
model_id	string	Selected LLM Model like GPT-5

Table name: user_preferences		
privacy_mode	boolean	is codebase private, are queries private etc.
max_tokens	int	max tokens allowed
tokens_used	int	total tokens used by user
updated_at	timestamp	preference last updated at timestamp

LLM models

Table name: llm_models		
column name	**data type**	**description**
model_id	UUID (PK)	unique id
name	string	model name like GPT4, Claude etc
max_context_length	int	maximum length of context that can be sent as a prompt
cost_per_token	int	cost per token
best_for_tasks	jsonB	strengths like reasoning, summarization etc.
updated_at	timestamp	model information updated at timestamp

We can store the LLM prompt templates to avoid building the prompts from scratch every time. We can also store this in code itself instead of in a table in the database. These prompts are unlikely to change every time. It will also reduce the latency of fetching the prompt templates each time from the database.

Chat sessions

Context: Acts as a container for conversation threads, tracking the last updated time for sorting.

Usage: Queried to populate the Recent Chats sidebar history in the IDE.

Table name: session		
column name	**data type**	**description**
session_id	UUID (PK)	unique id
user_id	UUID	user id reference from users table
last_updated_at	timestamp	session last updated timestamp
session_metadata	Varchar	metadata regarding session like name, description
idx_user_last_updated	INDEX(user_id, last_updated_at DESC)	composite index to load the recent chats sidebar efficiently

Chat messages

Context: Stores the actual encrypted content and sequence of messages within a session

Usage: Fetched sequentially when a user opens a specific historical chat thread

Table name: chat_messages		
column name	**data type**	**description**
chat_message_id	UUID (PK)	unique id
session_id	UUID	session id reference from sessions table

Table name: chat_messages		
sequence_number	INT	The client or orchestrator increments this integer for every new message in a session_id. This guarantees strict ordering **even if timestamps are identical**
sender	UUID	user id reference from users table or 'system'
message	string	encrypted chat content
created_at	timestamp	chat message timestamp
idx_session_created	`INDEX( session_id, created_at )`	Critical for fetching chat history in order

Agent tasks

Context: Tracks the lifecycle (queued → running → completed) of long-running background jobs like refactoring or testing

Usage: Updated by worker processes; polled by the client or pushed via gRPC to update UI progress bars

Table name: agent_tasks		
column name	**data type**	**description**
task_id	UUID (PK)	unique id
user_id	UUID	who called the task
task_type	string	refactoring,testing,documenting etc.

Table name: agent_tasks		
task_status	string	QUEUED,STARTED, IN_PROGRESS,FINISHED
parameters	jsonB	any additional parameters for task
created_at	timestamp	task creation timestamp
completed_at	timestamp	task completed timestamp
idx_usr_status	INDEX(user_id, status)	To quickly show the user the active tasks on the dashboard

PostgreSQL vs. turbopuffer

We see that most data is relational, and high read traffic needs to be supported. Both can be served by a PostgreSQL database.

For embeddings, we can use PostgreSQL with the **pgvector** extension since it's integrable into our postgres database. Alternatively we can use a serverless choice of vector database like **turbopuffer** that scales seamlessly.

Postgres pgvector extension

- Strengths:
    - Integration with PostgreSQL: Allows to store vector data alongside structured data, simplifying architecture
    - Hierarchical navigable small worlds (HNSW) Indexing: The HNSW index type offers good performance for approximate nearest neighbor (ANN) search, significantly speeding up queries compared to exact search
    - Cost-effective: More cost-effective for users already within the PostgreSQL ecosystem, especially for small to medium-sized datasets
- Potential drawbacks:
    - Scalability management: While it can scale, achieving massive scale – hundreds of millions or billions of vectors with high QPS (queries per second) – may require more manual sharding and partitioning compared to purpose-built distributed systems

turbopuffer

- Strengths:
    - Purpose-built architecture: Designed from the ground up for vector search at scale, optimized for low latency and high QPS
    - Stateless nodes: Uses object storage as a write-ahead log, which allows for cost-effective horizontal scaling and high throughput
    - Scalability: Can scale to trillions of documents across millions of namespaces, handling very large datasets more efficiently than general-purpose databases
    - Performance: Offers competitive or superior performance to other specialized vector databases
    - Managed service: Reduces operational complexity, which can be a significant factor in maintaining high performance at scale
- Potential drawbacks:
    - Not open-source: It is a commercial-only model
    - Separate infrastructure: Requires managing a separate system from the primary relational database (pgsql)

While PostgreSQL with pgvector is an architecturally sound choice for its simplicity and data consolidation, the non-functional requirement of 200ms latency and the ~1666 Peak RPS pushes the preference toward a specialized, performant, and horizontally scalable solution like turbopuffer [2].

Deep dive into design

So far, we have made the following design decisions:

Requirement	**Design solution summary**
Codebase awareness	Client context engine: Chunks code using ASTs locally. Vector DB: Indexes embeddings with obfuscated IDs for privacy.

Requirement	Design solution summary
Code completes	Hybrid sync: Uses gRPC streams for real-time typing Context: Injects file history + cursor position into the prompt
Chat mode	Scope awareness: Users select current file vs. codebase Retrieval: RAG pipeline fetches relevant chunks via vector search
Data persistence	Polyglot store: PostgreSQL for relational data (users/chats) Turbopuffer: Vector storage for code embeddings
Low latency (< 200 ms)	Next section focus: implementing semantic caching to skip LLM calls and speculative decoding to generate code faster than typing speed [5].
Reliability	Next section focus: designing circuit breakers to handle outages and exponential backoff to prevent cascading failures during high load.

Now let's examine a few of the non-functional requirements and consider how we can achieve them in our design.

Reducing latency

The server needs to respond quickly to requests for completions, chat and agent tasks so that the developer is not frustrated. This can be done in a variety of ways:

- Caching strategies
- Scalable architecture
- Optimized datastores
- Efficient change detection

- Race-to-response
- Semantic caching for code explanations
- Normalized cache keys
- Advanced pattern: speculative decoding

We'll now briefly look at each of those in turn.

Caching strategies

Caching-based approaches are perhaps the most important way to reduce latencies. Commonly searched vector embeddings and recent chat sessions can be indexed on the server; this will to reduce the load on the database as well as reduce latency, and commonly retrieved code completes and explanations can be cached for faster retrieval.

Cached item	Caching key	Description
Vector embedding	most frequently used text called for embedding	
Vector search	user_id:team_id: query_hash	Calculating the query_hash and running the vector search are CPU-intensive and necessary for every context-aware query. Caching the relevant chunk IDs saves milliseconds and reduces database load
Code complete for boilerplate snippets	team_id:model_id :model_version:fil e_id:code_snippe t_hash	Cache only exact, high-frequency boilerplate snippets that are static and widely used (e.g., common import statements or context-free method signatures), or cache only on the Client-Side (locally) for short-term session recall.

Cached item	Caching key	Description
Explanation / summarization	team_id:model_id :model_version:q uery_hash	Caching common questions about a project's architecture avoids the high cost and latency of rerunning the LLM.

Figure 3.11a illustrates typical caching dataflows. We can use a cache-aside pattern using Redis/memcached for distributed, low-latency caches and employ cache invalidation on source modification, LLM model upgrades etc.

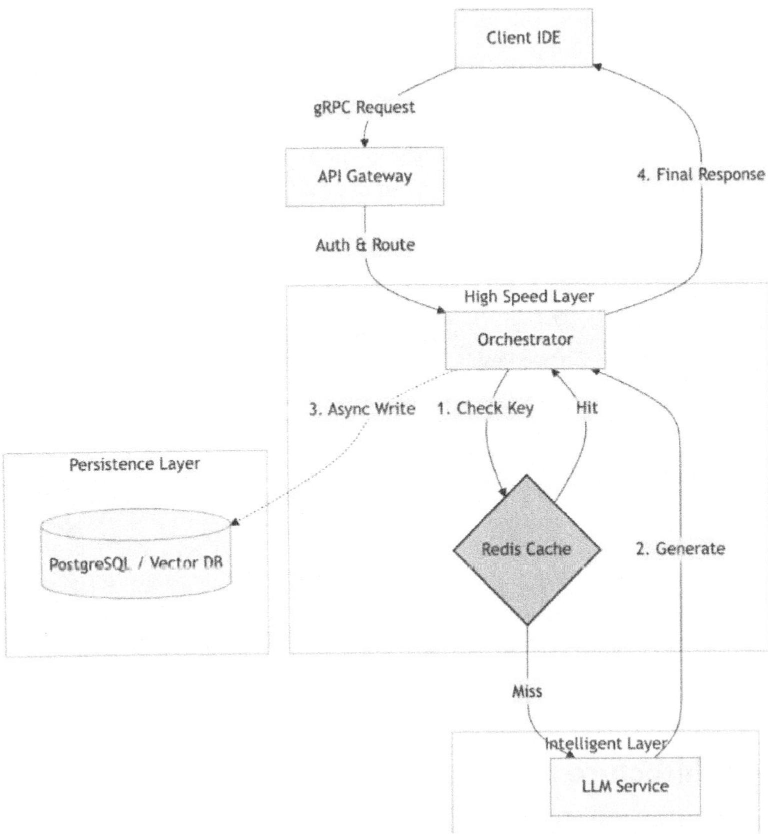

Figure 3.11a: Caching design

Figure 3.11b demonstrates how a cache-aside strategy works:

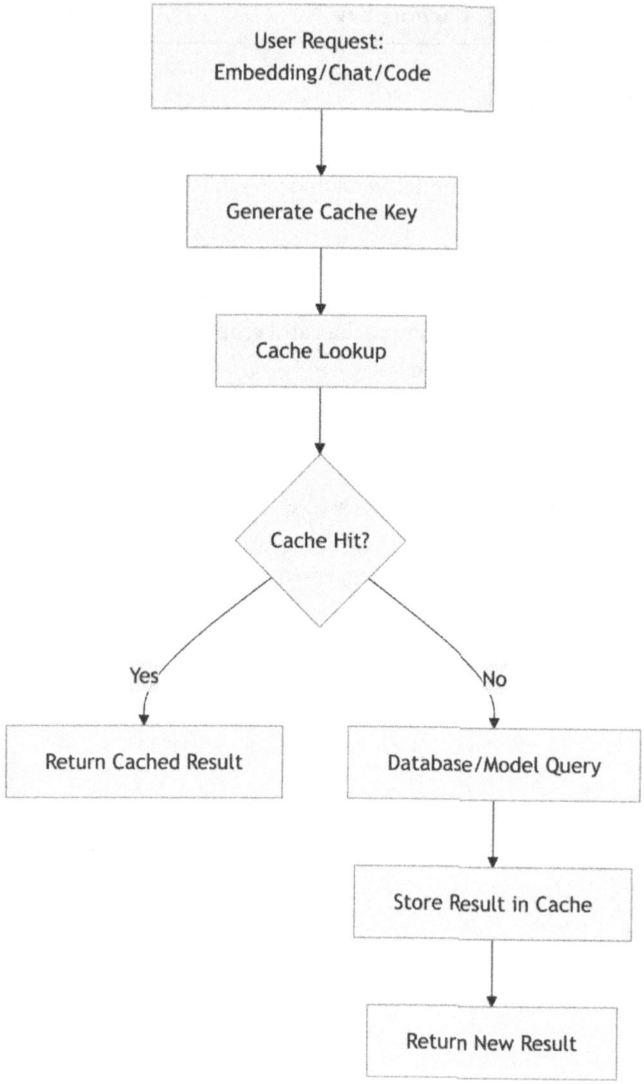

Figure 3.11b: Cache-aside pattern

Scalable architecture

Auto scaling: The orchestrator engine can be configured with horizontal scaling policies. This can be done monitoring the CPU and memory usage on the orchestrator engine

Async task queues: Queue long-running agentic tasks so that the system is available to respond to user requests and queries faster.

Optimized datastores:

Read replicas: Distribute load across PostgreSQL by adding read replicas for faster response.

Vector database scaling: Low-latency serverless solutions like turbopuffer help auto scaling without operational overhead.

Efficient change detection

Using Merkle trees for codebase syncing improves latency with partial updates without reindexing entire files. However, the Merkle indexer needs to be optimised for IDE performance. Calculating Merkle hashes for a massive monorepo is CPU-intensive. The client context engine must implement idle-time execution.

Debounce: Only trigger hash calculation after the user has stopped typing for > 2 seconds.

CPU cap: Restrict the indexing thread to a maximum of 10–15% CPU usage to ensure the IDE remains responsive to keystrokes.

Race-to-response

The orchestrator engine can fall back to lightweight models with lower latency whenever the optimal LLM is too slow.

Since our target is < 300 ms per response, if the primary provider takes longer than 200 ms, we also trigger a request to a backup provider that can respond in ~100 ms (though with less accuracy). We then wait up to 100 ms for the optimal provider's answer, and if it arrives in time, we return the optimal result; otherwise, we return the backup response to the client.

Semantic caching for code explanations

Developers often ask the same question with slightly different phrasing (e.g. 'How do I filter a list?' vs. 'Syntax for list filtering'). Exact match caching fails here. Here **semantic caching** can be pretty useful.

We embed the user's prompt and check our cache for any previous prompt with a cosine similarity > 0.95. If found, we serve the cached explanation immediately, bypassing the GPU inference entirely.

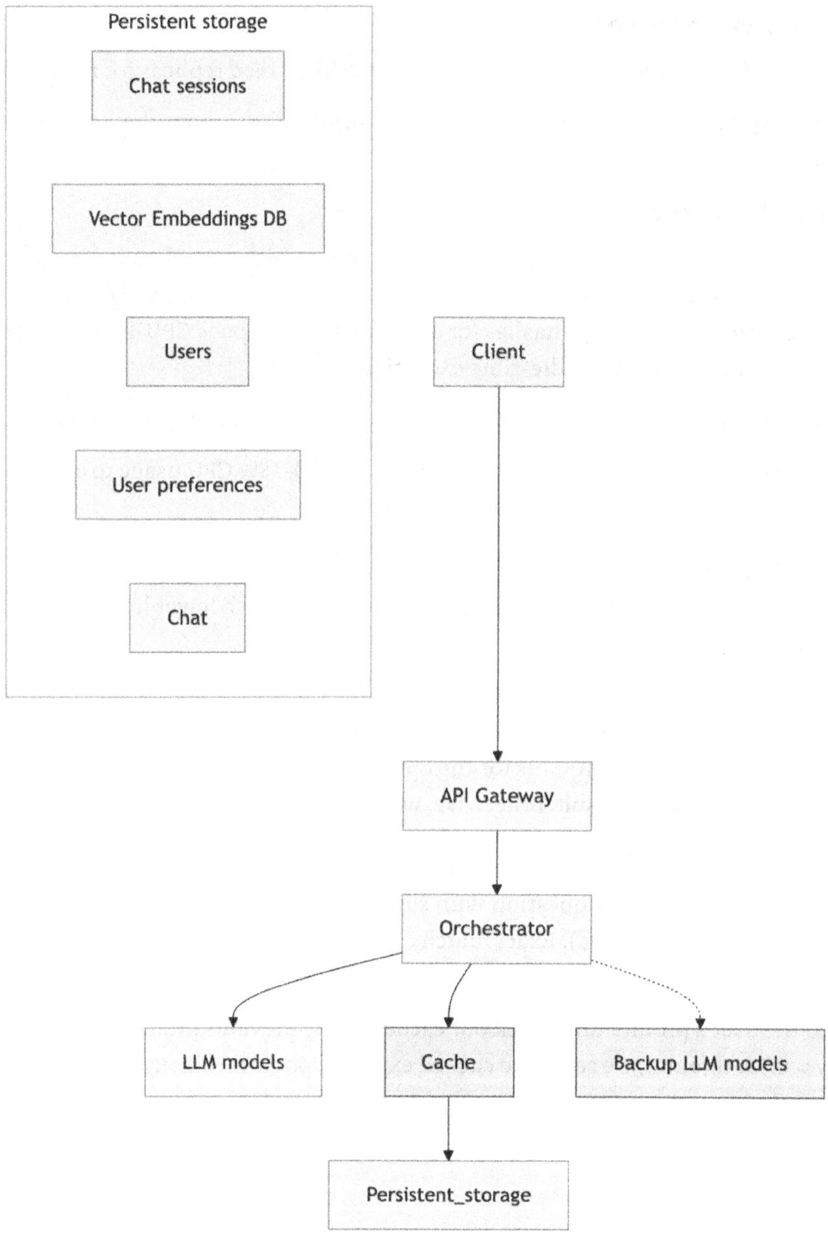

Figure 3.12a: Flow for code explanations

Normalized cache keys

A naive hash key (*hash*(*prompt*)) results in cache misses for trivial changes. Implement **prompt normalization** before hashing:

- Whitespace trimming: "Hello " to "Hello"
- Case insensitivity: "Python" to "python"
- Stop word removal: "What is the status" to "status" (to be used with caution, depending on domain)
- Embedding cache: Do not just cache the final text response. Cache the vector output from the embedding model. The embedding API costs money and adds latency; if the same text chunk is seen twice, reuse the vector.

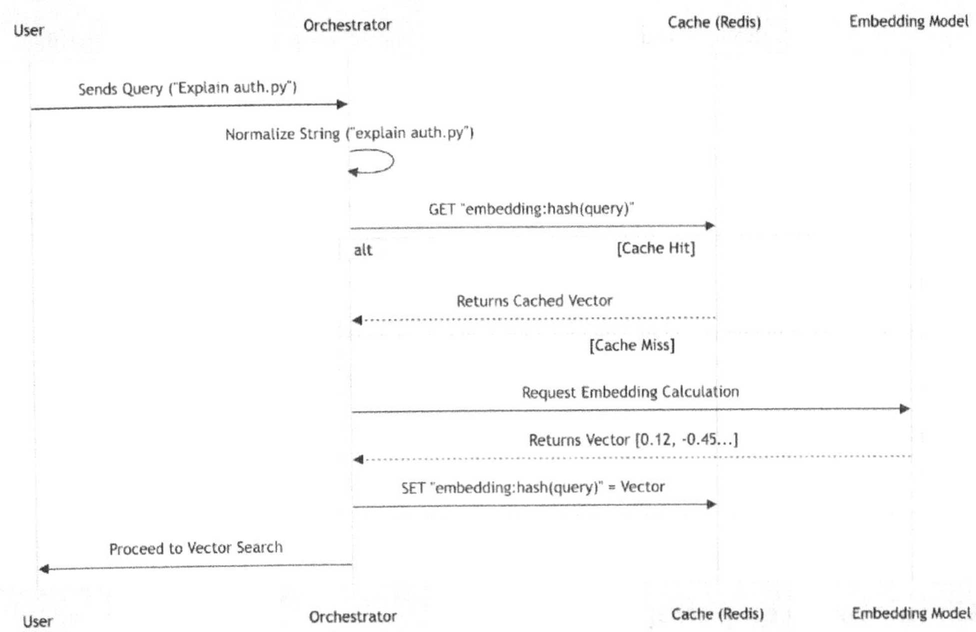

Figure 3.12b: Avoid redundant embedding calculations by caching

Advanced pattern: speculative decoding

Standard LLM inference generates one token at a time, which is often too slow for the < 200 ms target required for a native feel. To achieve the sub-second latency seen in modern AI editors, we must move beyond simple caching and implement **speculative decoding**. This is how it works:

- Large models (e.g. Llama-3-70B) are memory-bound. Reading the model weights for every single character generated adds significant latency [5].
- So we run two models, a draft model and a verification model.
- We use the draft model to predict the next few tokens, and feed that prediction into the verification model as a batch [5]. This allows the large model to verify 5 tokens in a single GPU operation, rather than generating them one by one.
    - Draft model (small): A tiny, hyper-fast model (e.g., a 7B parameter distilled model) speculates the next 10–20 tokens (or a full diff) instantly.
    - Verification model (large): The powerful model processes that entire drafted sequence in a single pass to verify it.
    - If the draft is correct, the user sees 20 characters appear instantly, achieving effective speeds of 1000+ tokens per second. This creates the Tab-to-jump sensation where the cursor moves over predictable code.

Improving reliability and availability at high load

We can use a variety of approaches to improve resilience at high load:

Strict timeouts for calls

- Maximum allowed time for the LLM to generate a response (inference)
- If model exceeds this timeout, cancel the request to the LLM to free up orchestrator thread

Circuit breaker pattern

- Monitor LLM model response time and failures rates, if they exceed the threshold, open the circuit
- Automatically stop sending traffic to slow or error prone models until they recover, and utilize healthy alternatives instead

Retrying with backups

Given the resource demands of LLMs, response delays or failures can occur during high loads, network issues or provider outages. A retry and backup strategy ensures graceful degradation and avoids service disruptions. Delays beyond a second can cause developer frustration and potentially reduce our system's value.

So it is important to configure retry with exponential backoff in the orchestrator engine while calling LLM models in case of failures or slowdowns in LLM model providers.

Circuit breaks should also be in place to route the query to backup LLM providers in case the optimal LLM model provider is unavailable.

Retry strategies

- Interactive (code completes): Do not use aggressive exponential backoff. If a user is waiting, a 60-second retry is effectively downtime. Use Capped Backoff (start 500 ms, max 1 s) or fail fast to a fallback model.
- Asynchronous (batch Jobs): Use Exponential Backoff (wait 1 min, 2 min, 4 min). Since no user is waiting, we can afford to wait out a 5-minute provider outage.
    - Exponential backoff with jitter: On failure/timeout, the system retries requests after waiting intervals that increase exponentially, e.g. 50 ms, 100 ms, 200 ms ...
- Retry limits: We retry thrice to avoid unnecessary load and extensive delay

Backup model strategy:

We keep a multi-model fallback strategy. This works as follows:

- We keep backup models which might not be optimal for accuracy but are faster
- If the primary model doesn't respond within 200 ms, call the backup models
- Present the first completed response to the user
- Inform users that the response is from a non optimal model
- Alternatively, we can also send the same query in parallel to multiple models utilizing the first response and cancelling the others. This increases resource usage, though, so usage needs to be balanced

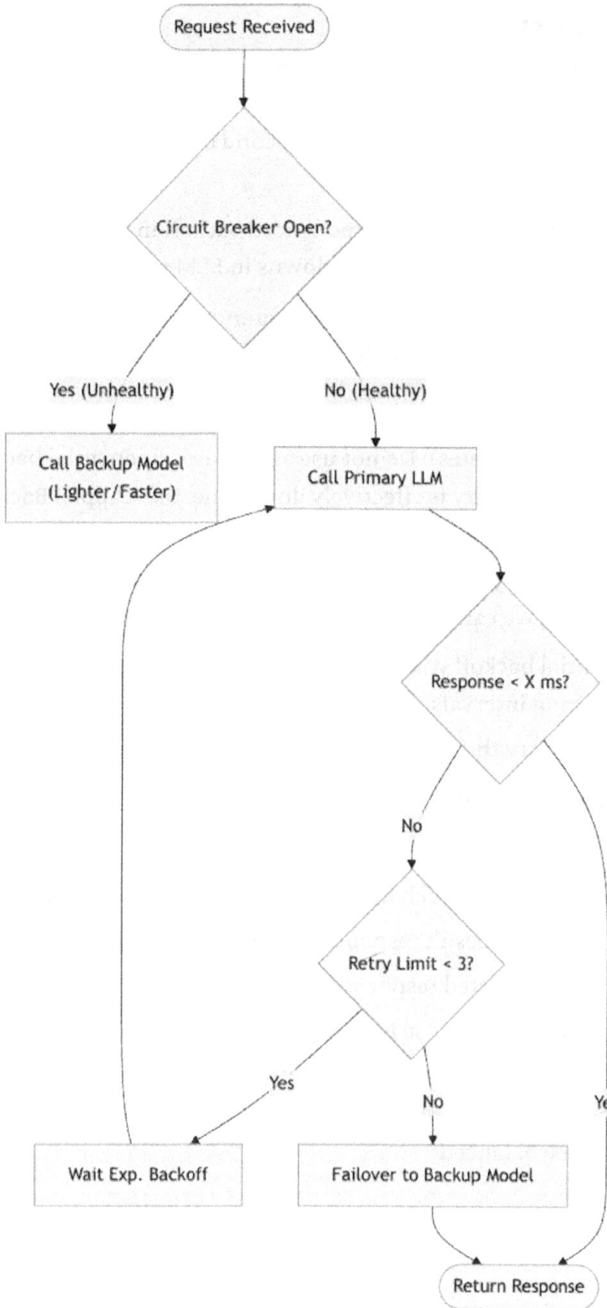

Figure 3.12c: Decision tree for timeouts, circuit breakers, and retries

Synchronous/asynchronous hybrid processing model

We employ hybrid processing models for different use cases of our IDE.

Sync: code complete (low latency, immediate response).

Async: chat/agentic tasks (high latency, long-running, handled by task queue and workers with retries).

Queuing and async processing for chat and agentic tasks

We can further queue and asynchronously process chat responses and agentic tasks to make the system available for code complete queries, which require sub-200 ms latency.

Workers can pick up tasks from the queue, send them to LLM model providers, and retry in case of failures.

Task queuing

- The chat prompts and agentic tasks are pushed to a messaging queue (like SQS) by the orchestrator.
- Requests are picked by the worker processes which then store these requests in an events table and subsequently call the LLM provider.
- If the LLM response times out, the worker can retry with exponential backoff and track the same in the table. The orchestrator sends chat prompts and agentic tasks to a messaging queue (e.g. SQS).
- Worker processes retrieve these requests, record them in an events table, and then contact the LLM provider.
- If the LLM response times out, the worker can retry with exponential backoff, updating the number of attempts in the table for the event.

Async response delivery

- User sees loading status on the IDE for these tasks
- Since we maintain an open gRPC bi-directional stream (established in the *Code context* section), the server pushes the task complete event directly to the client down this pipe.

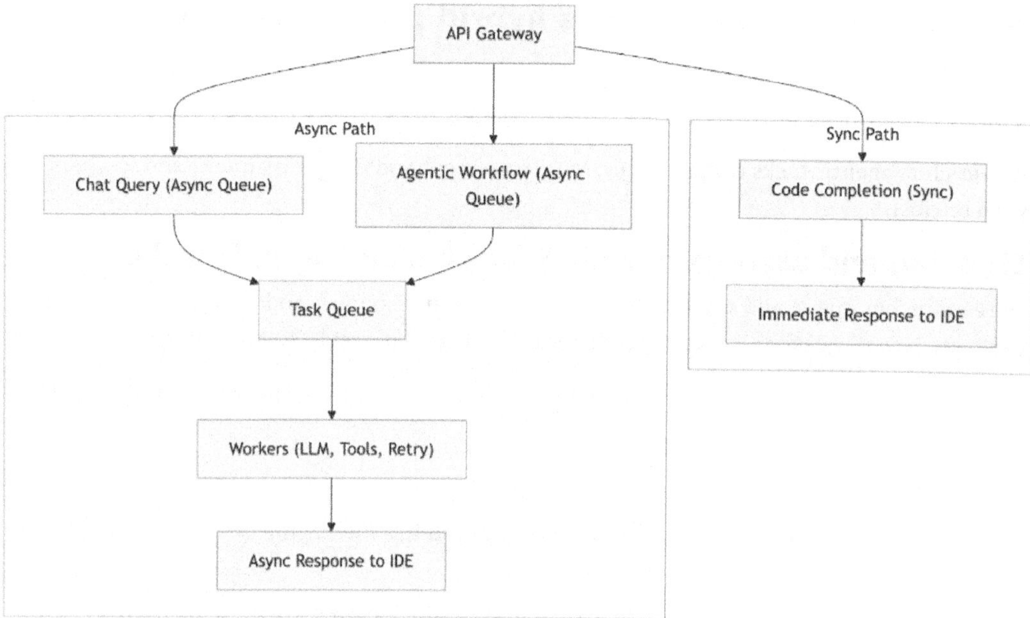

Figure 3.13: Async flow for code explanations and sync flow for code completes

We can ensure chat queries are prioritized and processed faster than agent tasks even in the queue by adding weights to the type of tasks. So chat queries have higher priority and will be consumed faster from the queue by the workers.

Rate limiting and throttling

To protect the system from overload or DDoS attacks, rate limiting and throttling are enforced at the API gateway layer. This restricts the number of requests any user or client can send over a fixed time window (e.g. 200 requests/min).

So our updated design now looks like this:

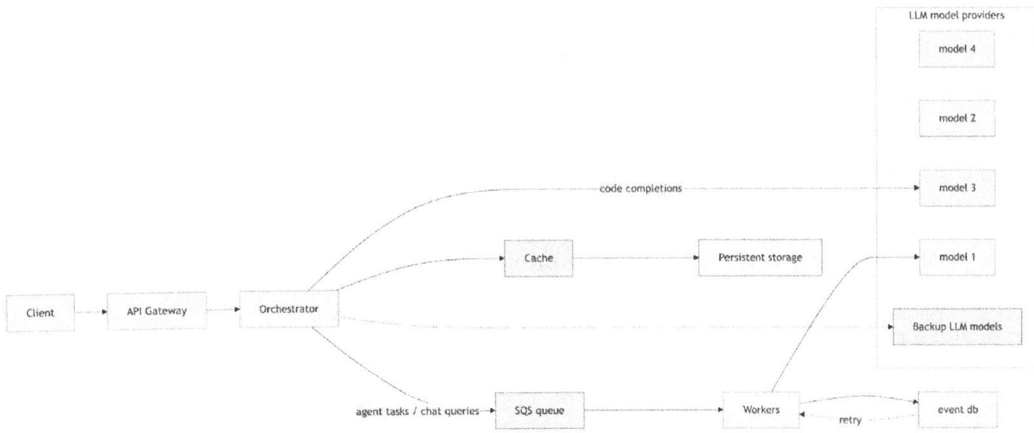

Figure 3.14: Adding rate limit and retries

Improving accuracy

A comprehensive list of instructions is required to be provided to the LLM to reduce hallucinations and errors. To achieve this, we can follow:

Advanced prompt engineering

Structured instructions: Prompts should specify desired formats, content boundaries and exceptions

```
{
"role": "system",
"content": "You are a coding
assistant. You must format your   response as a valid JSON object. Do not include
markdown formatting."
"schema": {
"type": "object",
"properties": {
"explanation": "string",
"code_diff": "string"
    }
  }
}
```

Using formats like JSON mode ensures the IDE can parse the answer programmatically, rather than using Regex to scrape text.

- ***Contextual knowledge***: Surrounding code, history of file changes and other relevant metadata should be provided to minimize ambiguity
- ***Extensive examples***: Provide examples of good and bad responses to instruct the model on expected behavior and avoid unwanted behaviors
- ***Negative prompting***: Clearly define unwanted behavior ("Do not add db migrations", "Do not hallucinate API names", etc.)
- ***Model-specific optimizations***: Different LLM models benefit from specified prompt tuning

Dynamic feedback loop

Developers should rate and annotate suggestions for better responses so that model prompt can be tuned.

Post-processing after tasks are run can be done to flag anomalies, check syntax correctness etc.

Multi-model use

Multiple models can be used in case of ambiguous requests to offer alternative responses

Compiler-as-a-judge

For code, we have a ground truth: the compiler. For automated evaluation, we attempt to compile/interpret the generated code. If it throws a syntax error, the score is automatically zero. This deterministic feedback loop is faster and cheaper than asking another LLM to review the code.

Applying privacy patterns

Privacy can be protected using a range of techniques:

Ephemeral guarantee

- ***In-memory decryption***: All encrypted code snippets sent to the server should be decrypted in memory and discarded post processing [3]
- ***No persistent code storage***: All sensitive data including codebase chunks and associated metadata like filenames are never stored on disk or on databases [3]
- ***Memory hygiene***: Variables holding plaintext code are explicitly overwritten or garbage collected immediately after the embedding vector is generated.
- ***No-logging policy***: We implement strict middleware that strips all request bodies from observability logs to prevent accidental leakage of code snippets into Datadog or Splunk.

Code cannot be reconstructed

- ***Semantic index search only***: The code chunks are converted into vector embeddings and then stored in the database, ensuring the code cannot be reconstructed from the database. There are limits to embedding-only privacy however:
    - While storing only vector embeddings prevents casual reading of source code, it is not a cryptographic guarantee of privacy.
    - Adversaries can potentially reconstruct original text from high-fidelity vector embeddings using model inversion techniques.
    - Mitigation: Encryption keys are rotated regularly and access controls are strictly scoped.
- ***Metadata obfuscation***: Real file and symbol names are not used, instead hashed ids are stored [3]

Minimizing attack surface

- ***Minimized code transfer***: Only code context required for a query or code complete is sent to the server, not the entire codebase
- ***Encryption policies***: All requests sent to/from the client are encrypted, and all data stored on server side is encrypted

Middleware PII scrubbing

Encryption protects data in transit, but it doesn't prevent the model from seeing secrets if a user accidentally pastes them. We implement **data cleaning middleware** on the client side before the payload is encrypted.

This middleware uses regex and entropy detection to identify potential API keys, hardcoded passwords, or AWS credentials. These are replaced with tokens (e.g. <SECRET_REMOVED>) before the context is ever sent to the server.

This ensures that even if our server logs are compromised, user secrets are never persisted or exposed to the model provider.

Training with test data

Now let's consider some of the factors to consider when training with test data.

Sourcing datasets

A good approach is to curate a diverse set of open source projects with varied languages, sizes and domains. Refresh the dataset regularly to incorporate up to date coding style and practices.

In addition, create custom open source repos with intentional gaps, edge cases to stress test behaviors.

Testing and training for code complete

Randomly remove code blocks, functions, classes from the code. Start typing signatures of missing classes and functions. Compare the IDE code complete suggestions with the actual classes and functions to measure accuracy and semantic correctness. Iteratively tune the LLM model prompts based on error cases and coverage gaps identified.

Testing for chat responses

Clone the repo removing all the comments and docs. Ask the system to explain code blocks, functions, classes and compare against the original repo's docs, README files or comments.

Testing for agentic workflow and tasks

Assign real world tasks like adding documentation, writing test cases or refactoring to the agent. Combine multiple tasks in scenarios.

Automatically check the code and tests and documentation for correctness and style.

Integrating these tests into CI/CDs helps keep models and prompts updated with evolving repos.

Mutation testing

Add logic and syntax errors to your code. Evaluate if the system can identify and fix these errors.

Negative prompt testing

Give confusing or risky actions like 'Delete all database migrations'. Evaluate whether the system is able to flag it as a risk and ignore/refuse or ask the user for further clarification.

Monitoring and user feedback

It is essential to implement robust feedback pipelines that allow users to provide input on their experience, especially for chat interactions. Users should be able to easily indicate whether a response was helpful or not, and this feedback should be collected and utilized to improve the LLMs, enabling better future responses.

We should monitor user engagement metrics. Tracking the number of active users and observing trends in how frequently and extensively they interact with the AI system helps gauge adoption and effectiveness over time.

Summary

LLMs make the already intelligent development environments even smarter, helping developers offload menial tasks and intelligently assist them like a coding assistant or a pair programmer.

References

[1] Orosz, Gergely. 'Real-world engineering challenges: building Cursor'. *The Pragmatic Engineer*, June 10, 2025. `https://newsletter.pragmaticengineer.com/p/cursohttps://newsletter.pragmaticengineer.com/p/cursor`

[2] Turbopuffer reduces costs: `https://turbopuffer.com/customers/cursor`

[3] Cursor – security: `https://cursor.com/security`

[4] Asif, Sualeh. 'Our problems'. Cursor blog, October 12, 2023. `https://cursor.com/blog/problems-2023`

[5] 'How Cursor Serves Billions of AI Code Completions Every Day'. *ByteByteGo Newsletter*, July 29, 2025. `https://blog.bytebytego.com/p/how-cursor-serves-billions-of-ai`

[6] Orosz, Gergely. 'Building Windsurf with Varun Mohan'. *The Pragmatic Engineer*, May 7, 2025. `https://newsletter.pragmaticengineer.com/p/building-windsurf-with-varun-mohan`

[7] Quastor. 'How GitHub Copilot Works'. Quastor, April 4, 2024.

Get this book's PDF version and more

4

Case Study: Adaptive Learning Platform

The future of **learning platforms** lies in personalization. An effective learning platform adapts to each user's unique pace. It helps reduce time spent on mastered concepts while focusing on lessons that are challenging but not discouraging, which is crucial for learner engagement.

The lessons or exercises need to be updated frequently to keep up with the nuances of the language and introduce new lessons based on user feedback and usage.

This is where large language models (LLMs) become transformative. LLMs can be leveraged on two primary fronts: curating a personalized curriculum for the user and generating new exercises.

In this chapter, we will design the core AI-driven enhancements for a platform rather like Duolingo (*Figure 4.1*) [1][2]. Our focus will be on the systems that enable personalized lesson progression and interactive exercises, so features like detailed scoring systems, although vital to the overall platform, are out of scope to concentrate on the fundamental AI architecture.

The chapter follows the same general structure as *Chapter 3*, so we'll be covering the following topics:

- Functional requirements
- Non-functional requirements
- Scale estimates
- API design
- The blueprint
- Data selection and data modelling

- Deep dive into design
- Testing scenarios
- Monitoring and alerting

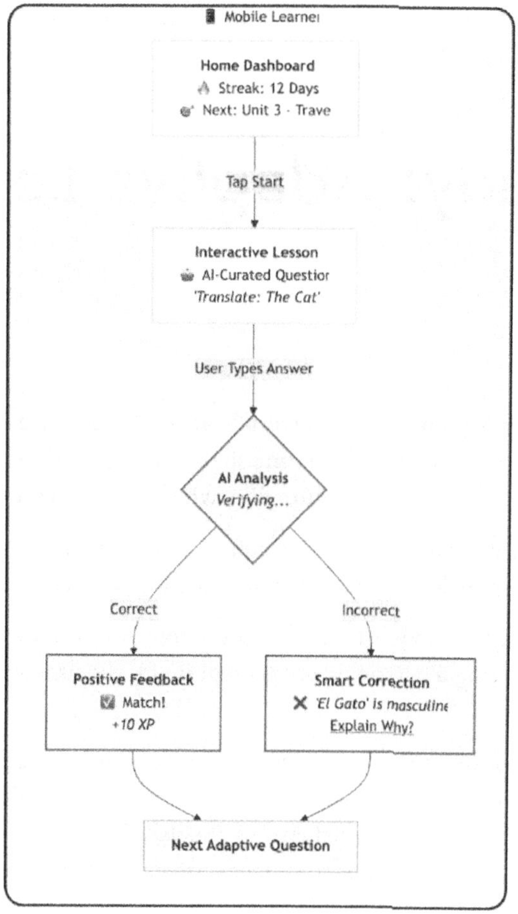

Figure 4.1: An AI-powered language learning platform

Functional requirements

In this Case Study we'll focus on requirements relating to two main functional areas:

- ***Lesson generation***: Design entire exercises and lessons of different levels of a language for different levels. This ensures a constantly fresh and relevant content stream.
- ***Lesson curation with adaptive difficulty***: The system should look at a user's past answers and figure out the perfect next question to ask - not too hard, not too easy.

Non-functional requirements

The main NFRs are:

- Low latency: The system must have a P99 latency of < 500 ms for the round-trip from submitting an answer to receiving the feedback or the next question.
- High accuracy: This is about trust. Our platform shouldn't give wrong answers or bad explanations.
- High availability: The system should be resilient. Even when there's an outage in an LLM provider, it should not bring down the entire learning platform.
- Highly personalized: Lessons should be highly tailored to the users' needs – it shouldn't be too challenging or too easy.
- Cost effectiveness: LLM API calls are expensive. There should be a good strategy for when and where to use LLM interactions.
- Scalability: The system should be scalable to allow for peak loads during timezone overlaps in learners.

Scale estimates

Before jumping into the design, let's get a feel for the sheer size of this platform.

The platform has 50 million daily active users [1][2]. There are 4 most popular languages, most learned by users. The platform supports 50 languages in total, with 250 lessons for the most spoken ones and up to 70 for the least spoken ones. Each lesson has up to 10 questions.

How many requests per second (RPS) do we need to support?

Daily active users (DAU): 50M

Lessons per user per day: 3

Questions per lesson: 10

RPS = (DAU * lesson per user per day * questions per lesson) / seconds in a day

So for serving lessons to users we need to support: 50M*3*10/ (60*60*24) = ***17,340 RPS***

Now each question requires 3 core API calls (minimum):

1. `GET` question content
2. `POST` user answer
3. `GET` feedback / results

Average RPS = 17K RPS * 3 API calls = 51K RPS

Peak RPS is 5 times ~= 51K * 5 = 255K RPS

Additional load considerations:

- Conversation practice sessions: +20% RPS [3]
- Real-time feedback and analytics: +15% RPS

Therefore total peak load = ~350K RPS

API design

Let's look at the APIs our system requires.

Admin lesson generation and review APIs

Under this head we have seven APIs to consider, for:

- Generating questions (sync)
- Generating questions (async)
- Retrieving question generation status
- Retrieving generated questions
- Reviewing a question (retrieving metadata and question)
- Bulk edit (question approval or rejection)
- Editing questions

We'll now consider each API in turn.

Generate questions (sync)

This API generates a small batch of questions (e.g. < 5) for rapid testing or low-volume needs, without queuing.

URI	/api/v1/admin/questions
Method	POST
Authorization	Bearer {admin_token}

Body	{
	"format" : "fill-in-the-word"
	"count" : 2,
	"level": "A2",
	"language" : "Spanish",
	"topic": "prepositions"
	}

Response	{
	"metadata": { "count_requested":
	2,
	"count_generated": 2,
	"initial_status": "IN_REVIEW",
	},
	"questions": [
	{
	"id": "question_137293",
	"text": "El libro está la mesa.",
	"type": "FILL_IN_THE_BLANK",
	"choices": ["en", "sobre",
	"hacia", "entre", "según"]
	},
	{
	"id": "question_137294", "text":
	"Caminamos el parque.",
	"type": "FILL_IN_THE_BLANK",
	"choices": ["en", "sobre",
	"hacia", "entre", "según"]
	}
	]
	}

Generate questions (async)

Submits a bulk generation job (e.g. 100+ items) to the background queue to avoid blocking the Admin UI.

URI	/api/v1/admin/question-generation-jobs
Method	POST
Authorization	Bearer {admin_token}

Body	`{`
	`"format": "fill-in-the-blank",`
	`"count": 10,`
	`"level": "A2", "language":`
	`"Spanish", "topic": "prepositions"`
	`}`

Response	`{`
	`"job_id": "job_d9e8f7a6",`
	`"status": "PENDING",`
	`"message": "Question generation`
	`has been queued.",`
	`"status_check_url": "/api/v1/`
	`admin/question-generation-jobs/`
	`job_d9e8f7a6"`
	`}`

Retrieve questions status

Polls the progress of a specific long-running generation job to show 'Processing...' states on the dashboard.

URI	/api/v1/admin/question-generation-jobs/job_d9e 8f7a6
Method	GET
Authorization	Bearer {admin_token}

Response (while still processing)	{
	"job_id": "job_d9e8f7a6", "status":
	"PROCESSING",
	"message": "Generating questions..."
	}

Response (when complete)	{
	"job_id": "job_d9e8f7a6", "status":
	"COMPLETED",
	"message": "Successfully generated
	10 questions.", "results_url":
	"/api/v1/admin/questions?job_id=job_d9
	e8f7a6"
	}

Retrieve questions

Fetches the final list of AI-generated content once the asynchronous job status is COMPLETED.

URI	/api/v1/admin/question-generation-jobs/job_d9e8f 7a6
Method	GET
Authorization	Bearer {admin_token}

Response	[
	{
	"question_id": "q_101",
	"text": "What is the capital of France?",
	"type": "multiple_choice",
	"language": "French",
	"lesson_id": "lesson_1",
	"job_id": "job_d9e8f7a6"
	// ... other question fields
	},
	{
	"question_id": "q_102", "text": "Translate 'Hello' to Spanish.",
	"type": "translation", "language": "Spanish",
	"lesson_id": "lesson_1", "job_id":
	"job_d9e8f7a6"
	// ... other question fields
	}
	// ... up to 10 questions
	]

Review question

Fetches the full metadata and content of a single generated question for human expert validation.

URI	/api/v1/questions/{questionId}
Method	GET

Response	{
	"id": "question_137293",
	"text": "Fill in the blank with:
	en, sobre, hacia, entre, según. El
	libro está la mesa.",
	"type": "FILL_IN_THE_BLANK",
	"choices": ["en", "sobre",
	"hacia", "entre", "según"],
	"answer": "sobre", "status":
	"IN_REVIEW", "language":
	"Spanish", "level": "A2",
	"topic": "prepositions"
	}

Bulk edit status

Allows experts to 'Approve' or 'Reject' multiple questions simultaneously to accelerate the curation workflow.

URI	/api/v1/questions/batchUpdateStatus
Method	POST

Body	{
	"question_ids": ["question_1",
	"question_2"],
	"status": "ACCEPTED"
	}

Response	{
	"question_ids": ["question_1",
	"question_2"],
	"status": "ACCEPTED"
	}

Edit question

Updates the text or difficulty of a specific question to fix AI errors before final approval.

URI	/api/questions/question_137293
Method	PATCH
Body	`{ "question": "Fill in the blank with: en or hacia. El libro está la mesa.", "options" : ["en", "hacia"], "status": "in-review" }`
Response	`{ "id" : "question_137293", "question": "Fill in the blank with: en, sobre, hacia, entre, según. El libro está la mesa.", "options" : ["en", "hacia"], "status": "in-review" }`

Curator APIs

Here we have just one API to consider ...

Generate a new lesson session API

This endpoint creates and returns a complete, personalized lesson for the user. Requests a fully personalized lesson plan (10–20 questions) tailored to the user's current proficiency and learning history.

URI	/v1/lesson-sessions
Method	POST

<table>
<tr><td>Body</td><td><pre>{
"skill_id":
"skill_verb_conjugation_past_tense",
"type": "PRACTICE", // Could also be
"TEST", "REVIEW", etc.
"preferred_question_count": 10
}</pre></td></tr>
<tr><td>Response</td><td><pre>{
"lesson_session_id": "session_a4b1c2d3",
"skill_id":
"skill_verb_conjugation_past_tense",
"estimated_duration_seconds": 300,
"questions": [
{
"question_id": "q_12483240",
"type": "MULTIPLE_CHOICE",
"prompt": "She to the store yesterday.",
"options": [
{"option_id": "opt_1", "text":
"go"},
{"option_id": "opt_2", "text": "went"},
{"option_id": "opt_3", "text":
"gone"}
]
},
{
"question_id": "q_43854", "type":
"FILL_IN_THE_BLANK",
"prompt": "We   the movie last night."
}....
]
}</pre></td></tr>
</table>

The blueprint: high-level design

In an online learning platform, safety and quality of lessons are non-negotiable. On-the-fly lesson generation from raw LLMs is risky – it could introduce errors, inconsistencies, or inappropriate content. So the LLM can produce lessons offline and those can be reviewed and vetted by experts before being available to the question bank. The LLM can curate them in real time for each user. So we will decouple quality and real-time service architecture.

Therefore our design is split into two distinct systems:

The offline content pipeline: A question bank factory where we leverage AI to generate a vast pool of content that is then vetted by human experts [1]:

Quality control --> LLM for scale/creation --> human-in-the-loop --> question bank

The online serving path: A real-time tutor that intelligently selects questions from this high-quality pool to create personalized lessons for each user.

This dual approach gives us the best of both worlds: the scale and creativity of AI and the quality and safety of human oversight.

System I: the offline content pipeline

The single goal of this system is to populate a central question bank with a large volume of high-quality, approved educational content. This process is handled offline and does not impact live user traffic.

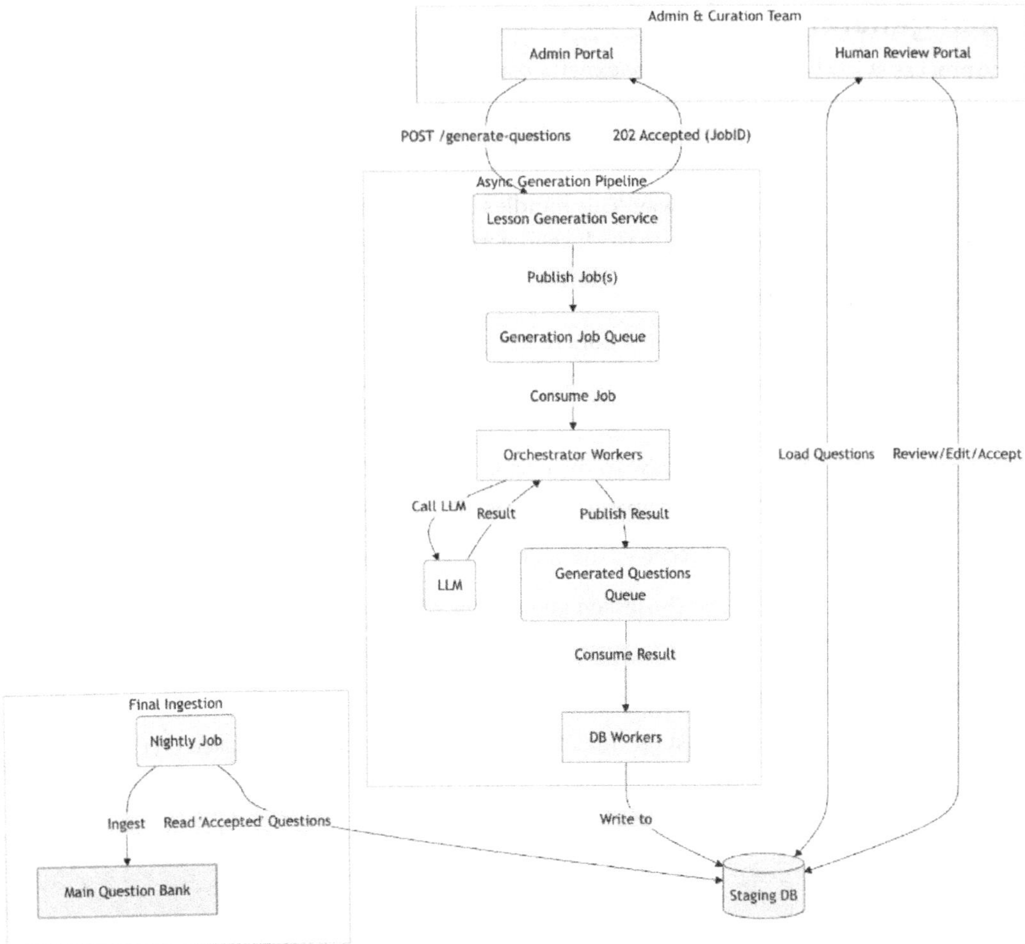

Figure 4.2: Offline content pipeline

Seed generation

The process starts with the language experts using internal tools that call the admin API to request a batch of questions. This query specifies language, level, topic and format.

API gateway

The client app calls the API gateway. This handles the authentication/authorization of the requests before forwarding them to the **lesson generation service**.

Lesson generation service

This admin component is responsible for creating lessons and enabling them to be reviewed and vetted, etc. These lessons can go through various stages of iteration by manual review until they are perfect. This is the staging area where lessons being developed are managed.

Once a lesson is perfected for release to the users, it is marked as accepted. A weekly (or daily) cron job adds these lessons to the lesson database via the lessons service.

The lesson generation service receives the set of lessons in the required question format.

For the lesson generation flow, the lesson generation service forwards the request to the **orchestrator engine**.

Orchestrator engine

This component selects the most optimal model to route the request to based on the kind of request (i.e. simple query, lesson generation or complex conversation). It then generates the required prompt before passing it to the LLM model.

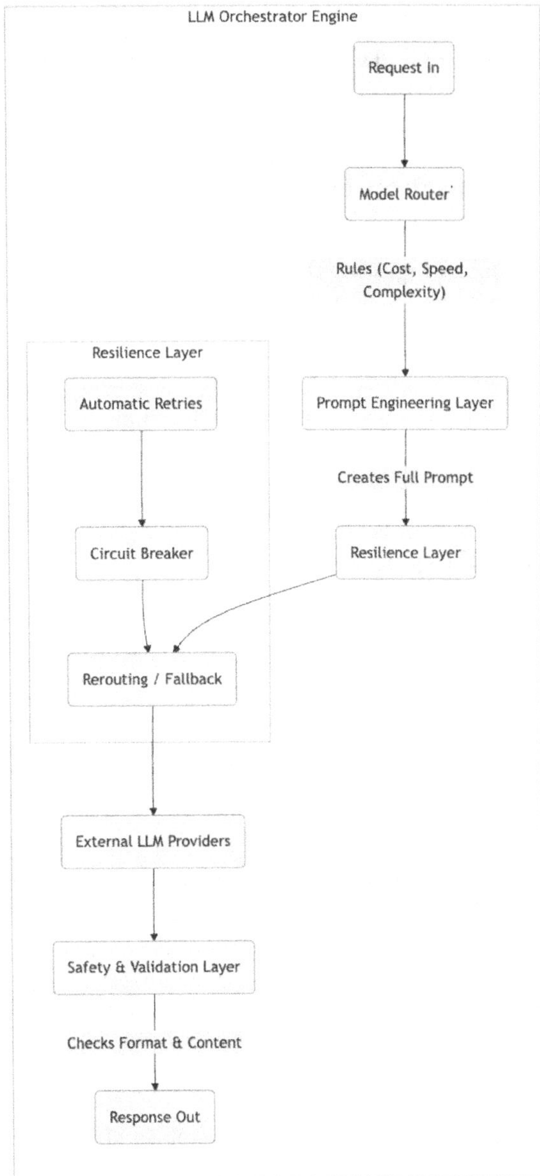

Figure 4.3: Orchestrator engine

Prompt example

Generate 10 lessons for Spanish A2 learners to practice future tense. The sentences should be about food. For each sentence give one answer and three distractors. Tag the question with the correct grammar tag. Output as a JSON array.

Human-in-the-loop review

Experts go through the questions and validate them, correct any mistakes in grammar, difficulty or question format and ensure they adhere to the platform's standards. They then modify and accept or reject these questions.

Ingestion into the question bank database

The accepted questions are ingested into the **question bank** by a scheduled nightly job that does more quality checks before ingesting them into the database. It takes all the newly accepted questions, runs validations, and ingests them into the main question bank database, making them available to the online serving system. The question bank is a database table maintained by the lesson service, which has a collection of a vast variety and number of lessons for different languages. The question bank is the single source of truth for all approved content.

System II: the online serving path

User request and API gateway

The user's app makes a call to our API gateway to request a new lesson (e.g. `POST /v1/lesson-sessions`). The gateway handles authentication and routes the request to the lesson curator service.

Lesson curator service

This is the real-time component that works behind the scenes to get the next lesson for the user from the pre-approved exercise bank.

Serving a lesson to the user entails selecting one of the pre-existing lessons, based on the user's level and understanding and learning progress. This is adapted dynamically as the user progresses through the lessons.

The lesson curator service maintains the question bank database table, which stores all lessons along with their different types, levels and tags, etc.

Fetching user context

The **user context service** maintains the user progress table, which has user lesson completions and scores in different kinds of lessons. This is used to gather information/context on the user's level and understanding while trying to serve the next perfect lesson for the user. This includes the user's known vocabulary, the strength score and their recent mistakes.

Proactive curation

We cannot run a slow, expensive LLM call for every user in real-time. Therefore our online path is built in accordance with a proactive curation (warm/cold path) pattern.

Proactive lesson curation

Waiting for the user to complete a question and then triggering the **lesson curator service** for getting the next question best suited to the user's abilities increases the latency and wait time of the user to get the next question.

We can do this instead asynchronously in batches for a better user experience.

Warm path: instant lesson delivery

This is an active user flow.

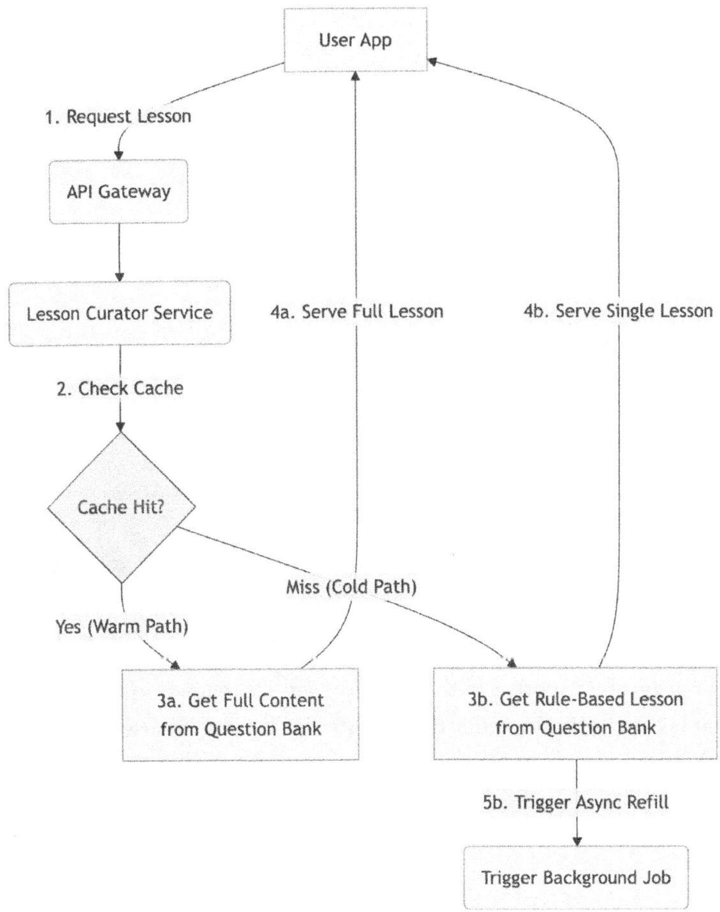

Figure 4.4: Instant lesson delivery

Instant fetch from cache: When a user requests a lesson, the curation service fetches the set of questions required from the `precomputed_lesson_playlists` cache (by using the `LPOP` operation on the Redis list) and serves it to the user instantly.

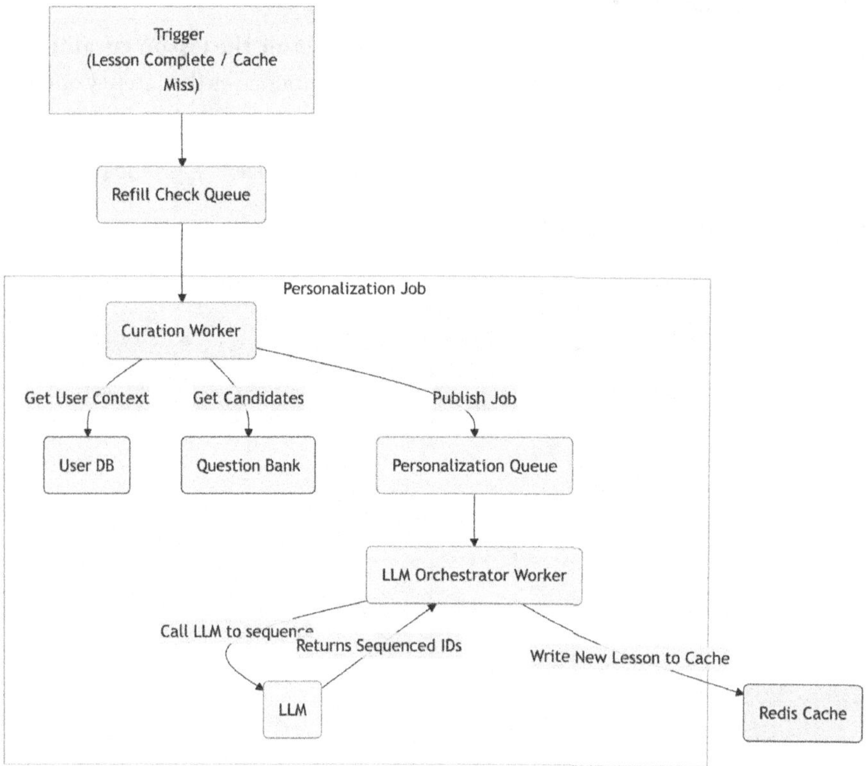

Figure 4.5: Personalized lesson flow

Event-driven trigger: When a user completes a lesson (or any other action that indicates user is active on the app), the service handling that action also publishes a lightweight message, like `{ "userId": "user_123" }`, to a dedicated, low-priority refill_check_queue queue.

Buffer check: A background worker in the curation service reads from this refill_check_queue and checks their lesson buffer in Redis. If the buffer is running low (e.g. fewer than 5–10 lessons remain), it initiates the refill process.

Asynchronous curation: This background worker grabs a big chunk of context on the user – their recent progress, history from the last 50 lessons, and a pool of a few hundred unseen questions from the bank. It bundles all of this into a payload and fires it off to an SQS queue.

LLM orchestrator: Then, our orchestrator worker picks up jobs from that queue at a controlled pace to avoid overwhelming our services. It takes the payload and hits the LLM with a clear prompt, saying, 'Based on this user's history, pick and sequence the best 20-30 questions from this candidate pool'.

Once it gets that list of question IDs back, it pushes it into the user's `precomputed_lesson_playlists` in Redis, ready for their next session.

Cache refill: When the user wants to start the next lesson, the Curator service directly fetches the next exercise from the `precomputed_lesson_playlists` cache by doing an atomic `LPOP` operation on the Redis list.

- The `LPOP` command successfully retrieves and removes the next lesson's ID from the cache in a single, atomic operation
- This lesson is now used. It cannot be served again from the cache
- The service then fetches the full lesson content from the Question Bank and serves it to the user

This pre-fetched buffer of lessons ensures that minor processing delays in the background are not visible to the end-user.

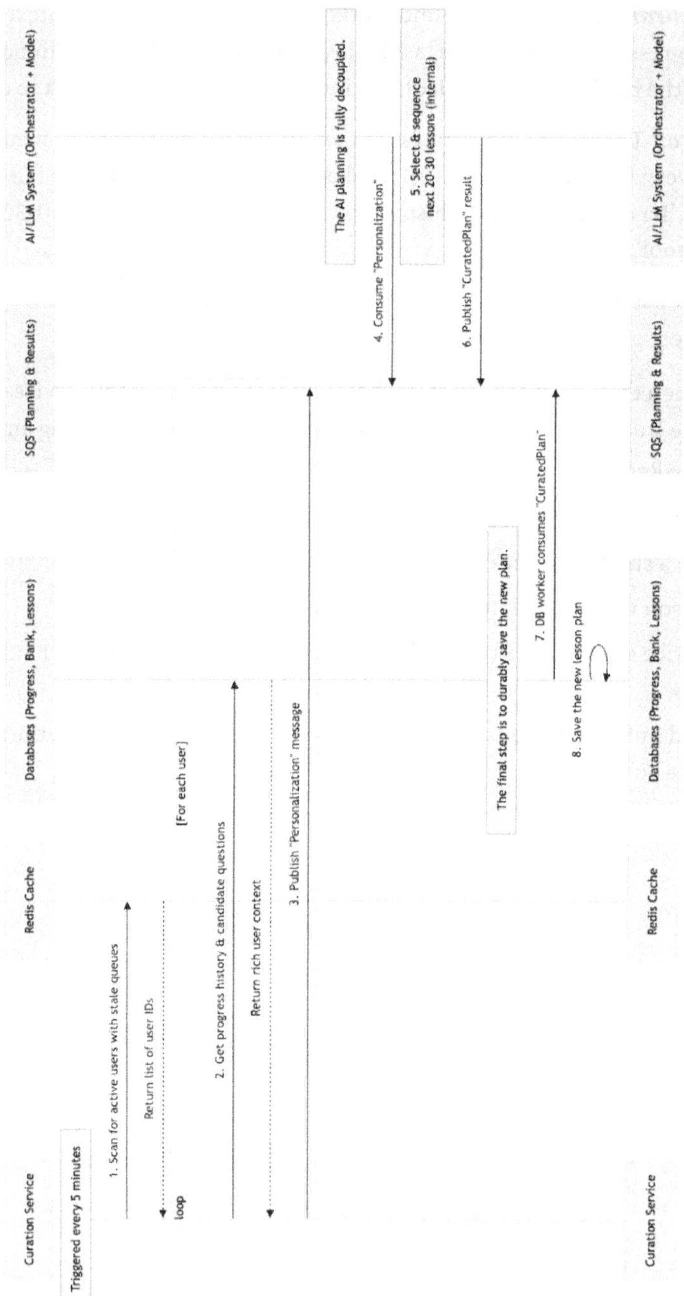

Figure 4.6: Curated lesson flow sequence diagram

Cold path: handling new and returning users

This flow handles users who don't have a pre-fetched lesson buffer.

Cache miss: When a new or returning user requests a lesson, the curation service checks Redis LPOP and finds that it returns nil.

Synchronous fallback: Instead of making the user wait for the background process, the service immediately performs a real-time, synchronous curation for just that single lesson. For this fallback, the curation service can bypass the LLM orchestrator and run a fast, rule-based query directly against the question bank. This query would filter for questions that match the user's skill level and language, while also excluding any they have seen recently using the `lesson_history` table. While not perfectly optimized, this initial lesson offers a faster, more reliable user experience.

Serve and trigger: The service sends this first lesson to the user. At the same time, it triggers the asynchronous refill process to start building up the user's buffer in the background, ensuring all subsequent lesson requests will be on the warm path.

This helps in several ways:

1. Decoupling the personalization engine from the user's actions
    - Smooth out the load on the LLM services, since we get a steady predictable stream instead of a burst of requests
2. Buffering
    - Pre-fetching 20–30 lesson ids acts as a buffer, making the system resilient to temporary delays in the pipeline
3. Graceful degradations

   If the LLM providers are down or taking a lot of time to respond, we can just fetch the lesson ids for the same level questions which the user hasn't seen in the last 20 lessons instead of sending the request to the orchestrator.

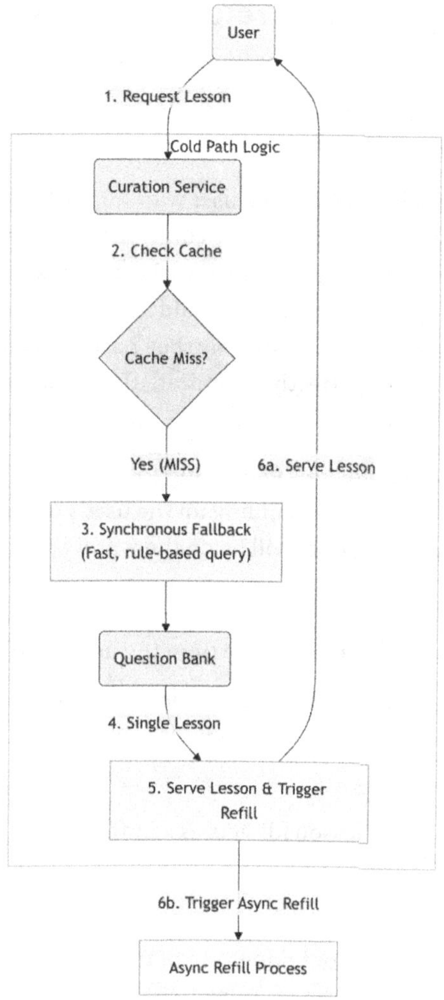

Figure 4.7: Cold path

Now, let's take a closer look at the orchestrator engine:

Orchestrator engine

This is responsible for making the detailed prompts for serving to LLMs.

It also decides which LLMs it should serve, based on the availability of the LLMs and the response times and the use case, whether accuracy is required or low latency is more preferred. The response goes through a safety and validation check before sending it back to the calling service (i.e. lesson curator service or lesson generation service).

Model router

This is an important layer responsible for reliability and cost effectiveness.

It runs a rule engine to decide which model is best suited for the job at hand. This prevents us from using an expensive, powerful model for a simple task.

Rule 1 (simple task): Is it a simple grammar check? Route to a small, fast, internally-hosted model.

Rule 2 (complex task): Is it a part of a complex conversation? Use a model like Gemini 2.5 or Claude.

Rule 3 (premium feature): Is it a premium user asking for a deep explanation and analysis for a question? This is where we can use a top-tier model like GPT 4.0 [2]

Prompt engineering layer

This creates the prompt based on the LLM being routed to and the user progress context. This includes guidelines and guardrails for the LLM along with the format of the response expected. This also includes examples to ensure we get a response as expected.

Resilience layer

The orchestrator is dependent on external, third-party APIs. These APIs are subject to:

- ***Transient network failures***: Brief hiccups, TLS handshake issues, or momentary packet loss.
- ***Service overload/rate limits (429)***: The provider is busy or usage quota is exceeded.
- ***Provider outages (5xx)***: A major failure, high-latency, or full downtime of the external service.
- ***High latency/timeouts***: The model takes too long to generate a response, exceeding the system's required response time

The orchestrator adopts several techniques to mitigate these issues:

Automatic retries

When an initial API call fails with a transient error (like 429 Rate Limit or 503 Service Unavailable), the layer automatically re-submits the request.

- ***Purpose***: To solve temporary, short-lived glitches without involving human intervention or switching models.
- ***Strategy: exponential backoff***: Instead of retrying immediately, the orchestrator waits for an exponentially increasing amount of time between attempts. This prevents your

system from overwhelming an already stressed external provider, which can lead to a Retry Storm.

- ***Limitation***: Retries are typically capped at three attempts to avoid adding excessive latency. If all retries fail, the issue is considered non-transient, and the circuit breaker is triggered.

Circuit breaker

The circuit breaker pattern prevents the orchestrator from sending requests to an LLM provider that is clearly and persistently failing.

State	Condition	Action in orchestrator context
Closed (normal)	Everything is working.	All requests go to the primary LLM provider.
Open (failing)	A threshold of failures (e.g. 5 consecutive 500 errors, or 20% error rate in 60 seconds) is met.	The orchestrator immediately stops sending traffic to this provider and returns an immediate failure/reroute. This prevents wasting time and tokens on a doomed request, and protects the failing service.
Half-open (testing)	After a timeout period (e.g. 30 seconds), the circuit breaker transitions to this state.	The orchestrator allows a single test request to the blocked provider. If the test request succeeds, the circuit closes (back to normal); if it fails, the circuit re-opens.

Rerouting

This mechanism provides continuity by routing the request to a different provider or model when the primary one is unavailable.

- ***Trigger***: The circuit breaker is in the 'open'state, or the primary LLM is consistently timing out after retries.

- ***Action***: The orchestrator switches the request to a *backup LLM provider* (e.g. if the primary is OpenAI, rerouted to a cheaper or alternative model from Anthropic or Google).
- ***Intelligent rerouting***:
    - ***Tiered fallback***: Reroute to a high-cost, high-performance backup first, then to a low-cost, lower-quality model for graceful degradation.
    - ***Context preservation***: The orchestrator ensures the prompt, context, and conversation history are correctly translated and formatted for the new provider's API.

This layer is responsible for reliability. Calls to external LLM providers can fail or time out. It uses circuit breakers to stop sending requests to a failing service and automatically retries or reroutes the request to a backup model if the primary choice is unavailable.

Safety and validation layer

This is crucial to validate the structure of the response sent back from the LLM provider. This also helps discard responses that are inappropriate or do not follow the guidelines. This checks for the structure, parsing, and content and updates the feedback loop for the response.

Data lake for analysis

We've built a standard analytics pipeline to learn from user interactions. Events from our services are sent to a central event streaming platform, which feeds our data lake built on cloud object storage. By using a modern open table format, we can reliably run large-scale data processing jobs on the collected data. This creates the feedback loop we need to continuously improve our AI models and content.

Database selection and data modelling

Let's look at the different data we need to store. Our architecture will use different types of databases for different jobs. This ensures we have the best performance, scalability, and reliability for each part of the system.

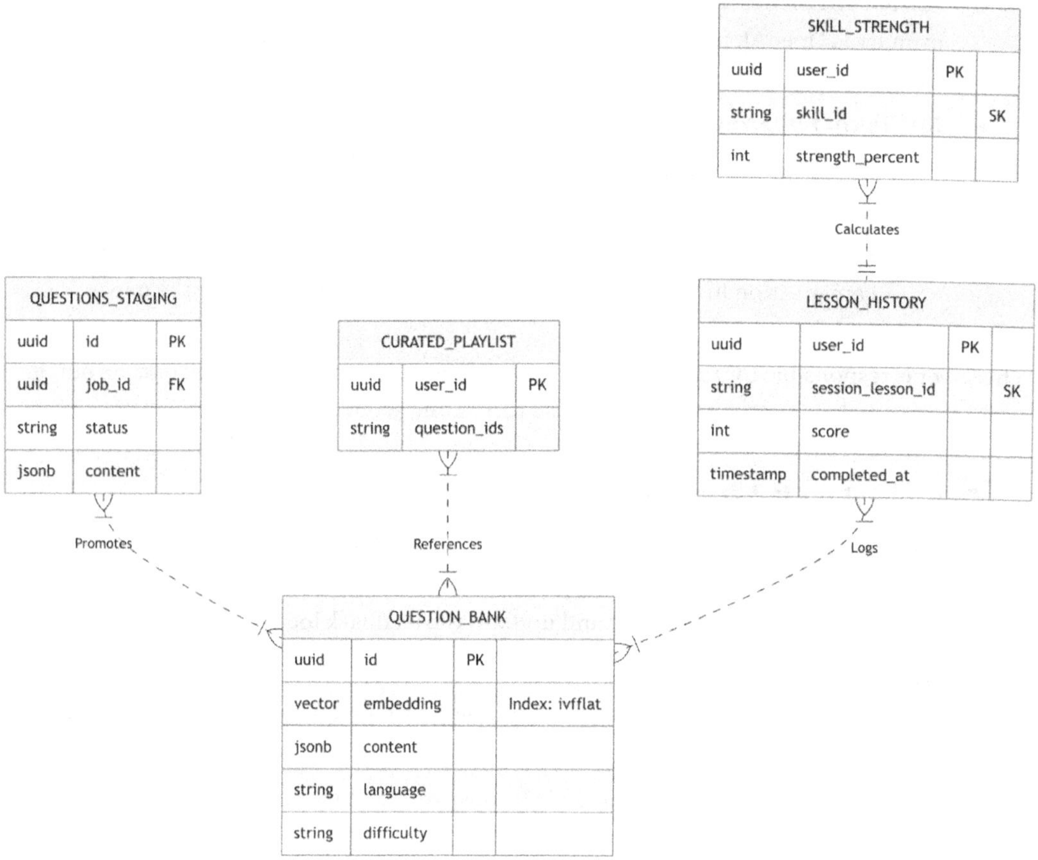

Figure 4.8: Database relations

User progress data

User progress data is stored in a high-throughput **NoSQL database** (like Cassandra or DynamoDB) to handle the massive volume of writes from user activity at per peak load 255K RPS. It's separated into two main models to separate the raw history from the calculated summary.

Lesson history

The lesson history is an append-only log, serving as a permanent record of user activity. This data feeds the offline analytics and personalization pipelines.

Context: An immutable, append-only log of every lesson session completed by a user.

Usage: Written to in real-time upon lesson completion; streamed via DynamoDB Streams to the Data Lake for offline model retraining.

lesson_history

Name	Type	Description
user_id	UUID (partition key)	UUID or unique id
session_id#lesson_id	STRING (sort key)	
evaluation_score	INTEGER	User's score for the lesson
completed_at	TIMESTAMP	When the session ended

However, storing an infinite append-only log of user history in a high-performance database (DynamoDB) is a financial antipattern. We utilize a lifecycle strategy:

The hot store (DynamoDB + TTL)

- Stores only the last 90 days of lesson history
- Used by the cold path for sub-millisecond duplication checks
- TTL: automatically deletes old records without consuming write capacity

The cold store (S3 data lake)

- DynamoDB Streams capture every write and delete
- Kinesis Firehose batches these events into Parquet files on S3
- Used by the offline pipeline for model retraining and long-term analytics

Skill strength

Context: This is a summary table, like `user_skill_strength`, that tracks a user's current calculated proficiency for each specific skill (e.g. 'Spanish future tense').

Usage: Read heavily by the lesson curator to decide difficulty and updated asynchronously by background aggregators. This table isn't updated in real-time; instead, it's periodically recalculated by an offline processing job that analyzes the raw data from the `lesson_history` table.

skill_strength

Name	Type	Description
user_id	UUID (Partition Key)	UUID or unique id
skill_id	UUID (Sort Key)	course joined time

Name	Type	Description
strength_percent	INTEGER	
updated_at	TIMESTAMP	

Since we need to support up to 90k writes per second, we can use a high write-throughput database like Cassandra or DDB (or other NoSQL databases)

Curated lessons cache

We store the curated_lessons in a Redis lists cache with light RDP snapshotting for faster recovery in case of failures in Redis nodes. We use Redis for its millisecond latency, which is essential for the user's real-time experience.

precomputed_lesson_playlists/curated_lessons

Context: A temporary buffer containing a list of question IDs curated specifically for a user's next session

Usage: Accessed via atomic LPOP operations when a user starts a lesson to ensure < 50 ms start times

Name	Type	Description
user_id	Text	UUID or unique id
question_ids	Text	A list or queue of question_ids for the user's next several lessons.

Admin review lessons data

questions_staging

Context: A holding area for AI-generated questions awaiting automated validation

Usage: Written to by the LLM orchestrator, polled by the admin portal for review dashboards

Name	Type	Description
id	UUID	Unique question id
difficulty_level	Text	Question difficulty level

Name	Type	Description
language	Text	Language the question is testing
content	JSONB	JsonB data of the actual content
question_type	Text	fill in blank, match, dialogue
concept_tags	Array	The concepts that the question is testing
score	Integer	
status	Text	New/In-Review/Accepted/Rejected

This can be stored in a relational database. However, we might need to search for semantically similar questions, using vector embeddings. We can use a dedicated vector database like turbopuffer or Pinecone or just use PostgreSQL with the pgvector extension. We will go with the last approach as we're already using PostgreSQL for storing user data as well.

Lessons data

We need to store structured question data but also support semantic search to find similar questions during content creation. We have structured data but we need to support semantic search for similar content during lesson creation. We can use PostgreSQL with pgvector extension which lets us handle relational data, flexible JSON, and vector embeddings in one database, avoiding the complexity of a separate vector DB.

Context: The single source of truth for all approved, live educational content, including vector embeddings

Usage: Read-heavy. Queried by ID (hot path) or by semantic similarity/tags (cold path/content creation)

question_bank

Name	Type	Description
id	UUID	Unique question id
difficulty_level	Text	Question difficulty level

Name	Type	Description
language	Text	Language the question is testing
content	JSONB	JsonB data of the actual content
question_type	Text	fill in blank, match, dialogue
concept_tags	Array	The concepts that the question is testing
embedding	Vector(768), Index	Vector embedding of the question for semantic search queries
score	Integer	

We'll use PostgreSQL for storing this data, as it too has high read throughput. It's easy to scale reads on RDBMS like PostgreSQL using read replicas. Since we do not have too much write throughput here, we don't have that concern.

Deep dive into design

Let's quickly recap the architecture we have discussed so far.

Functional requirement	Design solution summary
Lesson generation	Offline pipeline: Decoupled Factory model using LLMs for bulk creation. Human-in-the-loop: Expert review portal ensures safety before ingestion
Adaptive curation	Proactive curation: Pre-fetches personalized lesson buffers into Redis (warm path). Hybrid fallback: Uses rule-based logic for cold-start users.

Functional requirement	Design solution summary
High availability	Orchestrator engine: Implements circuit breakers, retries, and model rerouting to handle LLM outages.
Data persistence	PostgreSQL (content), DynamoDB (user progress)
Scale	Next focus: designing async worker patterns to handle generation spikes and read replicas for the question bank
Grading accuracy	Next focus: implementing function calling (tool use) to prevent LLM math hallucinations during grading

Now, let's take a closer look at scaling some components and features.

Asynchronous processing for content generation

For heavy tasks like 100s of question generation requests by the admin, a blocking synchronous call is a poor user experience – it would lock up the user's screen and inevitably time out.

We can use an asynchronous processing pattern, which uses a message queue to decouple the initial request from the actual work being done.

Let's walk through how this would work:

1. ***Job submission***: The admin initiates a request to generate 100 questions. The client calls an API endpoint, which our API service handles.
2. ***Lesson generation service***: This validates the request, creates a job entry with a unique jobId, saves it in the database, and pushes a message with the job details onto a request queue (`generation_jobs_queue`). It then immediately returns a 202 Accepted response to the client, along with the jobId. Subsequent workers handle up to 10 questions, so if a request comes for 100 questions, lesson generation service will split those into 10 more messages in the generation_jobs_queue.
3. ***Decoupling via message queue***: The `generation_jobs_queue` acts as a buffer. It decouples the lesson generation service from the processing workers, handles backpressure during traffic spikes, and ensures that requests are not lost if a processing worker fails.

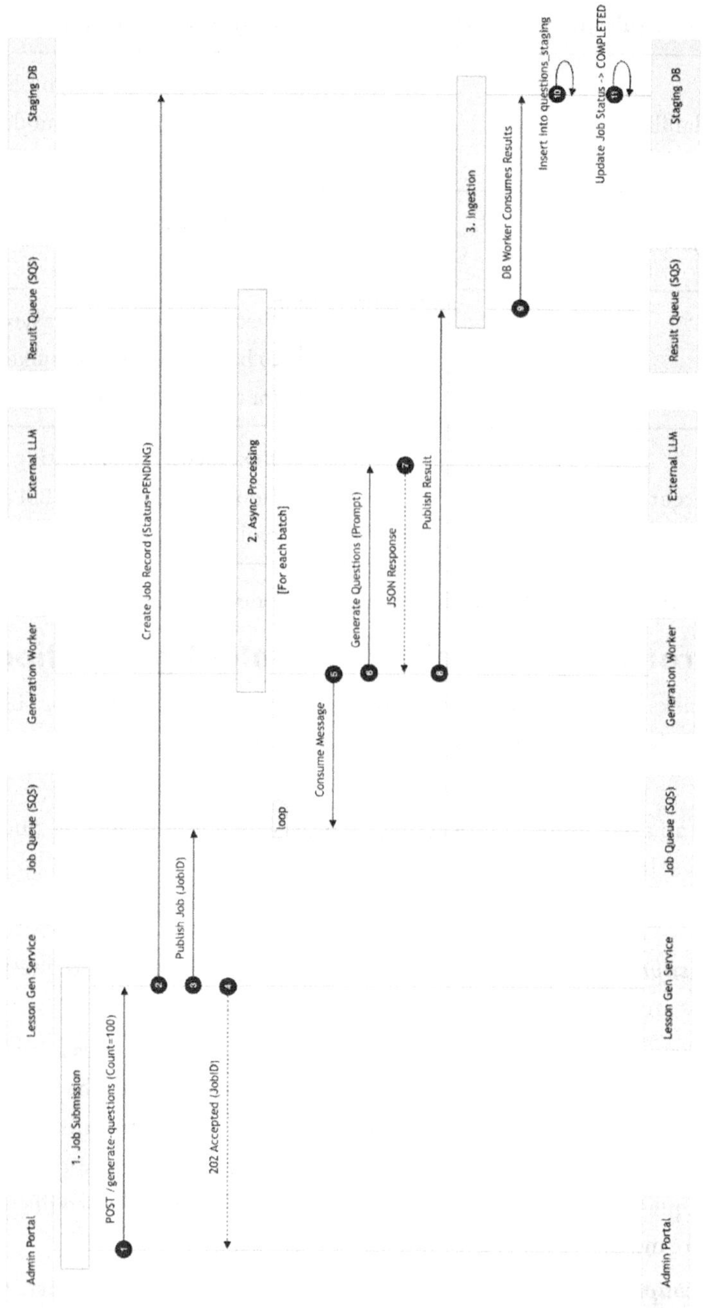

Figure 4.9: Async processing for question generation

4. ***Generation workers***: The generation workers within the LLM orchestrator are consumers of the queue. They handle the long-running CPU-intensive task of generating the new questions by invoking the LLM models and pushes it to the completed questions to a `generation_results_queue`.
5. ***DB ingestion***: The DB worker within the lesson generation service picks up these new questions from the `generation_results_queue` and populates the `questions_staging` database. This worker (or the lesson generation service itself) also updates the database, looking for the completion of all 10 child segments before marking the parent job as COMPLETED and compiling the final results URL.
6. ***Client Side Status check***: The admin UI, unblocked, can use the jobId from Step 1 to poll a status endpoint (e.g. `GET /api/v1/admin/jobs/{jobId}`). This allows for real-time status updates like "Processing..." or "Completed", improving user experience.

We also adopt a hybrid model if the admin requires immediate responses for trivial tasks. We switch to sync mode if the number of questions to be generated is less than or equal to 5. This avoids the overhead of an async model for trivial tasks and provides instant responses.

Scaling

Scaling our platform requires two sub-approaches: scaling our services to handle computational load and scaling our data tier to handle the flow of information.

Service scaling strategy

We will employ horizontal scaling (adding more server instances) for our services.

To support the 90k RPS scale, we can scale up the curation service instances and the orchestrator workers. Auto scaling on the orchestrator service should be done based on both messages pending on the queue and the level of CPU utilization. If many messages are pending, the workers should scale out. Similarly, if the service is seeing a lot of API requests, the curation service instances should auto-scale.

Data tier scaling and caching

We will employ different scaling strategies for each database type.

The question bank (PostgreSQL): This is a read-heavy database. To scale it, we can cache calls to the question bank database by maintaining the exercise object per exercise id key in a cache. We will also add read replicas, so that read traffic is distributed in different replica instances.

User progress data (DynamoDB): User progress data is tracked in DynamoDB which scales horizontally for write throughput. This database will see high write throughput as the curation service consumers add exercise IDs to user progress, and spiky read throughput as users fetch their next exercise.

The precomputed lesson cache (Redis): The precomputed_lesson_playlists is present in Redis cache. This can be scaled by running it in Redis clusters. If our Redis cluster were to fail and lose all its data, no user would lose their progress or history. The personalization pipeline would simply run again and repopulate the cache with fresh playlists. The worst-case scenario is a brief period where lesson delivery might be slower or less personalized while the cache is being refilled.

Dependency scaling

Handling the scaling and reliability of our external LLM dependencies is the primary responsibility of our LLM orchestrator engine.

Multi-provider redundancy

We should integrate with multiple LLM providers to avoid a single point of failure.

We should have circuit breakers and retries and rerouting to different LLM models for faster response in case the optimal one has too many requests.

Tiered LLM model

Orchestrators can route to different LLM models depending on urgency or complexity. For simple curation, it can use a simple and cheap model, reserving the use of GPT 4.0 models for conversational models.

Circuit breakers

Each LLM provider is wrapped in a circuit breaker. If a provider's latency spikes or returns too many errors, the circuit breaker trips. The orchestrator then instantly

- reroutes to a fast backup model
- or fails over to a non-AI response

Function calling for deterministic grading

LLMs are probabilistic and can struggle with precise math verification. Instead of asking the LLM 'Is this answer correct?', we use **function calling**.

When a user submits a numerical answer, the LLM is prompted to call a `verify_math_solution(user_answer, correct_formula)` tool [2]. The tool executes the math deterministically in a sandbox (e.g. Python) and returns a binary True/False. The LLM then uses this result to generate the feedback message. This guarantees 100% grading accuracy while retaining the friendly, conversational persona of the AI.

Testing scenarios

We can apply various testing strategies for checking the resiliency of the system.

Performance and load testing

The main goal here is to make sure our auto-scaling actually works. We'll use tools like k6 or JMeter to simulate thousands of users starting conversations at the same time. By cranking up the load (10k, 50k, 100k users), we'll find the system's breaking point, measure the wait times, and make sure we have the right auto-scaling rules.

Resilience and chaos testing

This is where we verify that the system is truly fault-tolerant. We use chaos engineering principles to deliberately inject failures while the system is under load to make sure our safety nets work:

Kill a service instance

Randomly terminate a conversation service instance. The test passes if a user's active conversation seamlessly continues on another pod by picking up the session from Redis.

Simulate network latency

We'll introduce network delays between services and Redis to confirm that our timeout and retry logic kicks in correctly.

Degrade the LLM

Simulate the LLM provider's API becoming slow or returning errors. This is the real test of our LLM orchestrator to see if it correctly trips its circuit breaker and fails over to a backup.

AI quality and regression testing

LLMs can be a bit unpredictable, so we need a way to make sure the quality of our AI's answers doesn't drift over time. We maintain a dataset of hundreds of common conversational questions and their ideal responses. Any time we tweak a prompt or upgrade a model, we run this test suite to make sure the AI's responses are still accurate, safe, and have the right tone.

Monitoring and alerting

Our whole monitoring philosophy is built around the following key signals. Watch them and we'll have a really good idea of the system's overall health.

P99 lesson serving latency: We track the end-to-end time it takes to serve a lesson, as this is our primary measure of the user's experience.

Cache hit rate: This is a critical alert. A significant drop in the Redis cache hit rate means more users are being forced into the slower, synchronous fallback path, and the team needs to investigate.

Queue depth: This is our primary alert. If the number of messages waiting in the queue grows consistently, it signals that our workers can't keep up and we need to scale them out.

End-to-end job duration: We track the P99 time it takes for a job to go from being enqueued to the final result being cached. This helps us spot bottlenecks in our LLM or database steps.

Worker and dependency health: We monitor the error rates of our consumer workers and our external dependencies. A spike in errors from our LLM provider is a key signal that our fallback logic might be kicking in.

Traffic: This tells us how much load the system is under. We're mainly watching the requests per second to downstream dependencies.

Errors: We track the HTTP 5xx error rates from all internal services and external API calls (especially the LLM provider). A sudden spike in errors is a key indicator of a problem.

Saturation: It tells us how close we are to hitting a capacity limit, like the CPU on our servers or, more importantly, the memory usage of our Redis cluster.

All of these metrics are fed into a central observability platform like Grafana or Datadog, giving the entire team a single, real-time view of the system's health.

Summary

So we see that LLMs are pretty potent tools for powering learning platforms in both content creation and content personalization flows.

On the content creation side, we've seen how platforms like Duolingo leverage LLMs to offload and accelerate lesson generation, while domain experts ensure quality by reviewing and refining. Learners benefit by getting lessons that are tailored to their learning style and pace.

Common to both flows are *retrieval and context injection*, like retrieving a learner's performance history to personalize the next lesson, or grounding a generated exercise in a validated curriculum. This same pattern, as we'll see, carries forward into other LLM-powered product domains.

Personalization is also extremely important in e-commerce search. Just as a learning platform adapts content to a learner's profile, an e-commerce search engine adapts results to a shopper's intent, preferences, and behavior. We will dive into this in the next chapter.

References

[1] Parker Henry, 'How Duolingo uses AI to create lessons faster'. Duolingo blog, June 22, 2023. `https://blog.duolingo.com/large-language-model-duolingo-lessons/`

[2] 'Introducing Duolingo Max, a learning experience powered by GPT-4'. Duolingo blog, March 14, 2023. `https://blog.duolingo.com/duolingo-max/`

[3] Parker Henry, 'Get to know the AI behind every video call with lily'. Duolingo blog, April 22, 2025. `https://blog.duolingo.com/ai-and-video-call/`

5

Case Study: AI-Powered Search for E-Commerce Platforms

Search has evolved from exact keyword and full-text matches to serving the precise needs of the user by understanding intent, creating new opportunities for **product discovery**.

Understanding the **user intent** behind search queries goes beyond simple spell checks; it's about understanding user emotions and context. A search for 'post-workout food' should be as well understood by the system as a simple query like 'butter chicken'. A search for 'cheeseburst pizza' should also show Coke and Pepsi, which pair well with the food. A search for 'old people home footwear' should show soft-soled slippers. We see this ability to handle ambiguous queries and go beyond exact keyword matching as one area where LLM really shines, due in large part to its vast knowledge of the world.

In this chapter we'll formalize the expectations of users of a generic e-commerce application and consider how to design intelligent search for e-commerce sites as exemplified by Amazon, Myntra, Nykaa, etc. The structure will be a variant of that employed in the previous case study, tailored here to our focus on search solutions:

- Functional requirements
- Non-functional requirements
- Scale estimates
- API design
- Background
- Blueprint high-level design
- Data modelling
- System design deep dive

- Efficient ranking
- Ensuring robustness
- Monitoring
- Alerting
- Testing and evaluation

Functional requirements

The main functional requirements we'll be considering are:

- *Natural language understanding*: The system must understand and process user queries in natural language, including complex and **long-tail queries**. For example, 'healthy snacks without nuts for kids' or 'a summer dress that's not too formal'.
- *Semantic search*: It should understand the user intent behind queries, serving relevant results with or without an exact keyword match.
- *Product recommendations*: The system should suggest relevant products, including complementary items commonly ordered by other users.
- *Personalization*: The search results should be based on the user's past behavior, preferences, and purchase history.

Non-functional requirements (NFRs)

On the non-functional side we have:

- *Relevance and accuracy*: The search results must be highly relevant to the user's query to ensure good conversions.
- *Low latency*: Search results must be delivered to the user in near real-time, typically within a few hundred milliseconds. P90 latency should be < 1 s, P99 latency should be < 5 s.
- *High availability*: The smart search must be highly available and resilient to failures (e.g. failures in LLM providers), as it's a critical component of the e-commerce platform.
- *Cost effectiveness*: LLM calls are highly expensive; the system design should be such as to optimize this cost.
- *Freshness*: The search index needs to be updated in near real-time to reflect changes in the product catalog, such as new products, price changes, and out-of-stock items.

Scale estimates

Assuming a mid-to-large size e-commerce platform then we could be looking at the following usage statistics:

Daily active users (DAU): 10 M

Average searches per user per day: 5

Total daily searches: 10M * 5 = 50 M

Queries per second (average) = 50 M / (60*60*24) = ~579 RPS

Peak queries per second (assuming 5x average rps) = (579 * 5) = ~2,895 RPS

Product catalog size: 10 M products

Data storage

Product data (1 KB per product): 10 GB

Vector embeddings: With 1536 dimensional embeddings (OpenAI Ada v2), and 4B per embedding = 1536*4* (10 M products) = 60 GB

User data: 10 GB

Total storage: 80-100 GB

API design

We can resolve our application's API requirements into the following endpoints.

Search results endpoint

The primary entry point for the storefront; executes the hybrid search strategy and returns a personalized, ranked list of products.

Method	GET
URI	/v1/search
Query params	q, userId, sessionId, page, filters, sortBy

Response


```
{
"searchId": "b4a8-f2c1-e9d0-a7b6",
"correctedQuery": "hill station outfits",
"results": [
  {
  "productId": "DEC-FLC-001S",
  "title": "Quechua Women's Hiking Fleece Jacket - MH120",
  "description": "A warm and breathable fleece jacket,
perfect for cool weather on your mountain hikes. Made with
recycled polyester.",
  "imageUrl": "https://example.com/images/
decathlon_fleece_blue.jpg",
  "price": {
    "amount": 1499.00, "currency": "INR"
  },
  "brand": "Decathlon", "rating": 4.7
  },
{
"productId": "DEC-WJK-015S",
"title": "Forclaz Women's Padded Trekking Jacket - MT100",
"description": "Compact and lightweight padded jacket
designed to keep you warm during your hill station treks.
Water-repellent.",
"imageUrl": "https://example.com/images/
decathlon_padded_jacket_black.jpg",
"price": {
  "amount": 2499.00, "currency": "INR"
},
"brand": "Decathlon",
"rating": 4.8
}
],
"relatedSearches": ["winter trekking clothes", "waterproof
jackets Decathlon", "thermal wear for women", "hiking
shoes"],
"pagination": {
    "currentPage": 1, "totalPages": 1, "totalResults": 2
  }
}
```

Parameter	Type	Description
q	string	The user's search query (e.g., "hill station outfits").
userId	string	The unique ID of the user for personalization
sessionId	string	unique ID assigned to the user in the current session
page	int	pagination page number
filters	string	A URL-encoded JSON string for filtering, e.g., {"brand":"Decathlon","size":"S"}
sortBy	string	Sort order. e.g., relevance, price_asc, price_desc

Background

Before we start with the design of an AI-powered search for e-commerce, let's discuss how search typically works in a traditional system. At the time of restaurant or store onboarding, the merchant uploads dishes or items, which are ingested as documents in a search database like **Elasticsearch** (ES) [2]. During this ingestion process, each dish or store item is thoroughly enriched with metadata attributes by our system, which helps in categorization and classification.

For example, when an item like a 'Diet Coke 500ml can' is uploaded, its attributes include:

Brand: Coca-Cola

Category: soft drink

Sub type: Diet Coke

Form: Can

Size: 500ml

Similarly, when a dish like 'spicy ghee rava masala dosa' is uploaded, its attributes include [2]:

Dish: Dosa

Flavour: ghee

Grain: Rava

SubType: Masala Dosa

Spice Level: Spicy

These attributes can be added either manually or (as done by larger companies) by using automated pipelines with rules-based systems, machine learning models, and data from suppliers to extract and normalize attributes. This automated pipeline runs on new or updated products to make them fully searchable. In short, it:

- ***Uses an LLM*** to read product info and automatically extract structured tags (e.g. color, material).
- ***Indexes for keyword search*** by adding the product's text and new tags into Elasticsearch.
- ***Indexes for semantic search*** by creating a vector embedding of the product's meaning and storing it in a vector database.

For the rest of the chapter, we will assume this ingestion and enrichment/annotation pipeline has already run. All products in our database are already indexed for both keyword and semantic search.

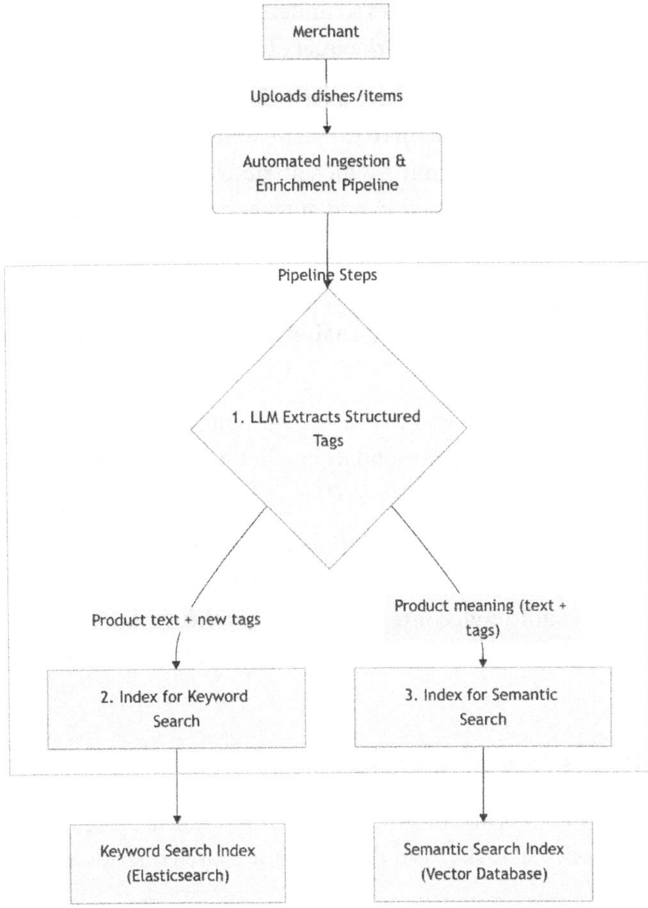

Figure 5.1: Ingestion and annotation pipeline

In a traditional search system, the user's query would be passed on to an Elasticsearch or search database where it would be used for retrieving similar documents. Traditional Elasticsearch, without additional plugins or a vector search setup, primarily uses lexical or keyword-based matching, not true semantic similarity. These documents would then be ranked by the score.

The query added by users can be at times vague and ambiguous, and does not point to a specific dish or item. Or other times it can be a bunch of words that make it hard to determine whether it refers to one dish or more. While techniques like adding synonyms, spell correction, and autocomplete are used for improving results for ambiguous or vague queries, and are useful to an extent, they are not foolproof.

LLMs can be pretty powerful in these cases to understand the intent behind the user queries. For example, with LLMs we can segment the query for a better understanding of the intent.

With the ingestion process, we already have a well-defined categorization and classification system. The user query can be passed on to the LLM along with the classification system context in order for the LLM to determine which attributes are present in the query. It will automatically also include spell correction and auto-complete steps. We can add in **guardrails** so that the LLM doesn't hallucinate and only returns the categories we're passing in the context.

We can further employ LLMs for **query expansion** as well, using alternatives that actually exist in our system.

For discovering new products, we send the same segmented and expanded query to the LLM. The LLM can then suggest related items and items that would pair well with the user's original search.

This process is enhanced by data from analytics pipelines that track user behavior, such as which items users buy together. These behavioral metrics, along with their conversion rates, can be fed to the LLM as additional context. These allow the LLM to make more intelligent suggestions, prioritizing related and complementary items that the users are likely to purchase.

Blueprint high-level design

We need to minimize latency while improving search intelligence. So, we separate the computationally expensive AI tasks from the real-time search queries. Our architecture will have

1. ***Offline query processing pipeline***: Our strict sub-second latency requirement is achieved by decoupling the computationally heavy AI work into an offline pipeline that populates a low-latency cache.
2. ***Real-time search flow***: This serves user requests in real time. We use a dual-path system designed for sub-second responses. It has a *fast path* for the majority of queries and a *fallback path*.
3. ***Product discovery flow***: Improve product discovery and conversions by retrieving complementary items.

Offline query processing pipeline

This runs in the background to form the intelligence that our real-time search relies on. It uses LLMs for computationally heavy tasks where latency is not a concern.

This pipeline runs daily (or more frequently as discussed in deep dive), analyzing user search behavior to continuously improve our search accuracy.

The queries searched by users over the past day are collected and sent in batches to the offline query processing pipeline. To understand the intent behind the user's search query, each past user query goes through a segmentation and expansion process.

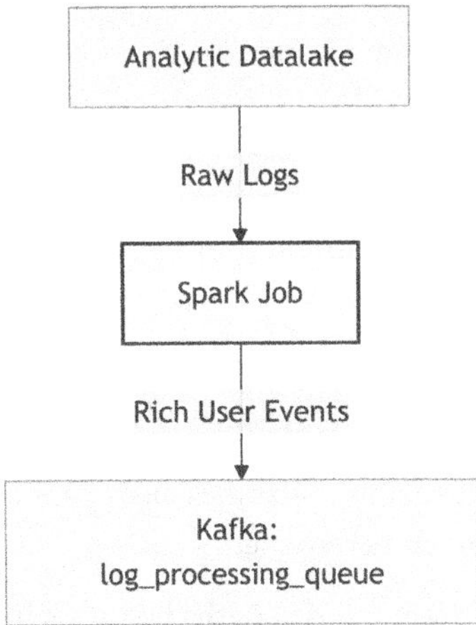

Figure 5.2: Log aggregation spark job

Log aggregation

A Spark job reads raw log files of user queries and their resulting user actions (clicks, purchases) from the analytical data lake storage, groups them by the user session and puts them into a processing queue like Kafka. It creates a rich list of events like this:

(UserID: "a", Query: "sofa", Clicked: "Product #123", AddedToCart: "Product #123")
(UserID: "b", Query: "couch", Clicked: "Product #123", Purchased: "Product #123")
(UserID: "c", Query: "hot dogs", Purchased: "Product #456" AND "Product #789")

This is the raw data, connecting user queries to what they buy.

During this aggregation phase the system explicitly counts the **query frequency**. This is a key part of the step. The frequency is used later to determine which queries to pre-process and where to cache them.

Parallelized enrichment

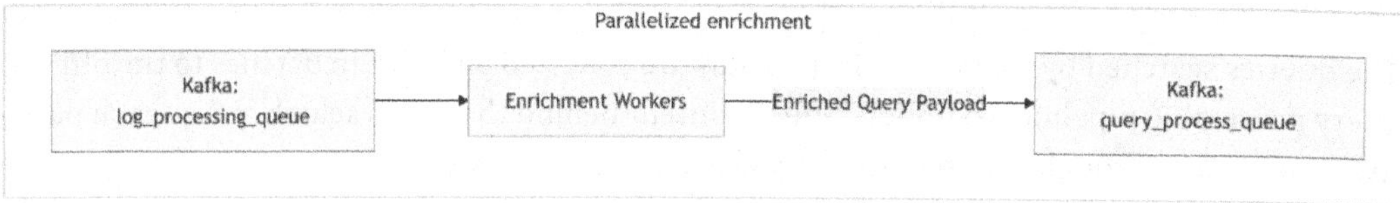

Figure 5.3: Parallelized enrichment

Millions of logs are processed concurrently by distributing the workload across instances.

The Spark job takes in batches of this structured data of user queries and processes it in parallel. The log aggregation and enrichment processes are decoupled via a Kafka queue. This helps scale both workers independently, whilst also providing resiliency in case an enrichment worker fails temporarily.

Each structured log entry undergoes several layers of parallel enrichment:

Query normalization: Common spelling mistakes and typos are corrected, and case is standardized and irrelevant characters removed.

User profile enrichment: We hydrate queries with the user's history, such as past purchases and brand preferences.

Contextual enrichment: This includes users' geolocation, time of day, device data, local trends, etc., that affect purchasing decisions.

Each user query is normalized and enriched with the above details and sent as a payload to a `query_process` queue (or Kafka topic).

Query segmentation and classification service

This is responsible for decoding user intent. The query segmentation workers consume the enriched payloads from the `query_process` queue.

This enriched query payload is sent to the GenAI service with additional details like the platform's classification structure, etc.

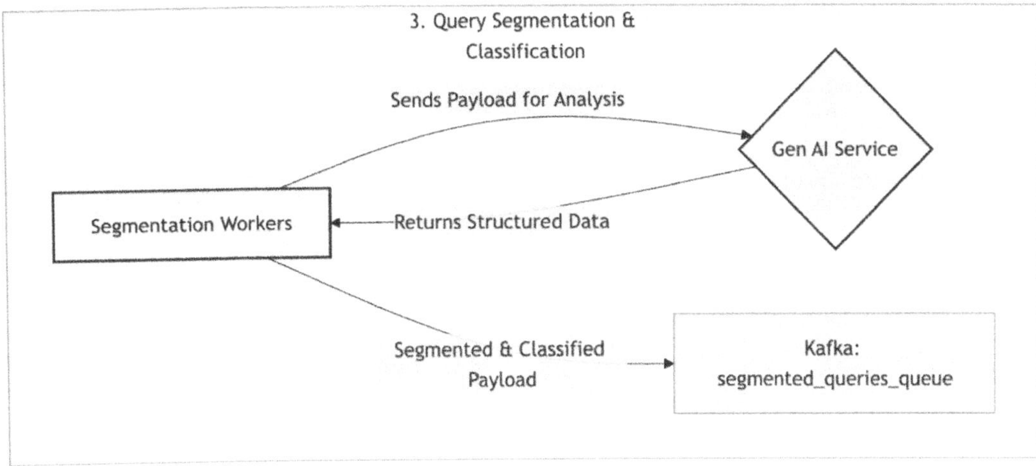

Figure 5.4: Query segmentation and classification

Segmentation: The GenAI service performs segmentation, structuring the query according to our platform's taxonomy. For example, the query "organic aged basmati rice" is segmented into:

organic: Attribute/Tag

aged: Attribute/Tag

Basmati: Product Quality

rice: Product Category

Classification: The model then performs **classification**. It takes the identified Product Category (rice) and maps it to the precise location within our internal product hierarchy, such as

Groceries > Rice, Flour & Pulses > Basmati rice

The output of this service is a new JSON payload containing this structured, mapped data. This payload, representing the system's deep understanding of the query's intent, is then pushed to the `segmented_queries` queue.


```
{
"original_query": "organic aged basmati rice",
"normalized_query": "organic aged basmati rice",
"user_profile": {
    "user_id": "user-abc-123",
    "past_purchases": ["p-987", "p-321"],
```

```
        "brand_preferences": ["OrganicIndia"]
        },
    "context": {
        "geolocation": "Mumbai",
        "time_of_day": "evening",
        "device": "mobile"
        },
    "segmentation_results": {
        "attributes": ["organic", "aged"],
        "product_category": "rice",
        "product_quality": "Basmati"
        },
    classification_results": {
        "taxonomy_path": "Groceries >Rice,Flour&Pulses> Basmati Rice"
        }
    }
```

Linking and query expansion service

This bridges the gap between what the user said and their true intent, while also proactively suggesting relevant alternatives they may not have considered.

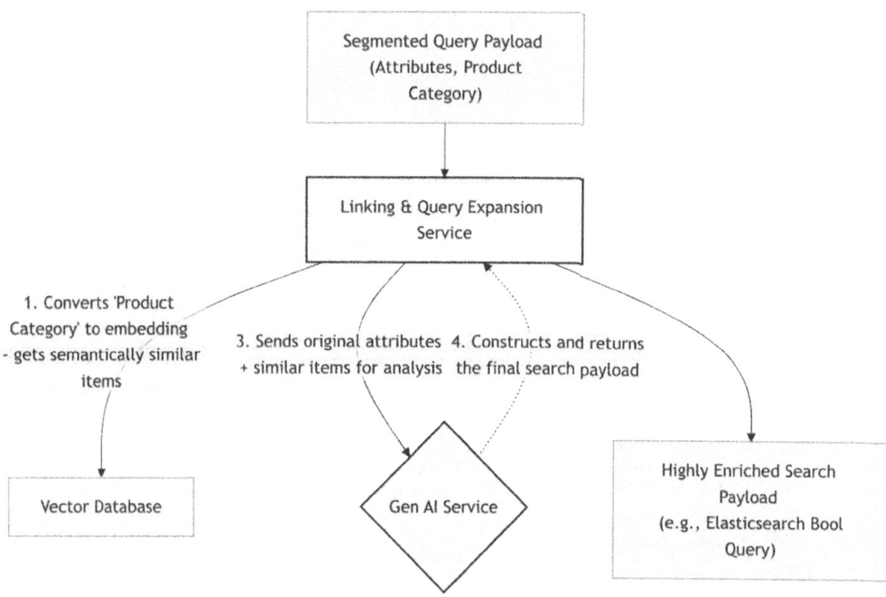

Figure 5.5: Linking and query expansion service

Now we want to link the user query to similar/alternate items in our system based on the intent of the user. The idea is to send the query as a prompt along with items from our catalog of products to LLM so that it can determine how to best expand the query with alternatives available in our system.

LLMs have a fixed short-term memory called the context window which is measured in tokens. This limit includes both input prompt and the model's generated output, so a large prompt leaves little room for an answer. So there is a restriction on the number of tokens being sent to in the prompt. We have a huge catalog of products, and it is not feasible to send the entirety along with the user query to the LLM for query expansion.

The system must first retrieve a small, relevant list of products that easily fits within the context window, allowing the LLM to intelligently refine it for query expansion.

Entity retrieval and linking: This is where vector database and **semantic search** come in.

The vector database called `semantic_search_index` stores the product description and tags in an embedded form along with the `product_id` to link it to [3][4].

The segmented query components (e.g. rice) are converted into **vector embeddings** (by calling the embedding model or cache) and used to perform a similarity search in our vector database.

Semantically similar items and products for each attribute value are searched. It will retrieve not only 'rice' but also semantically similar items like 'grains', 'poha' and 'millets'.

Intelligent query expansion: It sends these retrieved items to the GenAI service for the best query expansion with retrieved alternatives available in our system. The GenAI service picks the most relevant alternatives from the ones retrieved via semantic search, and combines the original user attributes (organic, aged) with these products.

```
{
"original_query": "organic aged basmati rice", "segmented_query": {
"attributes": ["organic", "aged"], "product_category": "rice", "product_quality":
"basmati"
},
"semantic_alternatives": [
{"product_id": "p-987", "name": "Organic Poha"},
{"product_id": "p-654", "name": "Barnyard Millet"},
{"product_id": "p-321", "name": "Brown Rice Flakes"},
{"product_id": "p-111", "name": "Aged Sona Masoori Rice"}
],
"instructions": "You are a search relevance expert for an e-commerce platform.
Analyze the semantic alternatives and select the most relevant ones for the
original query. Construct a search payload that combines the original attributes
```

```
with the base product and its best alternatives."
}
```

The output is a highly enriched search query payload that includes synonyms and alternatives. It looks like the following:

```
{
  "search_query_payload": {
    "bool": {
      "must": [
        {
          "match": {
            "attributes": "organic"
          }
        },
        {
          "match": {
            "attributes": "aged"
          }
        }
      ],
      "should": [
        {
          "match": {
            "product_type": "basmati rice"
          }
        },
        {
          "match": {
            "product_type": "sona masoori rice"
          }
        },
        {
          "match": {
            "product_type": "poha"
          }
        },
        {
          "match": {
            "product_type": "millet"
          }
```

```
          }
        ],
        "minimum_should_match": 1
      }
    }
  }
```

The output is a highly enriched search query payload that includes synonyms and alternatives.

Ranking and indexing worker

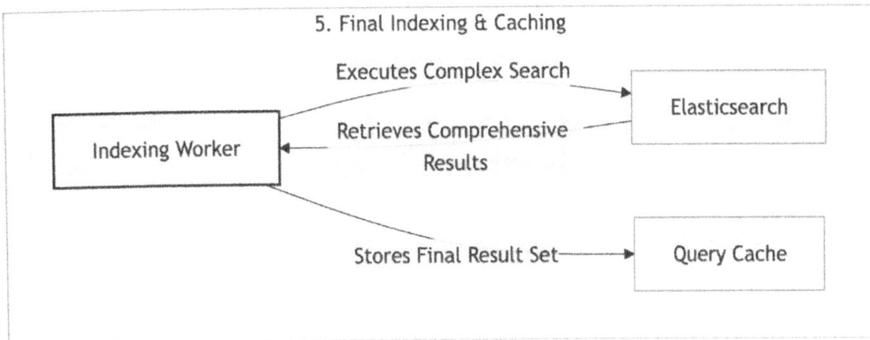

Figure 5.6: Ranking and indexing worker

The final segmented and expanded query is consumed by the Elasticsearch worker, which uses it to retrieve items from the Elasticsearch database by a **keyword search**.

We cache the enriched Elasticsearch query instead of the final list of product matches to solve two critical flaws: stale data and high memory usage.

Maintaining freshness

While caching the final list of product IDs offers the lowest possible latency, it risks showing users incorrect information. If a product's price changes or it goes out of stock, a cached product list would be wrong until the entire offline pipeline was run again.

By caching the ES query instead, the search service executes this query against the live Elasticsearch index every time. This ensures that the results returned to the user always reflect real-time price, stock, and rating information, satisfying the freshness requirement.

Memory efficiency

Storing the complete list of product IDs for millions of unique user queries would consume a significant and potentially unmanageable amount of memory.

Storing the Elasticsearch query is far more memory-efficient than storing a long list of product IDs for every possible search permutation.

Real-time search flow

This is the flow where the user interacts. It is designed for speed and uses a two-tiered approach, a fast path and a fallback path, as previously mentioned in the *Blueprint high-level design* section. The user enters an item or a query into the search bar, and the client app calls the server with the user's search query.

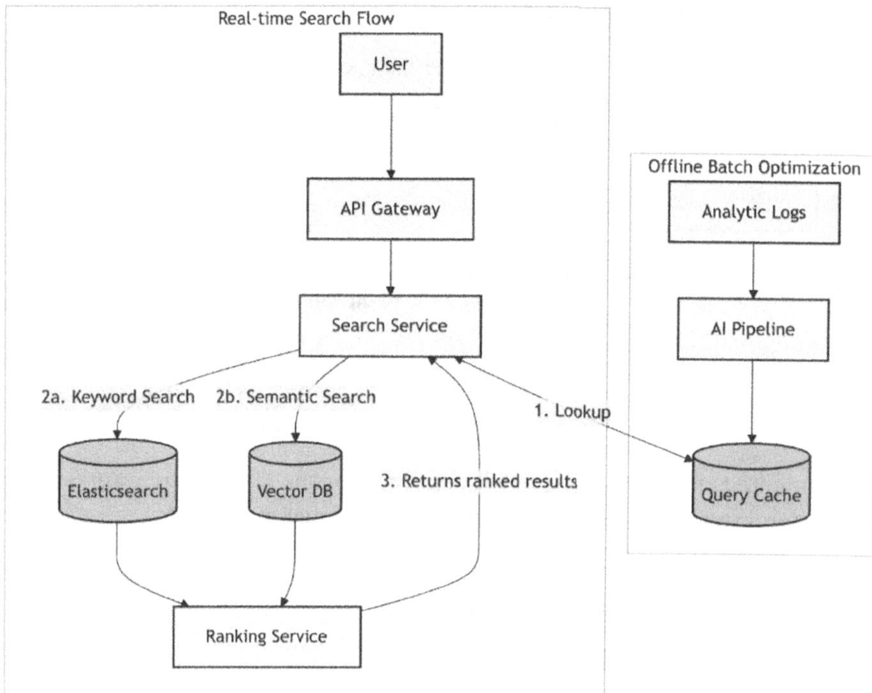

Figure 5.7: Real-time search flow

API gateway

User requests are validated for authentication and rate limiting at this component. It routes the request to the **search service**.

Search service

This service handles real-time search for sub-second responses. It checks the query cache first – a cache hit retrieves the ES query which is used to retrieve the set of relevant results, ranked and sorted. A cache miss leads to fallback on the fast path as below.

Fast path

The default for 99% uncached queries, this executes a hybrid search in parallel:

- ***Keyword search***: It calls the document search database with the query to retrieve the related documents.
- ***Semantic search***: It converts the user's query into a vector embedding on the fly (using the embedding cache or making a call to the embedding model) and makes a call to the vector database to search for semantically similar products.

Re-ranking: The responses from both searches are merged, de-duplicated, and ranked with light-weight ML re-ranking models. This uses criteria like keyword score, semantic score, and product popularity to create the final most relevant list.

Response: If the results have a high confidence score, they are returned to the user immediately.

Fallback path

This path is triggered for more complex queries, if the fast path returns zero results or results with extremely low confidence scores.

Trigger: When the Search service detects a failed search from the fast path.

LLM for query understanding: The Search service calls the GenAI service for query understanding. The goal is to rewrite the user's ambiguous query into system-understandable terms.

Example: A user's query 'stuff for my dorm party' is rewritten by the LLM to a structured query like `(category: "snacks" OR category: "drinks") AND (attribute: "party size")`

Retry search: This rewritten query is taken and sent to the fast path again.

Response: The results from this second, more successful attempt are shown to the user. This ensures that difficult queries also get a good response without slowing down the majority of the queries.

GenAI service (LLM gateway)

The **GenAI service** or **LLM gateway** is a centralized intelligent gateway for all interactions with large language models. This encapsulates the dependencies on third-party LLM providers from the rest of the system components, and is responsible for handling provider abstraction, implementing dynamic model routing, ensuring resiliency and reliability, and storing prompt templates. Taking those in turn:

Provider abstraction

It exposes a single unified API for GenAI tasks. Internal services like the search service and the offline query processors need to call only this generic endpoint. This makes it easy to enter and switch any LLM providers as required.

Dynamic model routing

This component routes the request to LLM providers based on the kind and type of request. It selects models based on:

Cost: For high-volume requests and simpler tasks, it switches to low latency and cheaper models like Gemini 2.5 Flash. For tasks like query rewrite, it can select more optimal LLMs like GPT-5o. The router also maintains a configuration that maps specific tasks to models.

Latency: For real-time online requests, it will prioritize the fastest available model that meets the quality threshold.

Resiliency and reliability

Since interacting with third party dependencies can be unreliable, we need a robust resiliency layer so it doesn't impact the rest of our system.

The GenAI service implements :

- ***Circuit breakers***: so that if one LLM provider is down, the request can be sent to the next optimal LLM provider
- ***Time-outs***: i.e. if a provider doesn't respond within a threshold duration, the request is cancelled
- ***Retries***: It performs intelligent retries with exponential backoff for transient errors

Prompt templates

It also stores prompt templates for fast generation of prompts

LLM providers

These are actual third-party services or self-hosted models that execute our prompts. They can be of several types:

- ***Managed AI platforms***: They offer access to a variety of models from different companies through a single API. Example: AWS Bedrock, Google Cloud's Vertex AI, etc.
- ***Direct model APIs***: These are the APIs provided directly by the AI research labs that create the models. Example: OpenAI (GPT models), Anthropic (for Claude models), etc.
- ***Open-source models***: These are models that can be downloaded and hosted on our own infrastructure for maximum control of privacy and cost. Example: Llama series, Hugging Face, etc.

Product discovery flow

We want to return related items or items that pair with the items searched by the user. This helps in new product discovery and conversion [1][2].

For example, a search for 'brownie' should suggest 'ice cream' as a complementary item. Our strict sub-second latency requirement is achieved by decoupling the computationally heavy AI work into an offline pipeline that populates a low-latency cache.

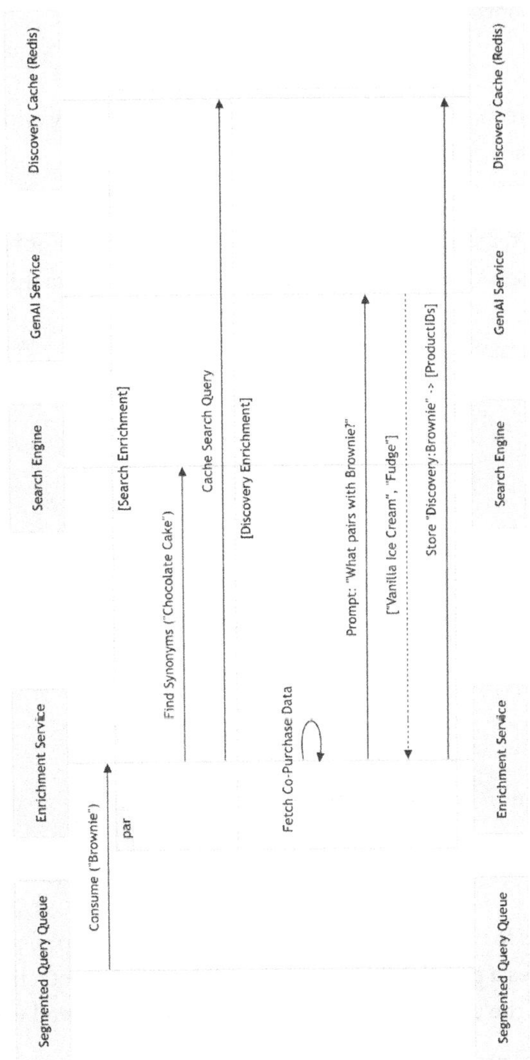

Figure 5.8: Product Discovery flow

Offline flow

We have discussed how the query segmentation and classification process helps in getting a clear mapping of the product entity and its attributes according to the platform's taxonomy (e.g. product: 'brownie').

Our offline pipeline is triggered after the query segmentation and classification service produces a message in the `segmented_queries` queue. The enrichment service consumes this message and performs both search and discovery tasks in parallel:

Search enrichment:

- The service performs the linking and query expansion flow and caches the resulting ES query in the `smart_query_cache` as discussed.
- Discovery enrichment: The service fetches co-purchase analytics for the product. The primary product, along with its rich analytics context, is sent to a GenAI service. The prompt in the GenAI service would look like something like this:

```
You are an expert e-commerce merchandiser. Given a primary product and data
on what customers often buy with it, generate a list of 3-5 complementary
products that would enhance the customer's experience. Return the output as
a JSON array.
**Input:**
{
"primary_product": "brownie",
"co_purchase_data": ["chocolate chips", "eggs", "vanilla extract", "vanilla
ice cream", ""chocolate sauce", ""whipped cream"]
}
**Output:**
["vanilla ice cream", "chocolate sauce", "whipped cream"]
```

The resulting list of items is saved in Redis in a `discovery_products` cache with the primary product name as the key.

Online flow

When the user searches for 'brownie', the primary search for brownie products happens as usual. The system makes a parallel call to the discovery cache to get a list of related products. This list is displayed to the user in a dedicated section, like 'Pairs well with' or 'Users also bought'.

Data modelling

There is a variety of data in our system. The storage and access patterns for each differs widely from others. Let's take a look at all the kinds of data we touched upon in the system design blueprint.

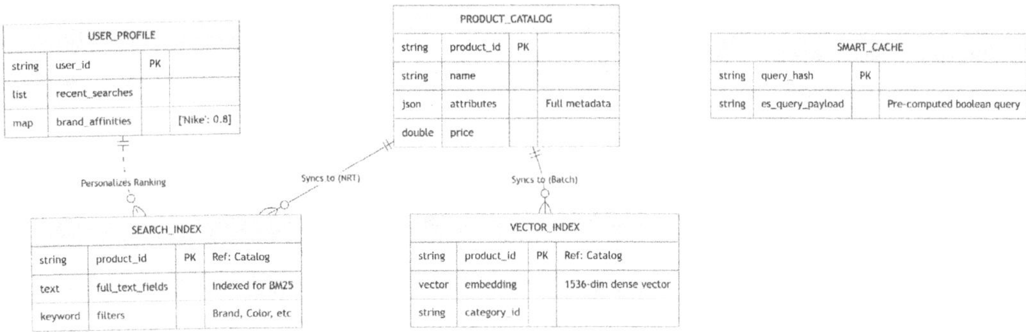

Figure 5.9: Table relationships

Product catalog

This handles all product details.

product_catalog

Context: The authoritative source of truth for all product data (pricing, descriptions, stock).

Usage: High read/write. Updated by merchant ingestion pipelines; read by the checkout service and search indexers to ensure data consistency.

Column	Type	Description
`productId`	String (partition key)	Unique identifier
`name`	String	Product name
`description`	String	Detailed product description
`attributes`	JSON object	Key-value pairs of product attributes (e.g. {"brand": "Nike", "color": "blue"})
`price`	Double (Sort Key)	Price of the product

Column	Type	Description
`imageUrl`	String	URL of the product image
`category`	String	Product category
GSI (Global Secondary Index)	`category_id` (Partition Key) `price` (Sort Key)	To allow efficient non-search retrieval like "Show me all items in 'Shoes' sorted by Price" without scanning the whole table

This product catalog will be populated during document ingestion, i.e. when new merchants are uploading stores or new restaurants are onboarding, etc. This sees a high write throughput when the ingestion pipeline runs. This also sees high read throughput as it is accessed by our search system during both online and offline flows. We can use a NoSQL database like DynamoDB for fast access in this case. The partition key is `productId`. This ensures all information for a single product is stored together.

Smart search cache

This is the cache that the search service queries first when a user query comes in.

Context: A specialized semantic cache that maps a user's natural language query (e.g. 'warm coat') to a pre-computed database query.

Usage: Extremely high read. Hit by the search service before any logic is executed. Maps user query hash -> Elasticsearch JSON payload

smart_query cache

Key	User query
Value	ES query

For the persistent tier stored in DynamoDB, the partition key would be the `user_query` itself.

Product search index (for keyword search and filtering)

This is a fast, traditional keyword-based search that handles all structured filtering.

It uses an **inverted index** to quickly look up products based on keywords in their title, description, and attributes. It's also highly efficient at applying filters (e.g. price < 100, brand = "Nike", color = "blue").

product_search_index

Context: An inverted index optimized for fast keyword matching, filtering, and faceting (counts).

Usage: This is the queried in the fast path. Executes logic (e.g. brand="Nike" AND price < 50) on sub-second timescale.

Field	**Type**	**Description**
`product_id`	Keyword	The unique identifier for the product. Mapped as a keyword for exact-match lookups.
`name`	Text	These are the primary fields for full-text search
`description`	Text	These are the primary fields for full-text search
`brand`	keyword	For filtering, sorting
`category_path`	keyword	
`price`	float	Allows for numeric range queries (e.g., price < 100) and sorting
`in_stock`	boolean	true/false
`rating`	float	
`review_count`	integer	
`attributes`	nested	Preserves the relationship between key and value for accurate filtering on multiple attributes at once

Field	Type	Description
`attributes.key`	keyword	For exact-match filtering on the attribute's name (e.g., "color")
`attributes.value`	keyword	For exact-match filtering on the attribute's value (e.g., "blue")
`imageUrl`	String	URL of the product image
`created_at`	date	for date based queries

We can use Elasticsearch or OpenSearch for querying.

Vector database (for semantic search)

For products that are semantically similar to the user's query, even if they don't share any keywords, semantic search is used. A vector database stores numerical representations (embeddings) of each product. For each product, several fields from the product catalog are combined into one semantic document before sending it to the embedding model.

For a product with these fields:

name: "Men's Terra Running Shoe"

brand: "Olympus Athletics"

category_path: "Apparel/Footwear/Running Shoes"

attributes: ["trail running", "waterproof", "breathable"]

The semantic document would be:

"Men's Terra Running Shoe by Olympus Athletics. Category: Footwear, Running Shoes. A waterproof and breathable shoe for trail running."

semantic_search_index

Context: Stores the high-dimensional vector embeddings of products to enable conceptual matching.

Usage: Queried during the hybrid search phase to retrieve items that match the intent but not necessarily the keywords of the query.

Column	Type
`productid`	To link back to the product data
`embedding`	The high-dimensional vector representation of the product
`category_id`	String
`metadata`	other metadata relevant to the product

When a query comes in, its embedding is calculated and the database performs an **approximate nearest neighbour** (**ANN**) search to find the closest product vectors in a high-dimensional space.

This vector database is used in the online search path for fast search. It sees a very high read throughput. During the offline enrichment for the search pipeline this will see fairly high write throughput as well. We can choose to go with a serverless option for vector databases like Turbopuffer to autoscale during load.

Product discovery cache

This is the cache that the **discovery service** queries for fetching related and complementary items from the user query.

product_discovery

Key	User query
Value	ES query to retrieve these product ids

Analytic logs store (datalake)

Context: An immutable append-only ledger of every search event, click, and purchase.

Usage: Write-heavy (streaming). Consumed by Spark jobs to train the ranking models and populate the Hot Queries list.

Column	Type	Description
event_id	STRING	Unique identifier (UUID) for each individual log entry.
event_timestamp		Precise UTC timestamp when the event occurred. Used for time-series analysis.
user_id	STRING	The unique identifier for the user who performed the action.
session_id	STRING	The identifier for the user's session, used to analyse a single user journey.
raw_query	STRING	The exact, unaltered search query as typed by the user.
filters_applied	MAP<STRING, STRING>	Key-value pairs of all filters applied to the search (e.g., {"brand": "Nike", "price_max": "100"}).
search_type	STRING	The type of search executed (e.g. 'hybrid', 'keyword_only', 'semantic_fallback').
displayed_product_ids	ARRAY<STRING>	An ordered list of the product IDs (SKUs) that were displayed to the user.

Column	Type	Description
clicked_product_id	STRING	The product ID the user clicked. NULL if no click occurred.
added_to_cart_product_id	STRING	Product ID added to cart from search results. NULL if none.
device_type	STRING	The type of client used (e.g. 'web', 'mobile_app_ios', 'mobile_app_android').

User profile

This is used by the search service to determine the user's buying preferences and history.

user_profile

Column	Type	Description
userId	partition key	Unique identifier
searchHistory		A list of recent search queries
purchaseHistory		A list of purchased product IDs
preferences		User preferences (e.g., favourite brands, sizes)

A NoSQL database like DynamoDB is used for fast access. The partition key is `userId`. This groups all data for a single user in one location for fast retrieval.

System design deep dive

Let's recap what we've discussed so far.

Functional requirement	Design solution summary
Natural language understanding	Query segmentation: LLM breaks queries into structured attributes (e.g. "red" -> Color, "dress" -> Category)
Semantic search	Hybrid retrieval: Parallel execution of keyword search (Elasticsearch) and vector search (HNSW) to capture both exact matches and intent
Low latency (< 1 s)	Tiered caching: L1 (Local), L2 (Redis), and warm tier (vector cache) to serve 80% of traffic without hitting the LLM
Personalization	Re-ranking service: Lightweight model re-orders the top 50 results based on user affinity (brand/price) in real-time
Product discovery	Offline enrichment: Batch jobs pre-calculate 'pairs well with' suggestions to enable zero-latency recommendations
High scale	Next focus: Lambda architecture for handling real-time trends and HNSW graph optimization for vector scale

For sub-second search results we decoupled the online path from the offline intelligence-building path. Let's explore how that offline pipeline and our caching strategy work to balance powerful, AI-driven results with low latency.

How often should the offline pipeline run?

Frequency depends on business needs and query patterns. While a daily run is standard, this frequency can be increased to hourly during high-traffic events like festivals or flash sales, when user query patterns change rapidly.

However, what if a query becomes a viral trend within a few minutes? Running the entire pipeline too often will become computationally expensive.

Near-real-time path

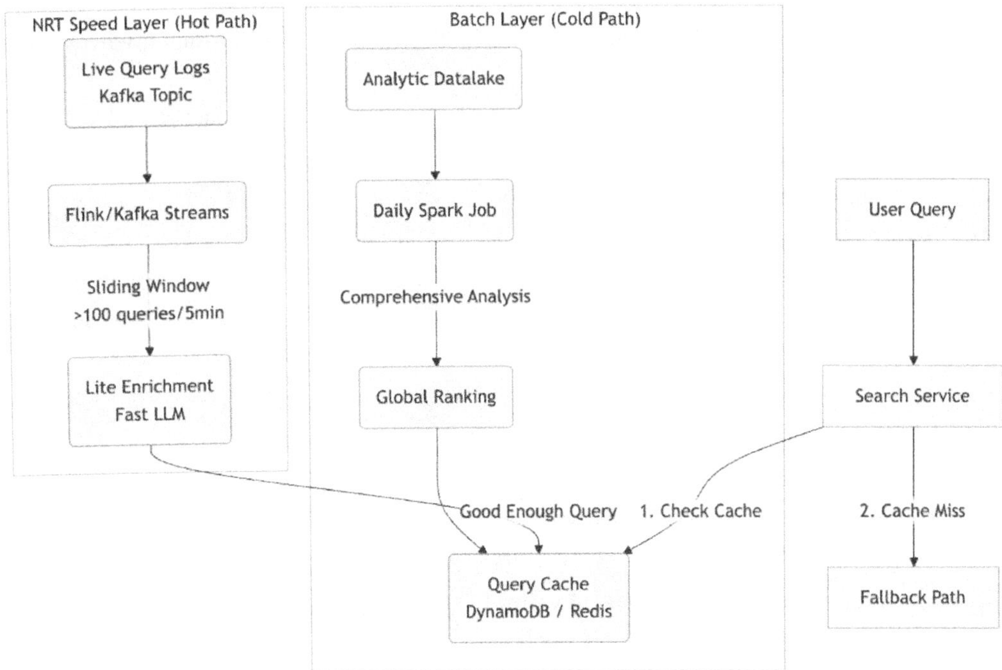

Figure 5.10: Near-real-time path

This is where a near-real-time path (**Lambda architecture**) could be useful.

We keep the daily job for deep, comprehensive analysis and global ranking and additionally:

1. ***Monitoring trends***:
   A separate, lightweight streaming path monitors query logs in real time by consuming directly from the `query_logs` Kafka topic. We use a stream processing engine (like Kafka Streams or Apache Flink) to perform **real-time aggregation**.

   To detect a **trending query**, the stream processor applies a sliding time window (e.g. a 5-minute window that slides every 10 seconds). It counts the occurrences of each unique `normalized_query`.

2. ***Lite enrichment pipeline***: When this near real-time (NRT) path detects a new, trending query (e.g. > 100 searches in 5 minutes), it sends just that query through a faster,

lightweight version of the segmentation/expansion pipeline. It skips the slow, expensive steps:

   a. It does NOT perform the full RAG-based query expansion (which involves vector lookups and complex LLM reasoning)

   b. It DOES perform a simple, fast segmentation. It calls a fast, cheap LLM model with a tight prompt (e.g. 'Extract product attributes from this query: ...') to get a moderately good structured query.

3. ***Populating the warm tier***: This 'good enough' enriched query is immediately written to our warm tier cache

   So a query that was new five minutes ago now gets a pre-computed result in the cache. The next user who searches for it gets a warm cache hit, and our search service can instantly serve relevant results instead of failing.

4. ***Handling data overwrites***: When the batch job runs, its writes must always overwrite any data previously written by the NRT speed layer. This ensures that the good-enough temporary results are eventually replaced by the perfect globally ranked results, maintaining the high quality of our search cache over time.

This ensures capture of any quick trends by the streaming pipeline and maintains the comprehensive analysis using the batch pipeline.

Handling caching

A core challenge is deciding what to cache (the value). Caching the final product list offers the lowest possible latency and reduces database load for common queries.

We will primarily cache the Elasticsearch query (the output from the LLM expansion). This ensures that any query run against the live index reflects real-time price, stock and rating information.

Storing the JSON query object is also far more memory-efficient than storing a long list of product IDs.

The trade-off is that this requires a round-trip call to Elasticsearch, which is slower than a direct cache hit and increases load on the search database.

Therefore, we use a hybrid approach:

- ***Default***: Cache the Elasticsearch query for all pre-computed long-tail and warm queries.
- ***Optimization***: For a small subset of hot generic queries with stable results, we will cache the final product list with a short TTL. This optimization layer shields our database, but the query cache remains our core strategy.

Cache tiers: hybrid strategy for speed and scale

We cannot pre-process and cache every unique query in expensive in-memory stores. We use the 80/20 rule, where 20% of queries generate 80% of traffic.

So, we use a tiered approach based on query frequency, which we obtained earlier during the log aggregation step. Our architecture uses two different cache types.

L1 and L2 caches (K-V lookups for hot queries)

During log aggregation, we count query frequency to determine which queries to pre-process and where to cache them:

- L1 cache (top 5%): Stored in-memory (in-JVM) for the lowest latency
- L2 cache (top 20%): Stored in a distributed cache like Redis

For these caches, the key is a simple, fast hash of the normalized user query. This is perfect for high-frequency, exact-match queries like 'iphone' or 'running shoes'.

Warm tier (semantic cache for the long tail)

For the long tail queries (e.g. 'winter wear for women'), it is unlikely two users will type the exact same query. A hash key is useless here.

We need a semantic cache. The warm tier is a vector database (like OpenSearch with the k-NN plugin, or a dedicated vector store) that stores the pre-processed ES queries.

The lookup flow is:

- On an L1/L2 cache miss, the search service creates a vector embedding of the user's query.
- It performs a semantic search against the warm tier vector store.

If a semantically similar, pre-processed query is found, the service retrieves its cached ES query payload.

This semantic cache lookup is far faster and cheaper than running the full fallback path (which involves a real-time LLM call) for every unique long-tail query.

Cache warming

The application instance can't just guess the top 5% of queries when it starts. It needs to warm its cache by fetching this list from a central, persistent source.

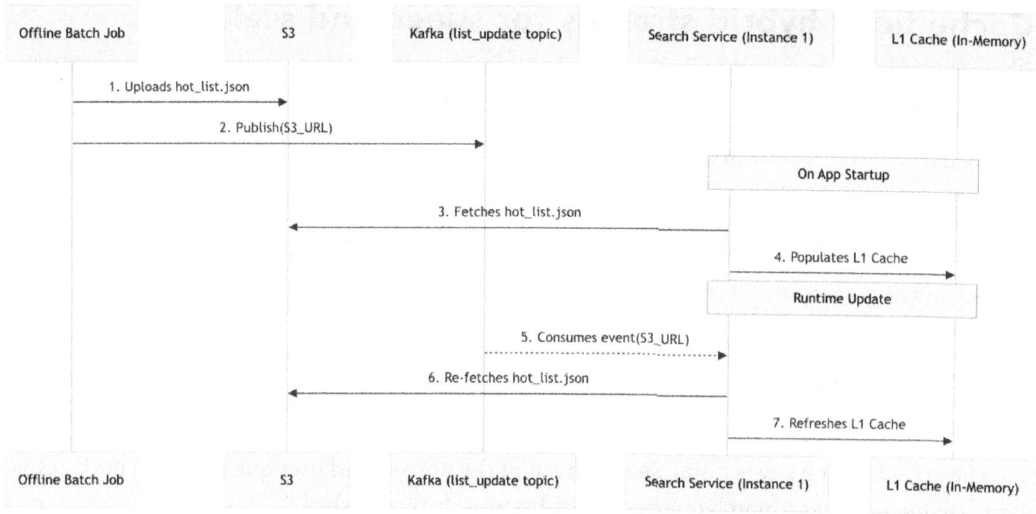

Figure 5.11: Cache warming

This is how it works:

1. Offline job: The log aggregation pipeline tracks the most frequent queries.
2. Generate hot list: As a last step of the pipeline, it creates a JSON/CSV file containing the top 5% queries and their corresponding pre-computed Elasticsearch queries. This list is uploaded to an S3 bucket.
3. Store hot list: It also sends a corresponding notification message (containing the bucket URL) to a `list_update` topic which is read by the search service application.
4. Application startup: At search service startup time it fetches this file from S3.
5. Populate cache: The service then parses this file and loads all the key value pairs into a local in memory store (like `ConcurrentHashMap`).
6. Runtime updates: All search service instances are subscribed to the `list_update` topic. Upon receiving the event, they trigger their internal logic to re-fetch and refresh their L1 cache.

This ensures the in-memory cache stays fresh and always represents the current top 5% of queries, making the system highly adaptive to changing user trends.

Cache invalidation

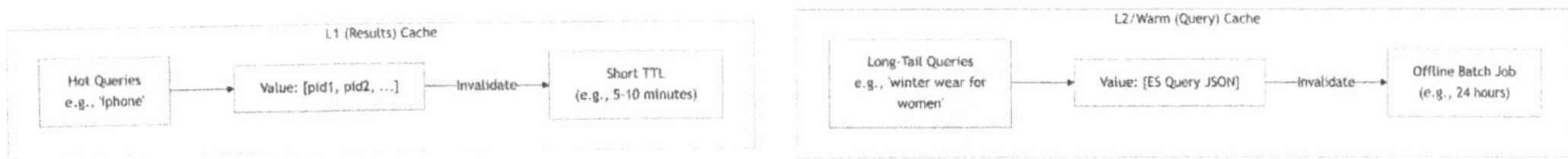

Figure 5.12: Cache invalidation

Our hybrid strategy requires two different approaches:

1. ***For the query cache*** (L2/warm tier): Invalidation is simple. The pre-computed query is just data; it only needs to be updated when the offline pipeline runs and generates a better query for that search term
2. ***For the results cache*** (L1/hot tier): This cache risks staleness. We will use a short **time-to-live (TTL)** (e.g. 5-10 minutes) as our primary invalidation strategy. A more robust, event-based invalidation (e.g. updates to the product catalog publish an event to invalidate cache entries) could be added for critical items, but TTL provides the best balance of simplicity and freshness

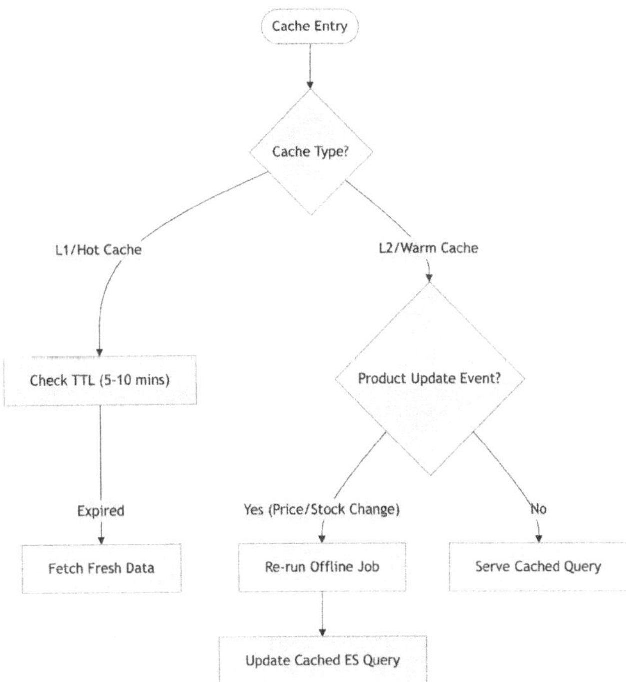

Figure 5.13: Cache update and expiry

Latency and the P99 trade-off

Our general P90 latency SLI (service level indicator) should be well under a second for the fast and cached paths.

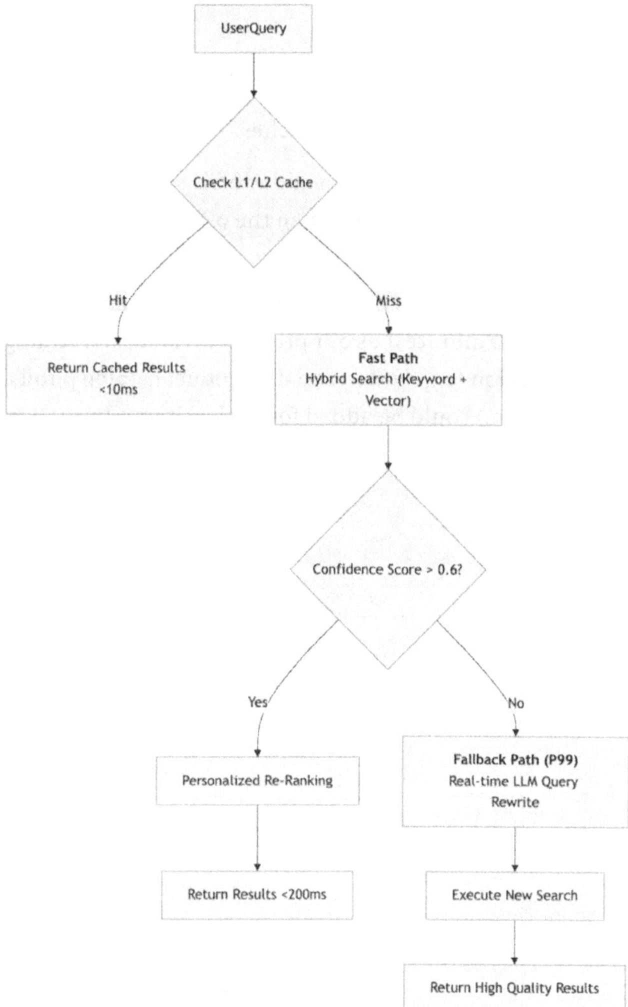

Figure 5.14: Long-tail queries served by LLM

For complex, long-tail queries that fail to match any cache tier or semantic search, the system triggers the fallback path (real-time LLM rewrite).

At this specific percentile (P99), we face a critical architectural trade-off: utility vs. latency.

Utility vs. latency

We must choose between two outcomes:

- Be fast: Fail immediately and return a 'No results found' page in under 200 ms.
- Show results: Execute a real-time LLM chain to understand the intent and rewrite the query, ensuring that the user finds what they need, even if it takes longer.

In this design, we prioritize showing results. It is a conscious decision to sacrifice speed to avoid a dead-end customer experience. While the standard search path (P90) is strictly optimized for sub-second latency, the fallback path operates on the principle that a slower, successful search is infinitely more valuable to the business and the user than a fast failure.

So, for complex, long-tail queries that are not present in any cache tier (and do not match semantically as well), we must use the fallback path (real-time LLM call). We can therefore accept a higher latency budget (e.g. < 3-5 seconds) for this P99 percentile case to avoid returning zero or low-confidence results.

This ensures that while 90% of users get instant results, the remaining 1% with difficult queries still convert, rather than bouncing off the platform due to a lack of results.

Optimized vector search: ANN

We have different algorithms for vector search using the approximate nearest neighbors.

We need to look at these key metrics while deciding on what algorithm to use:

- High recall or high accuracy
- QPS supported on a single core for throughput
- Low memory footprint
- Low latency

The algorithm we use also depends on where we store these vectors, i.e. in SSD storage or cloud storage, in memory or in secondary durable memory.

Figure 5.15: Optimized vector search techniques

We'll use two different algorithms: **HNSW** (**hierarchical navigable small worlds**) and inverted partitioning.

HNSW using graph-based partitioning

This creates a multi-layered graph structure using interconnected vectors. Searches start at the top sparse layer to locate the right neighborhood and then move to the compact dense bottom layers [3][4]. This graph is used to traverse nearby vectors, giving the method high recall and query performance. The downside is a large memory footprint, since it doesn't compress the vectors, and in addition to consuming a lot of RAM, index build times are high.

The method is suitable for low latency, high recall when we have a catalog of 1 M to 10 M items.

Inverted partitioning

This method groups vectors into clusters and then compresses the vectors in each cluster. This is useful when we need to significantly reduce the memory footprint. To find the nearest vectors, the method locates the best nearby clusters and then searches the compressed data inside them. This would be useful if our catalog had 1B+ items. The method has higher latency than the HNSW algorithm and lower recall, and is the preferred choice when memory cost is a constraint.

Algorithm family	How it works	Best for	Key weakness
Graph-based (HNSW)	Connects vectors in a multi-layered graph for efficient navigation	High accuracy & speed at moderate scale (millions)	High memory usage
Inverted partitioning	Group and compress vectors into clusters.	Massive scale (billions) where memory is the constraint.	Lower accuracy (recall)

Based on the above analysis, we decide to go with HNSW-based partitioning since our catalog size is within limits for a medium memory footprint. It ensures a highly accurate and low-latency experience for our users.

Efficient ranking

To deliver highly relevant and personalized results with low latency, we apply ranking twice.

We perform a generalized ranking in the offline search path to establish a baseline, and a lightweight, personalized re-ranking online to tailor the results for each specific user.

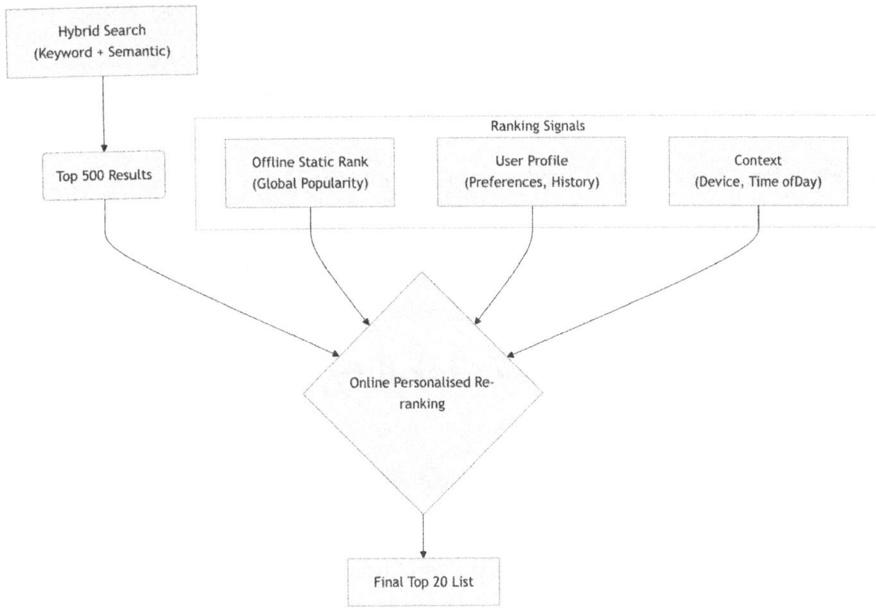

Figure 5.16: Personalized re-ranking

Offline static ranking (global relevance)

This assigns a ranking to every product—query pair based on the collective behavior of all users. This doesn't fit any particular user.

Key signals used to calculate this score include:

Collective user behavior: We analyze historical data to see which products perform best for certain queries. A purchase is given more weightage than an add-to-cart, which in turn is weighted more than a click.

Textual relevance: The semantic and keyword match between the query and the product's title, description, and attributes.

Product popularity: A product's overall sales velocity, number of views, and ratings, independent of any specific query.

The output of this phase is a global relevance score that is stored alongside the product in our search indexes and cache.

Online personalized re-ranking

This reorders the retrieved list based on the user who is searching. This lightweight model uses real-time user data to re-rank [3]:

Short-term intent: If the user has recently seen a brand's shoes, then we show more items from the same brand. So items of the same brand are scored more.

Long-term preferences: For historical data of users' past history and conversions, we give more score to the kind of items users have bought, i.e. 'organic' items etc.

Context: Other data, like the user's device, location, or time of day, can also be used to fine-tune the final ranking.

This final, personalized list is what the user sees, ensuring that the most relevant products for them are always at the top.

Ensuring robustness: availability, scalability, and resilience

High availability ensures our system remains available even if individual components of the system or entire data centres fail.

We use the following methods to make the system highly available:

Multi-AZ deployments: All critical components of our online path—including the application services, Elasticsearch clusters, vector databases, and Redis cache and DynamoDB—are deployed across multiple **availability zones (AZs)**. This eliminates a single point of failure in case the data centers of one AZ go down.

Scalability

Scalability is the ability of the system to handle growing amounts of load.

Horizontal scaling of services: Our microservices (e.g. search service, ranking service) are stateless. This means any instance can handle any request, allowing us to simply add more instances to handle more traffic. We use **Horizontal Pod Autoscalers (HPA)** in Kubernetes to automatically scale the number of instances based on real-time CPU and memory usage.

Scalable datastores: We choose datastores built for scale. DynamoDB and our serverless vector database automatically handle sharding and scaling to accommodate massive throughput. DynamoDB uses consistent hashing to scale efficiently.

Managed sharding

As data grows, it is not feasible to store it all in one server. The database automatically splits the data into shards and stores them on different servers.

Managed throughput

As the database load increases, the database needs to increase its compute power.

DynamoDB does this by automatically scaling up and down to match the traffic (in on-demand mode). In turbopuffer the necessary compute resources are automatically spun up to handle the load and then spun down, so you only pay for what you use.

Vector database scaling

A serverless vector DB generally scales using a decoupled storage and compute model.

Storage: The vector data and its index (like the HNSW graph) are placed in a highly durable, scalable object store (like S3). This storage can grow to petabytes without any manual management.

Compute: When a query is sent, turbopuffer's serverless architecture activates the necessary compute resources.

Parallelism: The query is sent to many stateless compute nodes in parallel. Each node loads only the part of the index it needs from the object store, searches its portion, and returns its top results.

Aggregation: A final service aggregates the results from all the parallel nodes to find the absolute nearest neighbors and returns them.

It scales because it can dynamically add more compute nodes as query volume increases, and we only pay for the compute-seconds we actually use for each query.

Asynchronous processing: The offline pipeline is designed for scalability through decoupling. By using message queues like Kafka, we separate the Spark jobs for log aggregation from the enrichment workers and the GenAI services. All these individual components can be scaled individually and independently. We can scale them according to CPU and memory along with queue size.

Resilience and fault tolerance

The resiliency of a system determines how it handles partial failures gracefully.

Load balancing

A **load balancer** sits before each service. It distributes traffic evenly across healthy instances for scalability. It also automatically redirects traffic away from any instance that becomes unresponsive, thus isolating failures.

Database failover

For stateful systems like our Redis cache, we operate in a primary-replica configuration across AZs. We have backup clusters for failover. If the primary node fails, a replica is automatically promoted to become the new primary with minimal disruption.

Kafka: Failover is handled by replication. For each partition, there is one leader broker and multiple follower brokers. Followers constantly copy data from the leader. If the leader broker fails, Kafka's controller (running in Zookeeper or KRaft) automatically promotes one of the in-sync followers to be the new leader. This happens in seconds, and producers/consumers are redirected to the new leader.

DynamoDB: Failover is automatic and managed by AWS. DynamoDB is deployed in a multi-AZ configuration. This means your data is synchronously replicated to at least three different physical datacenters (availability zones). If one entire datacenter fails, DynamoDB automatically routes all traffic to one of the healthy, replicated copies in another AZ with no data loss and minimal disruption.

Turbopuffer (serverless vector database)

Durable storage: The vector data is replicated across multiple AZs in an object store.

Stateless compute: The query-handling compute instances are stateless. If one fails, the load balancer simply removes it and routes traffic to healthy ones.

This combination ensures both data durability (no data is lost) and high availability (queries can almost always be served).

Circuit breakers

Interacting with third-party LLM providers is inherently unreliable. The GenAI service has circuit breakers for each LLM model. The circuit opens and traffic is re-routed to a fallback model in case the primary model encounters timeouts or failures. This prevents a single failing dependency from freezing our entire offline pipeline.

Monitoring

We need to monitor and alert our services, Spark jobs and other consumers along with our data stores.

We need to proactively understand the health of our system from both a technical and a user-centric perspective. We look at the health of our machines and the pulse of our users. Key metrics to monitor include:

Latency for the search API – We track the P95 and P99 latency of our search API. This tells us the experience of the slowest 5% and 1% of our users.

Error rate – We monitor the percentage of server-side errors (5xx). A sudden spike is our earliest warning that a service or dependency is failing.

Throughput – Measured in **queries per second (QPS)**, this helps us with capacity planning and identifying unusual traffic patterns, like a flash sale or a potential DDoS attack.

CPU and memory utilization – These are fundamental for cost optimization and triggering our autoscaling rules. Consistently high usage tells us it's time to scale up.

Click-through rate for discovery – This measures the percentage of searches where a user clicks on a result. It's a direct signal of relevance: 'Are we showing people things they find interesting?'

Conversion rate for search and discovery – This tracks the percentage of searches that lead to a purchase. This is our ultimate business metric, telling us if search is successfully driving revenue.

Alerting

We trigger alerts on anomalies that require human intervention:

Critical errors – A sharp increase in the API error rate

Performance degradation – When P99 latency exceeds our defined threshold (e.g. 500 ms)

Resource exhaustion – When CPU or memory utilization maxes out on our services or databases, indicating a scaling issue

Business metric drops – A sudden, unexplained drop in CTR or conversion rate, which could signal a problem with a new algorithm deployment

Testing and evaluation

LLM as a judge

We use a powerful LLM (like GPT-5) as an impartial expert. We present the LLM with a query and the search results from both the old and new algorithms. We then ask it: 'Which set of results is more relevant and helpful for the user's query? Explain your reasoning.' This gives us a large-scale, qualitative signal on whether our changes are directionally correct, helping us iterate faster. We use **golden datasets** to establish a baseline for what the ideal responses should look like.

Judge model: GPT-4o or Claude 3.5 Sonnet (high reasoning capability)

Scale: 1–5 (1 = irrelevant, 5 = perfect match)

Cost control: Run this on a random sample of 500 daily queries, not live traffic

Implementation

```
from pydantic import BaseModel
from openai import OpenAI client = OpenAI()
```

```
class RelevanceScore(BaseModel):
    score: int
    reasoning: str

    def evaluate_relevance(user_query, product_title, product_desc):
    """
    Uses GPT-4o to act as an impartial judge of search quality.
    """
        prompt = f"""
You are a Search Quality Rater. Rate the relevance of the product to the query.

Query: "{user_query}"
Product: "{product_title}" - {product_desc}

Scale:
1: Completely irrelevant (Query: "Phone", Result: "Socks")
3: Tangentially relevant (Query: "Nike Shoes", Result: "Adidas Shoes")
5: Perfect match (Query: "iPhone 15", Result: "Apple iPhone 15 Pro")

Return JSON with 'score' (1-5) and short 'reasoning'.
"""

    completion = client.beta.chat.completions.parse(
        model="gpt-4o-2024-08-06",
        messages=[{"role": "user", "content": prompt}],
        response_format=RelevanceScore,
    )

    return completion.choices[0].message.parsed
# Usage Example
# query = "winter hiking jacket women"
# product = "Quechua MH100 Fleece" (from our search engine)
# result = evaluate_relevance(query, product.title, product.desc)
# if result.score < 3:
```

Golden set regression suite

Before any code hits production, it must pass the golden set. These are non-negotiable, high-value queries where failure is not an option (e.g. 'iphone' must return Apple products).

Implementation

Use pytest to block deployments if core queries degrade.

```
# test_search_quality.py
import pytest
from search_client import get_search_results

# The "Golden Set": Queries that MUST return specific brands/categories
GOLDEN_CASES = [
    ("iphone", "Apple", "brand"),
    ("running shoes", "Footwear", "category"),
    ("protein powder", "Supplements", "category"),
    ("sony headphones", "Sony", "brand"),
]

@pytest.mark.parametrize("query, expected_value, field", GOLDEN_CASES)
def test_golden_set_accuracy(query, expected_value, field):
"""
Blocks deployment if top 3 results don't match the golden expectation.
"""
    results = get_search_results(query, limit=3)
    # Fail if 0 results - instant blocker
    assert len(results) > 0, f"Critical: No results for golden query '{query}'"

    # Check if the top result matches our expectation
    top_result = results[0]
    assert expected_value in top_result[field], \
    f"Regression: '{query}' returned {top_result[field]}, expected
 {expected_value}"
```

A/B testing

We roll out any significant change, like a new ranking algorithm, to a small subset of users (e.g. 5%). This group's behavior is then compared against the control group using the existing system. We closely monitor key metrics like click-through rate, conversion rate, and revenue per user. Only changes that show a statistically significant improvement are gradually rolled out to all users.

Control (A): Keyword search + simple vector (baseline).

Treatment (B): The new hybrid + re-ranking pipeline.

Metric to watch: Revenue per session (RPS)

Implementation

```
import hashlib

def get_experiment_bucket(user_id, salt="experiment_v2"):
"""
Deterministic bucketing. User X is ALWAYS in the same bucket
for the duration of the test.
"""
    hash_input = f"{user_id}-{salt}".encode('utf-8')
    # Hex digest to integer (0-100)
    bucket_val = int(hashlib.sha256(hash_input).hexdigest(), 16) % 100

    if bucket_val < 50:
        return "CONTROL" # 50% traffic
    else:
        return "TREATMENT" # 50% traffic

# In the API Handler
def handle_search_request(request):
    bucket = get_experiment_bucket(request.user_id)

    if bucket == "TREATMENT":
        return run_new_ai_search(request.query) # The new fancy system
    else:
        return run_legacy_search(request.query) # The old dependable system
```

Model routing and fallback logic

We do not send every query to an expensive LLM. We use a router to decide the path.

Fast path (P90): Elasticsearch + cached vectors

Slow path (P99): Real-time LLM query rewrite

Routing strategy

Exact match: If query exists in L1 cache -> return immediately.

High confidence: If vector search returns scores > 0.85 -> return immediately.

Fallback: If top result score < 0.5 -> Trigger LLM.

Implementation

```
def search_orchestrator(query, user_id):
# 1. Check Cache (Speed: < 10ms) cached = cache.get(query)
    if cached: return cached

# 2. Fast Path: Hybrid Search (Speed: < 200ms) # Uses cheap embeddings (e.g.,
OpenAI text-embedding-3-small)
    results = hybrid_search_engine.search(query)
    top_score = results[0].score if results else 0
# 3. Decision Gate: Is the result garbage?
    if top_score > 0.65:
        return results # Good enough, don't waste money

# 4. Fallback Path: The "P99" Rescue (Speed: 2-3s) # Trigger expensive model only
when necessary print(f"Low confidence ({top_score}) for '{query}'.Triggering LLM
rewrite.")

    rewritten_query = llm_rewrite_query(query) # Uses an SLM (cheaper, fast)
    rescue_results = hybrid_search_engine.search(rewritten_query)
```

Human evaluation

We have a team of human evaluators who review results for a curated set of challenging and ambiguous queries. They look for subtleties that automated systems can't – like contextual appropriateness, serendipity, and fairness. This human-in-the-loop feedback is invaluable for catching edge cases and ensuring our search experience feels truly intelligent.

Human-in-the-loop for NRT trends

The near real-time (NRT) pipeline detects viral trends. However, automatically promoting a trending query to the cache using a cheap LLM creates a viral hallucination risk.

- ***Guardrail***: Output from the NRT pipeline should go to a staging cache.
- ***Review***: High-velocity trends trigger a Slack alert to a merchandising manager who must click Approve to push the AI-generated search results to the public live cache.

Summary

Building an AI-powered search for e-commerce is a complex challenge. By leveraging the power of LLMs and vector search we can create an intelligent and personalized discovery experience for our users. The future of e-commerce search is not just about finding products; it's about understanding customers and helping them discover things they'll love.

The next chapter extends this thinking further, into an AI-powered Customer Support Agent. It shares a common foundation with this chapter: both e-commerce and customer support use cases rely on natural language understanding, retrieval-augmented generation, and low-latency LLM inference to serve users in real time.

However, while e-commerce search involves largely stateless interaction, i.e. one query / one response, the Customer Support Agent requires multi-turn conversation with users to drive towards a resolution.

As you will see, the design decisions change when the goal is answering a question rather than surfacing a product, with those decisions relating to such aspects as maintaining conversation history, having stricter guardrails and applying different success metrics.

References

[1] Sukel, Maarten. 'Enhancing Search Retrieval with Large Language Models (LLMs)'. *Picnic Engineering*, May 14, 2024. `https://blog.picnic.nl/enhancing-search-retrieval-with-large-languag e-models-llms-7c3748b26d72`

[2] Martinez, Eduardo. 'How DoorDash Leverages LLMs for Better Search Retrieval'. DoorDash, November 19, 2024. `https://careersatdoordash.com/blog/how-doordash-leverages-llms-for-better-search-retrieval/`

[3] Xiao, Xiao, et al. 'How Instacart Uses Embeddings to Improve Search Relevance'. *tech-at-instacart*, September 15, 2022. `https://tech.instacart.com/how-instacart-uses-embeddings-to-impr ove-search-relevance-e569839c3c36`

[4] Riyadh, Md, et al. 'LLM-assisted vector similarity search'. *Grab Tech Blog*. 'LLM-Assisted Vector Similarity Search'. Accessed December 5, 2025.

Get this book's PDF version and more

Scan the QR code (or go to `packtpub.com/unlock`). Search for this book by name, confirm the edition, and then follow the steps on the page.

UNLOCK NOW

Note: Keep your invoice handy. Purchases made directly from Packt don't require an invoice.

6

Case Study: AI-Powered Customer Support Agent

Companies can receive several thousand customer support tickets that executives need to handle within hours or days, creating a massive operational load. Relying just on human agents leads to huge turn around time (TAT) for the tickets which can create a poor user experience. To help customer support executives handle their loads, there are automated support agents [1][4].

Traditional support agents have predefined workflows and fail for queries that deviate even slightly from expected, typical categories or simple FAQs. Furthermore, a significant architectural constraint for these systems is the huge amount of data that companies maintain. They struggle to efficiently traverse a large, complex, and constantly evolving knowledge base, or deep-dive into a massive documentation portal to pinpoint a specific, context-relevant paragraph within a long article.

We can leverage LLMs in these use cases that drastically reduce load on human agents and create robust support flows.

In this chapter, we will design an AI-powered customer support agent for **MongoDB** [3]. We choose the MongoDB ecosystem as a case study due to its immense feature breadth and the massive scale of its official and community knowledge base, which perfectly illustrates the limitations of traditional support systems and the need for advanced GraphRAG solutions.

Developers engaging with MongoDB documentation might be facing any of a vast array of issues, such as trying to understand feature functionality or handling a frustrating connection problem. The AI agent should be smart enough to automatically handle queries that it can answer, and redirect to human agents otherwise. It should also summarize the chat history between the customer and the bot to help the human agent get a concise, actionable overview [2].

We will be engaging with the following topics:

- The standard RAG pattern
- Functional requirements
- Non-functional requirements
- Scale estimates
- High-level design
- API design
- System design blueprint
- Data modelling
- Deep dive
- Accuracy – avoiding hallucinations
- Monitoring and alerting
- Failure mode analysis

The standard RAG pattern

As established in *Chapter 2*, our foundation is a standard retrieval-augmented generation (RAG) pipeline. We ingest raw MongoDB documentation and historical support tickets, chunking them into semantic units. These chunks are embedded using an embedding model like `text-embedding-3-large` or the `text-embedding-ada-002` model and stored in our vector database (OpenSearch) to enable high-speed semantic retrieval.

Under normal circumstances this allows us to retrieve content that is semantically similar to a user's query, grounding the LLM and reducing hallucinations. However, in a complex technical support domain, semantic similarity is not the same as relevance. A vector search might find ten documents that seem like 'error E11000' (or whatever it is we happen to be interested in), but fail to find the one document that explains the root cause, because the phrasing is different. To solve this, we must evolve from standard RAG to GraphRAG.

Why is naive RAG not enough in this case?

There are several reasons why the performance of naïve RAG solutions often falls short. First, vector search excels at finding similarity, but that does not necessarily mean relevant, as we've already said. Several documents may be framed similarly, leading to the retrieval of several semantically similar chunks which may be related to the query. So the LLM receives redundant, overwhelming context, which makes it difficult to pinpoint the exact solution which is needed.

Second, retrieval may be inefficient due to poor chunking. Documents are often organized hierarchically (Title->Section->Sub section), and if a user query matches the title of a document, the system may retrieve the high-level summary but miss the critical information located five sections down. The core piece of content the user needs is missed because the embedding model didn't recognize the connection between the high-level match and the low-level detail [4].

Utilizing a knowledge graph

To mitigate the limitations of semantic-only retrieval, we introduce a knowledge graph (KG). A KG is a structured representation of data defining relationships between entities. Graph databases like Neo4j or Amazon Neptune can be used for this. A KG makes it easier to retrieve a particular entity based on its relationship with other entities.

Instead of relying on word similarity, the KG understands relationships such as:

document A -**[is_part_of]**-> section 3

or

ticket X -**[resolved_by]**-> code commit Y

This allows the retrieval engine to traverse complex, logical paths to find the definitive solution set. We utilize the GraphRAG pattern to traverse complex relationships between entities, to get relevant, inter-connected information for navigating structured and domain-specific data.

Functional requirements

As an initial list of functional requirements for our solution, we have the following:

- *Query intent detection*: The agent must accurately understand the **intent** and context of user queries expressed in natural language. It should remember the **conversation history** to handle back-and-forth dialogue.
- *Accurately retrieve solutions*: The system must use semantic search across the knowledge base and past tickets to retrieve relevant solutions and answer the customer accurately.
- *Intelligent escalation and handoff*: The agent must reliably detect when a query is unanswerable (i.e. low confidence score). In such cases it should seamlessly escalate/handoff to a human agent including a summarized context of the chat.
- *Maintaining freshness*: The knowledge base ingestion pipeline must ensure the system's training and retrieval data is kept fresh and synchronized with the company's documentation repo, latest patch notes, etc. within a definite period.

Non-functional requirements

Non-functional requirements (NFRs) include:

- TAT (turnaround time) for replying on tickets: Up to 3 seconds for the first reply on ticket. Up to 1 min for follow up / case resolution or escalation to human agents.
- Accuracy and hallucination control: Should be able to solve user queries accurately (avoid **hallucinations**).
- Reliability and fault tolerance: Should be able to answer queries reliably even when parts of the system are down.
- Scalability: The architecture must be capable of processing up to *N* concurrent sessions and handling projected peak load increases.
- Data security and privacy: The system must follow all relevant data privacy regulations (e.g. GDPR, CCPA) and implement masking or redaction protocols for any personally identifiable information (PII) before it is processed or stored in internal logs.

Scale estimates

We must quantify the expected load to properly size the infrastructure for the NFRs, particularly around latency and scalability.

Input metrics

Metric	Baseline estimate	Description
Peak support tickets/day	3000	
Agent containment rate (goal)	70%	Automate most basic and intermediate support tickets
Peak concurrent chat sessions	200	Peak hour traffic will be 5-10% of the daily total

Source document volume

Source component	Estimated count / volume	Description
Official MongoDB documentation	5000-7000 core pages / articles	Documentation, guides, tutorials, etc.

Source component	Estimated count / volume	Description
Internal support tickets (historical)	50k resolved tickets	Closed tickets with RCA and resolution logs
Community Forums / Stack Overflow / Github Issues/ Reddit	100k threads/posts	High-volume source of common issues
TOTAL RAW SOURCE ITEMS	≈160k	Amount of data that the ingestion pipeline must manage

Vector database volume

Metric	Estimate	Description
Average chunk size	256-512 tokens	Balance between retaining context and preventing the LLM's context window from being overwhelmed
Chunking ratio	10 chunks per item	Chunk counts vary widely, but we take 10 as average
Total vector chunks	~1.6 Million vectors [x2]	160k total source * 10 chunk per source
Vector dimensionality	768 to 1536 dimensions	Depends on the chosen embedding model
Estimated storage size	~9.8 GB + metadata = 20GB	1.6 Million vectors * 1536 dimensions * 4 bytes for float32

Let's calculate the total amount of chat message data in the database, assuming 3k customer support tickets per day and 20 messages per chat on average:

Per day data, assuming 500B per chat message: 3k*20*500B ~= 30MB

Daily number of documents ingested: ~2k (if 1% of the 160k total items are updated daily)

High level design

Here's what a high level overview of the system would look like. We will discuss this further in the *System design blueprint* section.

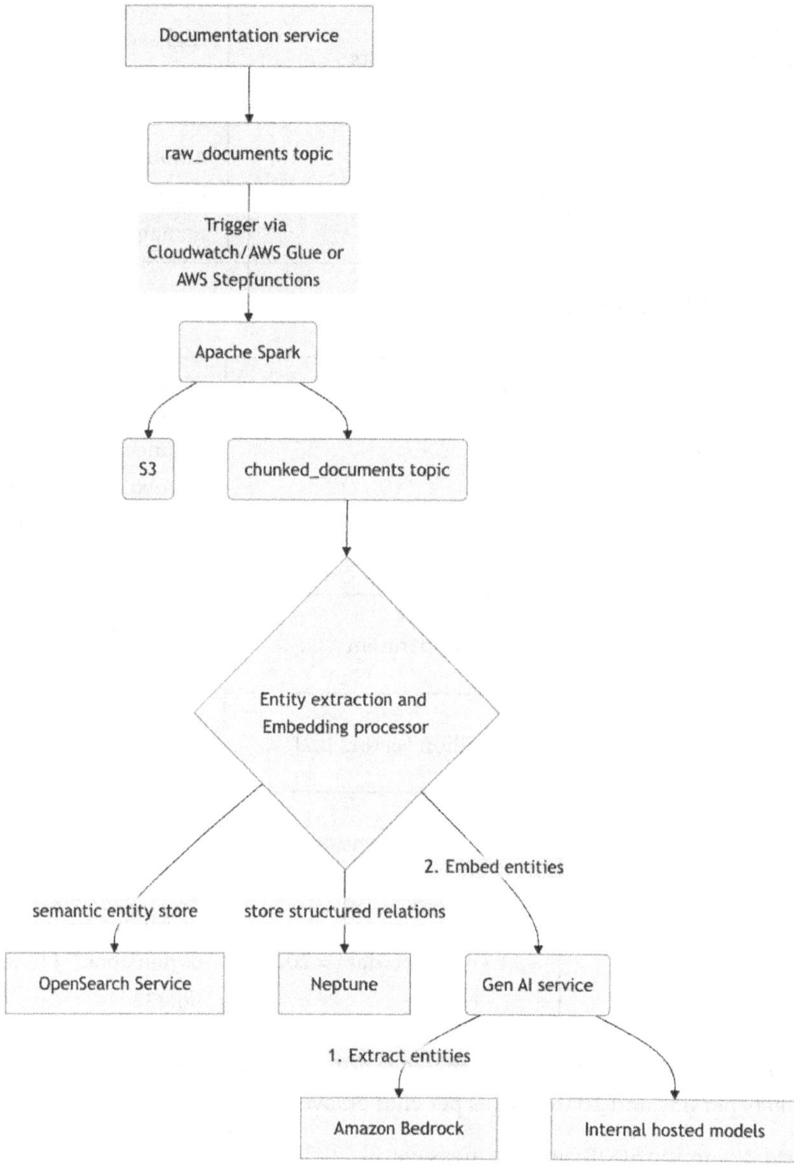

Figure 6.1: High level design

Here are some common components:

Chat service (Web/Slack): Manages user session, state and chat history GenAI service: A simple, resilient client (with circuit breakers) that only calls LLM APIs (like Bedrock)

RAG orchestrator: The backend brain that executes the tiered query logic

API design

To implement our solution we can define a trio of APIs, as follows.

Real time source webhooks

This API's job is to write to the `raw_documents` topic whenever any documentation is updated, or an issue or ticket is closed.

URI	/api/ingest/collect
Method	POST
Body	`{ "source_id": "TICKET-1990", "url": "...", "type": "TICKET" }`
Response	`{ "status": "QUEUED", "message": "Source item added to raw_documents buffer." }`

The Spark job is automatically scaled up (from 0 to *N*) when the Kafka `raw_documents` topic lag exceeds 200 messages, ensuring immediate freshness during spikes, and is otherwise guaranteed to run daily at 2:00am (via AWS step functions) for cost-efficient nightly cleanup.

User chats with customer support via Slack/Web

The service maintains a session state for each user session.

URI	**/api/v1/chat**
Method	POST

Body	`{`
	`"initial_query": "how to connect to db driver?",`
	`"channel":{`
	`    "ctype" : "slack",`
	`    "cid": "s3289710"`
	`    },`
	`"is_faq": false,`
	`"faq_id": null`
	`}`

Response	`{`
	`"session_id": "s1",`
	`"response": "Here is the relevant documentation to help you out..",`
	`"confidence_score": 7.2,`
	`"channel": {`
	`    "ctype": "slack",`
	`    "cid": "s1382ry3" ,`
	`    "sent": true`
	`  }`
	`}`

Embed chunked documents (internal API)

Accepts a text chunk and returns the high-dimensional vector.

URI	/internal/ingest/chunk/embed
Method	POST
Body	{ "chunk_id": "c12", "content": "this is a sample chunk...", "embedding_model": "text-embedding-ada-002" }
Response	{ "chunk_id": "c12", "vector" : [-1219,32432,35434,-4353,43534], "dimensions": 1536, "model_used": "text-embedding-ada-002", "processing_time_ms": "100" // time taken for vectorization }

System design blueprint

Now let's discuss the architecture for the system during the user query flow (i.e. chat or ticket creation by the user).

User query flow

This section details the architecture of the user query flow, focusing on the decision-making and hybrid retrieval-augmented generation (RAG) engine.

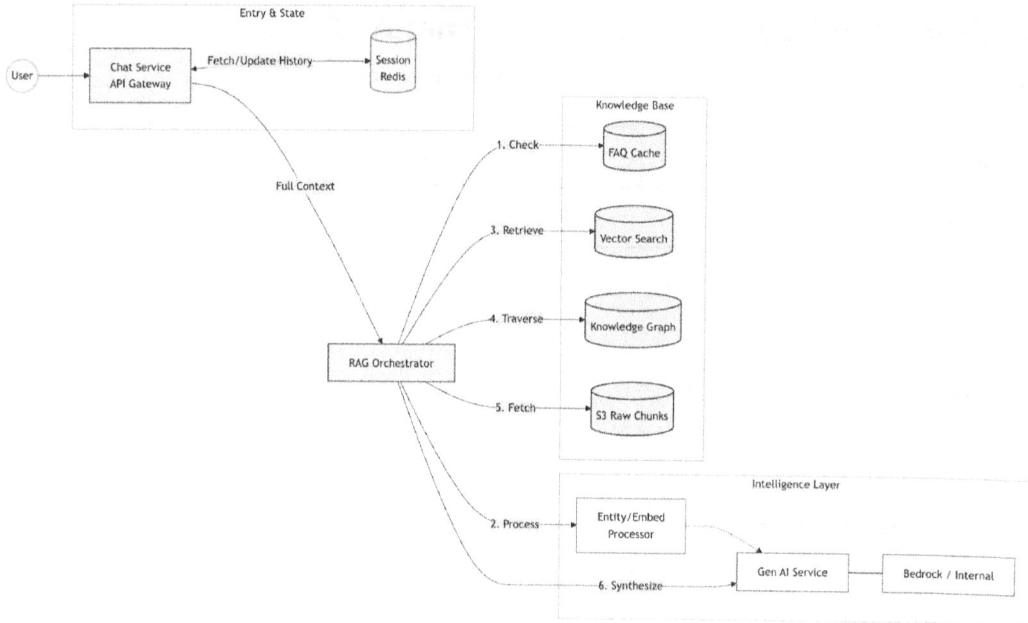

Figure 6.2: User query flow

Chat service and state management

Before a query is processed, the **chat service** (which handles the user-facing `/api/v1/chat` endpoint) must manage the conversational history. This **state management** is critical because we require analysis of the entire history of the chat, not just the single, most recent message. The system uses a `session_id` (returned in the initial chat response) to manage this. The `session_id` acts as a key for retrieving the full conversation history, which is stored in a dedicated, low-latency cache.

This way we avoid the inefficiency of passing the entire, potentially large, conversation history in the API call body for every single turn. This keeps the API request payload small. When a user sends a new message:

1. The chat service receives the new message and its `session_id`.
2. It sends a response back on the ticket stating it is working on resolving the query.
3. It retrieves the full chat history from the cache using the `session_id`.
4. It appends the new message to this history.
5. This complete, updated history is then passed to the orchestration layer for intent detection and RAG processing.

The history in the cache is updated with the new message and the subsequent response.

RAG orchestrator service

The chat service acts as a lightweight, user-facing API gateway. It is responsible for handling user authentication and session management (as described above). Once the user's query and full chat history are prepared, the chat service passes the request to the RAG orchestrator service. The **RAG orchestrator** is responsible for all downstream calls: checking the FAQ cache, performing vector search, executing graph traversals, and calling the GenAI service for final synthesis.

Tiered orchestration and intent routing

The system prioritizes speed and cost-efficiency through a tiered approach managed by the RAG orchestrator.

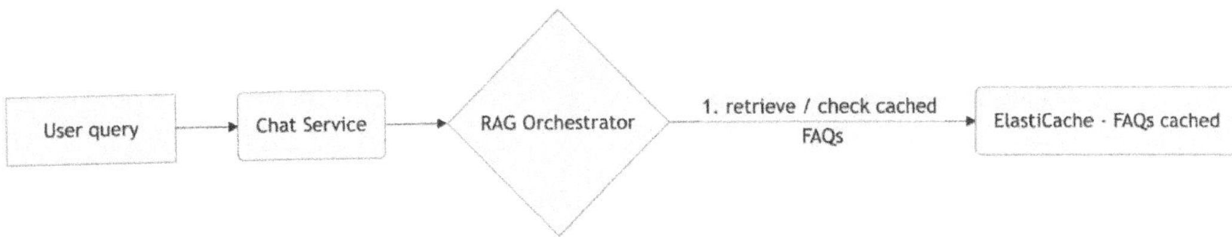

Figure 6.3: Rag orchestrator flow

Predefined workflow/FAQ redirect

When the RAG orchestrator receives a request from the chat service, it first executes a fast, low-latency check. It checks a high-speed cache for an exact match against known, simple FAQs [1].

Why do we need the entire history of the chat?

In a multi-turn support chat, the user's latest message is often incomplete on its own.

Turn 1 (User): "My app isn't connecting."

Turn 2 (Bot): "What error code do you see?"

Turn 3 (User): "E11000"

If we simply vectorize E11000, the search engine lacks context. (Is it a billing error? A connection timeout?) It effectively searches for a potentially ambiguous alphanumeric string.

So before performing vector search, the RAG orchestrator sends the full chat history to the GenAI service.

Entity extraction and contextual query rewriting

In case of a cache-miss, the RAG orchestrator sends the entire chat history to the GenAI service to analyze the context and extract the primary entities and intent of the user query. It generates a concise, context-aware internal search query and structured entities.

```
({Component: 'Auth', ErrorCode: 'E11000'})
```

Hybrid RAG approach

The RAG orchestrator takes this response and begins the hybrid retrieval.

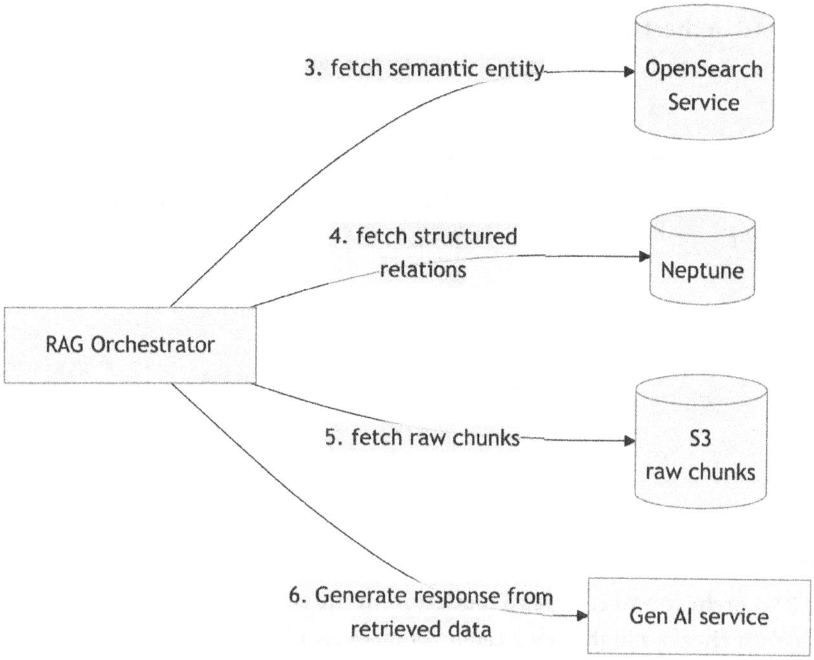

Figure 6.4: Hybrid RAG approach

Vector search: It first semantically searches the vector database (OpenSearch) for similar chunks, identifying the top-K relevant documents and support cases. The related `documentation_ids/case_ids` are scored according to their semantic similarity and relevance. The vector scores are summed per document to identify the top-K relevant documents, support cases etc.

Graph traversal: The RAG orchestrator then consults the knowledge graph (Neptune) to find structured paths (like root causes and resolution steps) connected to these retrieved items. The system then extracts their complete, structured solutions directly from the KG.

Chunk retrieval: It then retrieves the raw text chunks for the final context from S3 (since the s3 chunk URLs are attached to the nodes in the graph database). The raw text chunks for the resolution are then retrieved from S3.

Final synthesis: This comprehensive, grounded context is combined with the chat history and finally sent to the GenAI service which can synthesize a highly accurate response.

Ingestion pipeline

We build the ingestion pipeline as a multi-stage **event-driven architecture** to ensure that the knowledge base is constantly refreshed without impacting real-time latency.

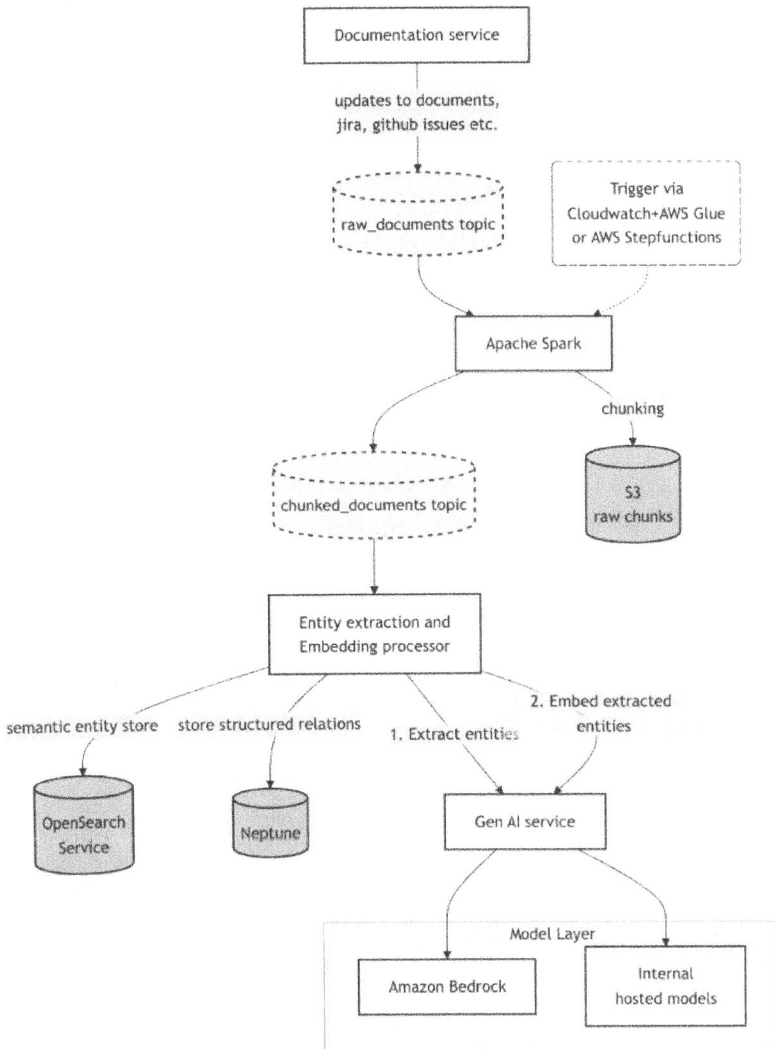

Figure 6.5: Ingestion pipeline

Asynchronous triggering and elastic scale

All updates start with a single event. When documentation is updated, or a support ticket/GitHub issue is closed, the event metadata is captured and published to the Kafka `raw_documents` topic. This topic acts as a durable buffer queue for all pending work.

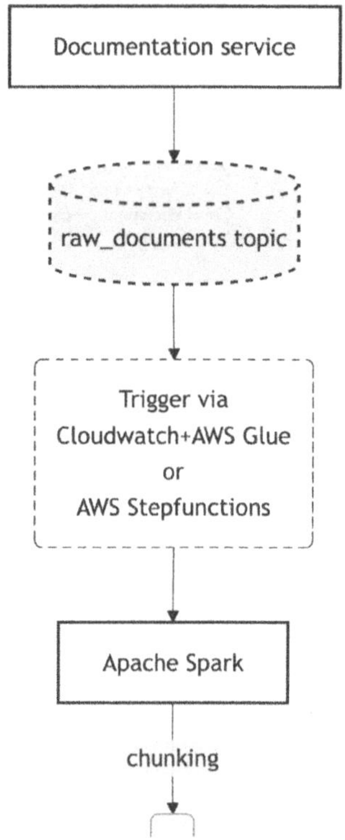

Figure 6.6: Async triggering

The load on the `raw_documents` topic will be bursty. To handle this load, we use a hybrid triggering model, involving load-based and time-based triggers.

Load-based trigger

The Spark streaming job is automatically scaled up (from 0 to *N* pods) by Cloudwatch monitoring when the `raw_documents` topic lag exceeds a message threshold (say 200). This ensures immediate processing during traffic spikes and optimizes resources by scaling to zero when idle.

Time-based trigger

An AWS Step Function job is guaranteed to run daily at 2:00am for a cost-efficient nightly cleanup, ensuring that any remaining small backlog is processed outside of peak hours.

Data ingestion and chunking (Spark)

The Spark streaming job consumes the backlog from the `raw_documents` topic. It reads the links for the updated documents, closed tickets, etc. This ensures processing is decoupled from source systems.

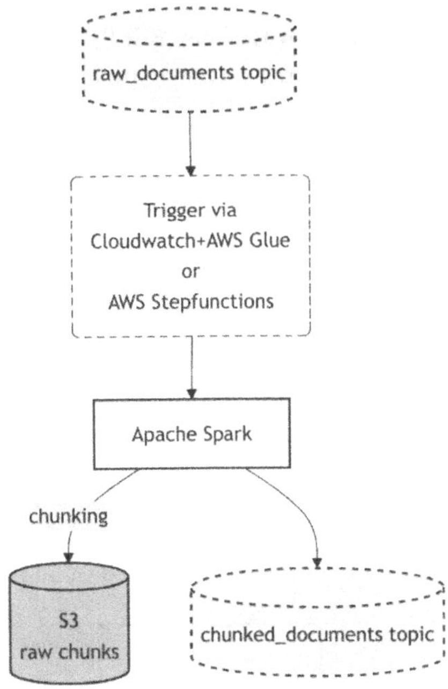

Figure 6.7: Data ingestion and chunking

The embedding model has a restriction on the size of the data being embedded. So we cannot just send an entire document (like the MongoDB manual) to be embedded by the model; it will be inefficient even if it is a smaller document.

So, the Spark job chunks the document into sections, or the JIRA ticket into components.

Chunking respects semantic boundaries (sections, paragraphs, JIRA components). This is crucial for retaining context and splitting content based on structure (sections, paragraphs etc. of a document or components of a ticket). Each chunk is assigned a unique id and retains a reference to the original document/ticket Id.

PII redaction in the Spark job

Before any document chunk is vectorized or stored in S3, it must pass through a **PII redaction filter**, since once PII is embedded in a vector it is extremely difficult to selectively delete it without re-indexing the entire corpus.

The Spark job then stores the raw chunks in blob storage such as S3 Raw Storage for durability.

The link to the chunks in S3, along with their metadata, is then published to another Kafka topic (`chunked_documents` topic) to signal downstream readiness.

Entity extraction and embedding processor

The **entity extraction and embedding processor (EEEP)** consumes the events from the `chunked_documents` topic. It downloads the raw S3 chunk and initiates calls to internal models for extracting entities and relations.

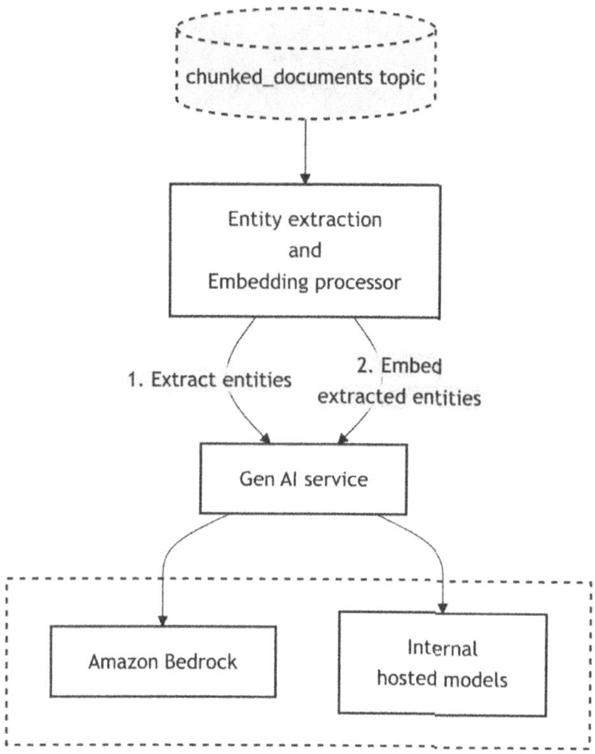

Figure 6.8: Entity extraction and embedding processor

Extract entities and relations

The EEEP sends the chunk to an internally hosted (and fine-tuned) model to capture the structural relationships (entities and relations) for further processing.

Suppose we have a sentence

"The MongoDB find() method returns documents from a collection"

the model would extract:

Entities: *find(), method, document, collection*

Relationships: *find()-[is_a]-> method, method -[returns]-> documents, documents -[are_in]-> collection*

Vectorization

The EEEP also has the responsibility for creating the high-dimensional vector embeddings for storage in the vector database, using the chunk id as the metadata. The EEEP sends the extracted entities and relations within the chunk before embedding to the embedding model. EEEP uses an internally hosted model for generating embeddings.

Vector and graph persistence

The chunk's metadata is persisted in both the vector database and in the knowledge graph for hybrid RAG retrieval.

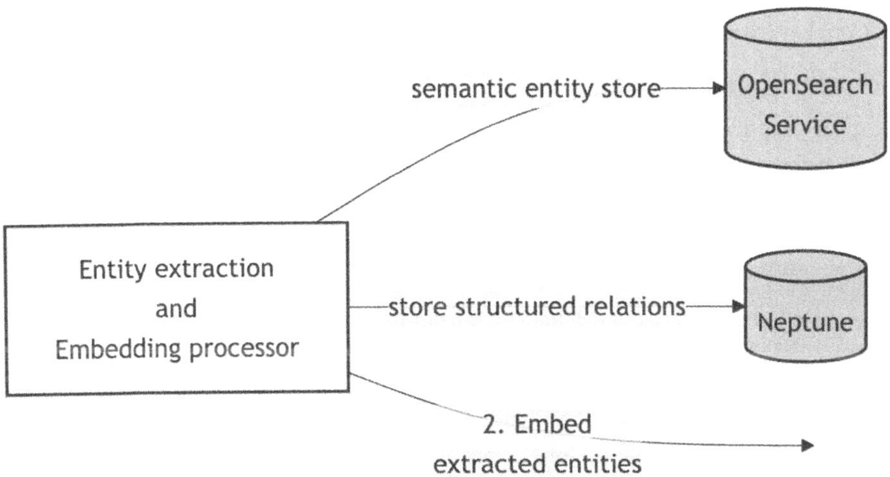

Figure 6.9: Vector and graph persistence

Vector database (semantic search)

The vector database stores high-dimensional vector embeddings along with metadata for fast semantic retrieval. Note that we also add the extracted entities and relations within the chunk before embedding.

An optimization for storage that is done here is that we don't embed the entire raw chunk in the vector database. Embed only dense, searchable content. We don't embed the raw text. The vector database's job is semantic indexing, not raw data storage. In fact, the extracted entities, relations and their reference to the parent document are what we need here, so only this metadata can be embedded. The metadata also has information about the title of the document or Jira ticket, etc.

This helps ensure better semantic search and better retrieval.

The actual chunk, which was stored in blob storage like S3, is referenced in the knowledge graph and the vector database against the embedded metadata.

Knowledge graph (structured relations)

Once the main entities and their relationships are extracted, they are used to build the knowledge graph.

Intra-connections (within-item)

These define the internal structure of a single item.

Every document can have different subsections discussing different points – title, sub-heading, Section 1.1, etc. The sub-sections are represented as nodes connected by hierarchical relations, e.g. *[Section 1.1]* ***-[is_part_of]->*** *[Section 1]*.

For a JIRA ticket (title, description, resolution), the internal components form the connections.

Inter-connections (between items)

These capture explicit links and structural dependencies across the knowledge base. This is vital for complex technical issues, such as capturing explicit links, e.g.

[Article A] ***-[references]->*** *[Article B]*

or mapping component usage:

[Ticket A] ***-[uses_component]->*** *[MongoDB Sharding]*

GenAI service

The GenAI service interacts with LLM vendors. It crafts prompts from templates and the context provided to it by the Spark job. Its primary purpose is to remain resilient in case of failures in a particular LLM provider and reroute tasks to back-up LLM providers. It also implements circuit breakers and exponential retries for this purpose. We will discuss how to expand this service in the *Deep dive* section.

OpenAI text-embedding-3-large and text-embedding-ada-002 models

These are embedding models provided by OpenAI, which take the data and convert it into vector format suitable for semantic comparisons.

Data modelling

Suppose we have these existing tables in a customer agent system:

tickets

Context: The central ledger tracking the lifecycle of a support issue from creation to resolution.

Usage: High concurrency. Updated frequently by both the AI (adding tags/summary) and human agents (changing status).

messages

Context: An immutable log of the conversation transcript, including metadata such as who sent it (bot vs. human).

Usage: Write-once, read-any. Used to build the prompt context for the AI and the chat history UI for the user.

Blob storage for chunked data

S3 raw storage serves as the immutable source of truth for all knowledge used by the RAG system.

Storage choice and durability

We leverage a Cloud-based blob storage solution such as Amazon S3 (or equivalent Azure Blob/GCP Cloud Storage), specifically utilizing a low-cost, high-durability tier (e.g. S3 Standard or Infrequently Accessed) for cost efficiency and reliability.

We store the finalized, raw text chunks generated by the Spark processing job in the S3 storage.

Access patterns and load

High-throughput batch writes: The system experiences high write throughput during the nightly (or threshold-triggered) batch execution of the Spark chunking job. The write access pattern is simple: append new files to the current bucket (date).

Low-volume, highly specific reads: The primary retrieval path is through the vector DB/KG, not S3. Reads only occur after the retrieval layer has identified the top-K relevant chunk_ids. The read access will be through a direct S3 immutable file path.

S3 bucket path

The path is defined by the globally unique `chunk_id` and is organized by the date of ingestion for efficient governance and lifecycle management.

Path:

```
s3://[bucket-name]/[source_type][/year]/[month]/[day]/[chunk_id].txt
```

Example:

```
s3://kb-storage/DOC/2025/10/01/c123456789.txt
```

Vector database

The vector database is the highly scalable, low-latency engine for semantic search. It is optimized for efficient index searching and metadata filtering, not raw text storage.

Technology choice

We require a solution built for high-dimensional, approximate nearest neighbor (ANN) search as a managed service like OpenSearch. We use AWS OpenSearch, which can store and search vector embeddings for entity metadata of chunked articles and tickets.

Workload

High-throughput batch writes: The database will see significant ingestion bursts when the Spark job processes the backlog, requiring the platform to scale its write capacity and indexing in real time.

High-velocity ANN search: The primary operation is ANN search (or cosine similarity) on the vector embeddings to quickly find the top-K semantically relevant chunk_ids in sub-second time. This search is often combined with metadata filtering (e.g. filter by `source_type`).

The Spark-driven processor calls the `/internal/ingest/kb/vector/add` API, creating a new index entry per chunk, associated with its embedding and metadata.

knowledge_chunks

Context: Stores vector embeddings of documentation, parsed into small, semantic snippets.

Usage: Read-heavy. Queried via vector similarity search on every user message to retrieve relevant context.

Field	Type	Required	Description
`id`	String	Primary key	The unique identifier of the chunk (chunk_id). Used to retrieve the vector and its metadata
`vector`	Array of floats	Required	The high-dimensional vector embedding obtained from the /embed service
`source_metadata`	Object	Required	Key metadata for search filtering and RAG grounding

Field	Type	Required	Description
doc_id	String	Required	The ID of the original document, ticket, or issue
source_type	String	Required	The type of knowledge: ("DOC", "TICKET", "GITHUB")
update_timestamp	String (ISO 8601)	Required	Timestamp of the last update; used for freshness checks
security_level	String	Optional	e.g. "PUBLIC", "INTERNAL"—crucial for filtering responses based on the customer's clearance level
chunk_url	String	Required	S3 path of the chunk

Knowledge graph

The knowledge graph (KG) provides the structural context necessary for the hybrid RAG approach with verifiable, interconnected entities.

Technology choice

We will utilize a dedicated, scalable graph database service such as Amazon Neptune or Neo4j, or a graph-optimized layer within our core data platform.

Amazon Neptune has a managed, serverless architecture, which automatically handles scaling and capacity provisioning. This removes the operational overhead of manually configuring instances according to capacity.

Workload

Heavy write throughput: Writes are based on adding new `entity_ids` and their relations (nodes and edges). These occur asynchronously during the ingestion pipeline's scheduled runs.

Targeted traversal: We retrieve the intra-relationships and structure for specific IDs in the RAG prompt.

The KG is composed of two primary entities: nodes (entities) and edges (relationships).

Node structure (entities)

Nodes represent discrete, identifiable concepts (within the MongoDB ecosystem as per our example).

Field	Data type	Constraint	Description	Example value
`id`	String	Primary Key	Unique identifier for the entity(can be doc id or jira id etc + type)	E-5f72a4c
`name`	String	Required	The name of the entity	"MongoDB Node.js Driver"
`labels`	Array of Strings	Required	type(s) of the entity, critical for graph traversal filtering.	["Driver", "Component", "Software"]
`attributes`	Object	Optional	Key-value pairs containing entity properties.	{"version": "4.5.0", "language": "JavaScript"}
`chunk_id_ref`	String	Conditionally Required	References the chunk_id in the Vector DB/S3	c12345

Edge structure (relationships)

Edges connect nodes and define the semantic meaning between them, allowing the system to reason across documents.

Field	Data type	Constraint	Description	Example value
`source_id`	String	Required	The id of the starting node.	E-5f72a4c

Field	Data type	Constraint	Description	Example value
`target_id`	String	Required	The id of the ending node.	E-9b3d1e0
`relationType`	String	Required	The type of relationship required for defining traversal paths.	"DEPENDS_ON "
`attributes`	Object	Optional	Properties of the relationship itself.	{"weight": 0.8, "verified": true}
`source_context`	String	Required	The ID of the document/chunk that explicitly stated this relationship. Required for RAG traceability.	c12345

Key RAG-optimized relationship types

This ensures that when the RAG engine executes its graph traversal step, it retrieves not just text, but structured answers that are easier for the final LLM to synthesize accurately.

Relationship type	Nodes connected	Purpose in RAG retrieval
IS_PART_OF	[Section] → [Article/Ticket]	Used to retrieve the entire parent context when a section is matched.
REFERENCES	[Article] → [Article]	Expands the retrieval search to highly relevant, related documents.

Relationship type	Nodes connected	Purpose in RAG retrieval
HAS_ROOT_CAUSE	[Ticket] → [Concept/Entity]	If a user mentions a concept, the RAG can traverse back to a ticket with the same root cause.
USES_COMPONENT	[Ticket] → [Driver/Service]	Filters retrieval to ensure the answer is relevant to the customer's stated version/ driver (e.g. "Node.js").
RESOLVES	[Resolution Chunk] → [Problem/Error]	Allows the RAG engine to retrieve the canonical "Resolution Step" for a known error ID.

Deep dive

Let's recap what we have discussed so far.

Functional requirement	Design solution summary
Knowledge retrieval	RAG pipeline: Vector search on documentation chunks + hybrid keyword search
Context awareness	Conversation buffer: Injecting the last *N* turns into the prompt so the bot remembers "My server version is 5.0".
Hallucination control	Citation enforcement: The UI only renders an answer if the LLM cites a specific Chunk ID from the knowledge base.
Ticket management	Statemachine:Trackstickettlifecycle(Open-> Bot_Active -> Escalated -> Closed) in PostgreSQL.
Smart escalation	Next focus: Sentiment analysis to auto-detect angry users and handoff for real-time agent takeover.
Action execution	Next focus: Tool use (function calling) to allow the bot to actually do things (e.g. "Restart Cluster") safely.

Let's now look closely at the design's NFRs.

Scalability

Scaling focuses on ensuring that the high-volume ingestion path and the real-time query path remain bottleneck free.

Spark ingestion jobs

Scaling is handled dynamically by Cloudwatch monitoring the Kafka topic lag in the AWS MSK. This allows the AWS Glue to manage the automated scaling of Spark clusters from 0 to *N* worker pods only when processing is required, providing immediate throughput increases during ingestion spikes. The scaling is driven by data volume, ensuring cost optimization.

OpenSearch Serverless auto-scaling

We utilize Amazon OpenSearch Serverless, which automatically scales capacity based on the workload's demands. This eliminates the need for manual sharding/instance management and guarantees that the high write throughput from the ingestion pipeline and high read concurrency during peak RAG queries are both handled elastically.

S3

Similarly, S3 is an AWS managed service and a thread pool can be used to manage connections to S3.

Graph database

We deploy Amazon Neptune Serverless for the KG. It adjusts compute resources based on the changing requirements of the complex traversal queries. It allows handling graph workloads at scale without the need for managing or optimizing database capacity.

GenAI service

The GenAI service can become a bottleneck if not scaled properly. When facing a huge load of requests, it needs to actively send the request to the LLM providers that are available, and trip the ones that are having delays. This can be done using circuit breaker configuration in the GenAI service. It monitors latency from external LLM providers, and trips the circuit for slow endpoints, automatically rerouting the request to available backup LLM models to maintain user-facing performance.

Reducing latency

Low latency is crucial for an AI-powered customer service agent to ensure a smooth user experience.

When the user creates a ticket, the AI-powered agent should start working on it and be able to respond with resolutions within a few seconds. The customer, who typically waits for a manual agent, would traditionally expect responses in hours. In the case of an enterprise agent, with dedicated support, it would still take minutes for manual response.

The overall system must meet the < 60 seconds NFR by optimizing the sequential and parallel steps in the RAG pipeline.

Retrieval optimization

The retrieval phase first runs vector search (OpenSearch) to identify the relevant IDs, followed by the specific ID-based lookups in the Neptune KG. Latency is minimized since expensive Neptune traversal is constrained to only the handful of verified, relevant document IDs retrieved from OpenSearch.

SLMs for pre-processing

Smaller, fine-tuned models are used for low-cost, low-latency tasks like intent detection and entity extraction, reserving the larger, slower generative LLM for the final answer synthesis.

This reduces the time spent on initial query analysis.

Response and prompt caching

The LLM orchestrator implements two caching layers: the response cache and the prompt cache.

Response cache

Caches the final LLM response using the hash of the contextualized query + LLM model ID as the key.

Prompt cache

Caches static prompt templates using the prompt ID as the key.

Co-location and connection pooling

All core services (orchestrator, OpenSearch, Neptune, and LLM providers' regional endpoints) must be co-located within the same AWS region. Connection pooling is used for all external LLM provider APIs to minimize HTTP overhead.

Coalesce caching (request coalescing)

Thousands of users often rush to support asking the exact same question simultaneously, e.g. in case of a partial outage. A standard cache will miss the first request for everyone, causing a thundering herd that can crash your LLM gateway.

We implement coalesce caching (or request collapsing) in the API Gateway. The gateway identifies identical in-flight requests. It pauses all subsequent requests, waits for the first LLM response to complete, and then serves that single response to all 10,000 waiting users at once. This reduces the load on the LLM provider by orders of magnitude during critical incidents.

Accuracy - avoiding hallucinations

For better customer satisfaction in handling tickets, we need to ensure our system returns the correct and relevant responses. Ensuring the system returns verifiable and correct responses is paramount to achieving a high customer satisfaction (CSAT) score. This relies on strategic guardrails within the hybrid RAG flow.

Explicit prompt guardrails

We implement strong, explicit guardrails within the LLM's system prompt. This instruction set mandates that the LLM must not hallucinate and should reply with a standardized fallback message (e.g. 'I cannot find the relevant information...') if the retrieved context from the knowledge graph or vector database is insufficient.

Validation and evaluation suite

System performance is evaluated using a variety of methods: with respect to a golden dataset, by using an **LLM as a judge**, and via human-in-the-loop methods.

Golden dataset evaluation

We maintain a dedicated golden dataset of verified queries and correct answers. Our system is continuously evaluated against this set.

Example 1: Simple FAQ / intent detection

Query: *"how to connect to db driver?"*

Golden answer (factual): *"You can connect to a MongoDB database using a connection string (URI) and a language-specific driver. For example, in Node.js, you would use the MongoClient class. Here is a basic code snippet: [Code Snippet]"*

This tests the system's ability to handle simple, common questions and provide accurate, helpful code.

Example 2: Complex query / RAG retrieval

Query: *"I'm trying to optimize read performance for a large collection, but my find() query with a sort() is slow. I already have an index on the sort field."*

Golden answer (synthesized): *"A slow find() with a sort() on an indexed field often indicates that the query is not using the index efficiently or that the index doesn't cover the entire query.*

Check the Index: Ensure the index also includes the fields in your query's filter, not just the sort field.

Covered Query: For best performance, create a 'covered index' that includes all fields used in both the query filter and the sort operation.

Use .explain(): Run db.collection.find(...).sort(...).explain('executionStats ') to verify that the query is using your index (look for IXSCAN) and not performing an in-memory sort (SORT stage)."

This tests the hybrid RAG engine's ability to retrieve, synthesize, and relate multiple concepts (find, sort, indexes, explain) to solve a nuanced performance issue.

Example 3: Error code / GraphRAG traversal

Query: *"My app is crashing, I see an 'E11000' error in the logs."*

Golden answer (contextual): *"An 'E11000 duplicate key error' means you are trying to insert or update a document that violates a unique index. This commonly happens when you try to insert a new document with a _id that already exists or a value in another field (like 'username') that is defined as unique. Please check the document you are trying to insert and ensure its unique fields have new values."*

This tests the system's ability to map a common entity (the error code) to its specific root cause and resolution steps, a key feature of the knowledge graph.

Example 4: Unanswerable / intelligent escalation

Query: *"I think my billing is wrong, you charged me twice this month."*

Golden answer (escalation): *"I see you have a question about billing. I am not equipped to handle billing information or access your account details for privacy reasons. I will escalate this to a human agent who can securely assist you."*

This tests that the agent correctly identifies a query it has low confidence on (or is out-of-scope) and hands off appropriately.

LLM-as-a-Judge

We employ a separate, powerful LLM instance configured as a Judge model to score the system's live performance against the golden dataset or against real-life user queries [1]. This provides a quantifiable metric (according to the Judge LLM) on the quality and helpfulness of the response.

Here are a few practical examples of how this LLM-Judge would be used in the context of the MongoDB support agent:

Example 1: Scoring for accuracy and correctness

This example tests if the agent's answer is factually correct by comparing it to a known-good golden answer.

Internal prompt to LLM-Judge:

```
User Query: "My app is crashing, I see an 'E11000' error in the logs."

Agent Response: "An 'E11000' error is a duplicate key error. This means you are
trying to insert a document with an _id that already exists. You should check your
code."

Golden Answer: "An 'E11000 duplicate key error' means you are trying to insert or
update a document that violates a unique index. This could be the _id field, or
another field you defined as unique (e.g., 'username'). You should check the
document you are trying to insert."
On a scale of 1-5, how factually accurate is the Agent Response compared to the
Golden Answer? Explain your reasoning.
```

LLM-Judge output:

```
Score: 3/5

Reasoning: The agent's response is partially correct but incomplete. It correctly
identifies the 'duplicate key error' but incorrectly assumes it only applies to
the _id field. The golden answer is more accurate because it correctly states that
the error is due to any unique index, which is a critical distinction for a
developer.
```

Example 2: Scoring for groundedness (detecting hallucination)

This example tests if the agent's answer is grounded in the factual context provided by the RAG system, or whether it's hallucinating (making up) information.

Internal prompt to LLM-Judge:

```
Retrieved Context: "[chunk_1]: ...For optimizing 'find()', the most important tool
is the index. Use '.explain('executionStats')'... [chunk_2]: ...If your query
filters on 'fieldA' and sorts on 'fieldB', a compound index on '{ fieldA: 1,
fieldB: 1 }' is most effective..."

Agent Response: "To optimize a slow 'find()' query, you should use an index. A
good first step is to run '.explain()'. You can also try using the
'setQueryOptimizer()' function, which often helps."
```

```
Is the Agent Response fully grounded in the Retrieved Context? Are there any
statements in the response that are NOT supported by the context?
```

LLM-Judge output:

```
Grounded: No (Partially)
Reasoning: The agent's statements about "index" and ".explain()" are grounded in
the context. However, the suggestion to use setQueryOptimizer() is not present
anywhere in the provided context. This is a potential hallucination that could
mislead the user. The Grounding Score for this response would be low.
```

Example 3: Scoring for helpfulness and tone (open-ended)

This example evaluates the agent's performance on a real-world user query where there is no golden answer.

Internal prompt to LLM-Judge:

```
User Query: "this stupid driver won't connect i'm just getting a timeout error"
Agent Response: "I understand you're frustrated. A timeout error when connecting
often means... [full response text] ..."
On a scale of 1-5, rate the quality and helpfulness of the Agent Response to the
User Query. Consider:
Did it address the user's technical problem (timeout error)?
Did it handle the user's frustrated tone appropriately?
Was the answer actionable?
```

LLM-Judge output:

```
Score: 5/5
Reasoning: The agent performed excellently.
Tone: It immediately acknowledged the user's frustration ("I understand you're
frustrated...") before becoming technical.
Technical: It correctly identified the likely class of problem (reachability) and
provided the three most common, actionable solutions (Firewall, IP Whitelisting,
Connection String). This is a highly helpful and high-quality response.
```

Human-in-the-loop

A dedicated team of domain experts constantly reviews cases flagged by low system confidence scores or negative user feedback. This feedback loop is essential for quickly identifying drift and retraining/refining the knowledge base.

This includes evaluating the performance of different models with different prompts and rating which one works best.

This also includes system evaluation for real life user queries and evaluating how the system fares.

Smart chunking and metadata

Accuracy starts at ingestion. We enforce smart chunking by including necessary continuity context (parent section, title) in every chunk's metadata. This ensures that the vector DB retrieval provides context that is not just semantically similar but is also well structured, leading to a higher quality generation step, where retrieved chunks are fused with the query and passed to the LLM.

Reliability

The system needs to be reliable so that even though dependencies like LLM provider models may be down, the whole system should still be functional. This is handled by the GenAI service, by implementing circuit breakers. The LLM provider models which are not performing well, are slow, or unavailable, trip the circuit. The GenAI service then reroutes the prompt requests to backup models which are available.

Privacy

We enforce strict data isolation to ensure that confidential or internal corporate knowledge never leaks into public responses, ensuring privacy.

Ingestion isolation

The initial ingestion pipeline configuration (Spark job/data source connectors) must be strictly defined to only crawl and process documents explicitly tagged as "PUBLICLY AVAILABLE" (e.g. MongoDB Documentation, public GitHub issues)

Query-time filtering

The vector database (OpenSearch/Neptune) is configured to filter search results based on the `security_level` metadata associated with the user's session, guaranteeing that even if internal data were present (e.g. for internal-facing agents), it would not be exposed to a public user.

Middleware PII masking

We cannot trust the LLM to ignore sensitive data. We implement a middleware layer before prompt construction that detects patterns (credit card numbers, SSNs) and replaces them with tokens (e.g. <CREDIT_CARD_MASKED>). This ensures that sensitive user data never enters the context window or the third-party provider logs.

Monitoring and alerting

We set up monitoring and alerting for different aspects of the system to identify their performance. A robust monitoring strategy is essential for maintaining the reliability and performance (< 5 sec NFR) of the hybrid RAG system. We define a tiered approach using observability platforms (e.g. CloudWatch, Prometheus/Grafana) to cover the entire pipeline, from ingestion to user response.

Ingestion pipeline metrics (freshness and cost control)

These metrics track the health and efficiency of the asynchronous knowledge update process, which runs on Spark and Kafka.

Kafka raw_documents topic

Alert: Lag > 200 messages (trigger autoscaling via Cloudwatch and AWS Glue) and > 5000 messages (high-priority alert)

Ingestion slowdown

Indicates source systems are producing data faster than the Spark cluster can consume it. Triggers AWS Glue to scale the Spark cluster.

End-to-end ingestion latency

Alert: Time to ingest a single document/ticket > 30 minutes (from source event to vector DB write)

Stale knowledge: The system is indexing old data. Requires investigating the Kafka–Spark connection or the GenAI service API's health.

Vectorization latency

Alert: P95 latency for `/internal/ingest/chunk/embed` > 500 ms

Embedding bottleneck: Indicates the dedicated embedding model inference endpoint is under-provisioned or congested. Triggers auto-scaling of the embedder service.

Query path metrics (user experience and performance)

We evaluate the query path performance by capturing different metrics as below.

End-to-end RAG latency

Alert: P90 latency for `/api/v1/chat/message` > 5 seconds

NFR breach: Immediate, critical alert. Triggers scaling review for LLM orchestrator and core retrieval services.

Retrieval latency (total)

Alert: P90 time for vector DB + KG lookup > 1.2 seconds

Retrieval bottleneck: Indicates the OpenSearch index or Neptune read replicas are saturated. Triggers automated scaling of read replicas/serverless capacity.

LLM inference latency

Alert: Individual LLM call time (time to last token – TTLT) > 4 seconds or time to first token (TTFT) > 1 second

Provider performance degradation: Triggers the circuit breaker in the LLM orchestrator to route traffic to a healthy backup provider.

Financial and quality metrics

We track the cost incurred due to LLM and other resources.

LLM token usage and cost

Alert: Daily cost exceeds *X* (e.g. 150% of baseline)

Monitor input/output token counts per query against the provider's API usage dashboard.

Detects inefficient prompts, infinite conversation loops etc.

Accuracy / grounding score

Alert: Grounding score < 90% (or user feedback is > 5% negative) LLM-Judge metric, human expert verification (via HITL), and user feedback (thumbs up/down)

Every user query is continuously scored by an LLM-Judge metric that evaluates whether the generated response is grounded in the retrieved context. User feedback is also continuously aggregated, by signs such as thumbs up / down.

When any of these thresholds are breached, it indicates that the RAG pipeline is not fetching relevant context.

Review of chunking strategy, vector database becomes necessary at this point.

Escalation rate

Alert: Escalation rate spikes > 20% above baseline

Tracks rate of redirects from system agent to human agent; indicates that the agent is failing to solve queries, possibly due to failure of the intent detection model.

System Health

We monitor and track the system metrics to understand the health of our system at any point.

Resource utilization

Alert: CPU utilization > 85% or memory usage > 90% for any service instance

Triggers horizontal scaling or capacity upgrade.

Error rate

Alert: 5xx error rate > 1% of total requests

Indicates a service is unhealthy.

Dependency health

Alert: Continuous failure of connections to dependencies like S3 etc.

Indicates network isolation issue or service failures.

Failure mode analysis (FMA)

We must design for the inevitable failure of the non-deterministic components.

Component	Failure mode	Impact	Mitigation strategy
LLM provider	Hallucination	The agent gives confident but incorrect legal/ technical advice.	Grounding and citation: The UI only shows answers if they cite a specific chunk ID from the Knowledge Base. No chunk = No answer.
LLM provider	Latency spike (> 10s)	User abandons chat; cascading timeouts in API gateway.	Streaming and fallback: stream tokens immediately to show activity. If TTFT > 5s, auto-failover to a less smart but faster local model.

Summary

This chapter walked through the end-to-end design of a production-grade, LLM-powered customer support agent. We saw how ingestion quality, increased through strategies like smart chunking and metadata enrichment, determines the retrieval quality.

We examined how a multi-step evaluation strategy, combining LLM-as-a-Judge scoring, user feedback aggregation, and human-in-the-loop verification, keeps the system reliable in production.

We saw how using intelligent integrations with LLMs we can help reduce human agent workload so that they can focus on escalated and complex issues, leaving the simple ones to the LLM customer agents.

Having made it to the end of this book, a few themes should now feel familiar:

Retrieval and context injection are foundational. Whether personalizing a lesson in *Chapter 4*, surfacing a product in *Chapter 5*, or resolving a support ticket here, the LLM is only as good as the context you retrieve for it. The pipeline around the model matters as much as the model itself.

Humans remain in the loop. From domain experts reviewing Duolingo lessons, to developers steering AI-generated code suggestions, to HITL reviewers flagging poorly grounded responses, all of them rely on human experts for the final validation and vetting of the quality.

Reliability is never assumed. Latency budgets, grounding scores, guardrails, and fallback paths are all first-class design decisions that separate a proof of concept from a production system.

Observability closes the loop. Every chapter has returned to the question: how do you know it's working? Metrics, feedback signals, and evaluation frameworks create confidence in the product.

The use cases explored in this book arise in different domains, but they share common patterns of architecture. As LLMs continue to evolve, the specific models will change. The design principles are the only constant.

References

[1] Jia, Zhe, et al. 'Path to High-Quality LLM-Based Dasher Support Automation'. Doordash Blog, September 17, 2024. `https://careersatdoordash.com/blog/large-language-modules-based-dasher-support-automation`

[2] Zhu, Chun, et al. 'Genie: Uber's Gen AI On-Call Copilot'. Uber Blog, October 10, 2024. `https://www.uber.com/en-HR/blog/genie-ubers-gen-ai-on-call-copilot/?uclick_id=92508acc-3a86-4fcc-bc5f-ba1799e3055e`

[3] 'Retrieval-Augmented Generation (RAG) with MongoDB'. MongoDB docs. `https://www.mongodb.com/docs/atlas/atlas-vector-search/rag/`(Accessed December 5, 2025)

[4] Unni, Keshav, 'Better Customer Support Using Retrieval-Augmented Generation (RAG) at Thomson Reuters'. *Thomson Reuters Labs* (Medium blog), August 8, 2023. `https://medium.com/tr-labs-ml-engineering-blog/better-customer-support-using-retrieval-augmented-generation-rag-at-thomson-reut ers-4d140a6044c3`

7

Glossary

A

Abstract syntax tree (AST): A structured, tree-like representation of source code that captures the hierarchical relationships between classes, functions, and methods. Used in system design for semantic code chunking.

Agentic AI: An autonomous system that uses an *LLM* to reason, plan, and execute a multi-step workflow (Reason + Act loop) to achieve a high-level goal without a pre-defined path.

Artificial intelligence (AI): A branch of computer science that aims to create machines and software systems capable of carrying out tasks that have traditionally required the application of human intelligence, such as learning and problem-solving.

C

Circuit breaker: A resilience pattern that detects when an external provider (such as an *LLM* API) is failing. It temporarily stops sending requests (opens the circuit) to prevent cascading failures, often rerouting traffic to a fallback model.

Coalesce caching: A concurrency pattern where middleware identifies identical in-flight requests during traffic spikes, pauses subsequent ones, and serves a single *LLM* response to all waiting users.

Context engineering: The strategic design of the data pipeline that assembles relevant information (history, *RAG* context, instructions) to fit within the model's *context window* at inference time.

Context window: The short-term memory of an *LLM*. It is the hard limit on the amount of text (measured in *tokens*) the modecan process at one time, including both the *prompt* and the generated response.

D

Deep learning: An advanced subset of *machine learning* using multi-layered neural networks to learn complex patterns from unstructured data such as images, audio, and text.

Deterministic: A system behavior where the same input always produces the exact same output. Standard software is almost always deterministic; *LLMs* are not.

E

Embeddings: High-dimensional numerical vectors that represent the semantic meaning of text or data. They allow computers to compare concepts based on meaning rather than keywords.

F

Fan-out: The pattern of taking one large task (e.g. generate 100 questions) and splitting it into many small tasks (10 workers generating 10 questions each) to run in parallel.

Fine-tuning: The process of increasing a pre-trained generalist model's expertise in a particular domain (e.g. medical or legal) by training it further on a specific, smaller dataset.

Function calling: A capability where an *LLM* outputs a structured request (e.g. JSON) to execute a specific tool or API function (such as `verify_math(2+2)`), rather than generating text.

G

Generative AI (GenAI): A type of *artificial intelligence* capable of creating novel content (text, images, code, etc.) rather than just analyzing existing data.

Golden dataset: A manually curated set of inputs and ideal outputs used as the ground truth for testing and benchmarking *LLM* performance.

GraphRAG: An advanced retrieval technique that combines *knowledge graphs* with *LLMs*, allowing the system to traverse relationships between entities rather than relying solely on vector similarity.

H

Hallucination: A failure mode where an *LLM* confidently generates false or nonsensical information because it is statistically plausible based on its training data.

HNSW (hierarchical navigable small world): An algorithm used by vector databases (like pg_vector) to find nearest neighbors (similar questions) extremely fast, without scanning the whole database.

Hybrid RAG: A retrieval architecture that queries both a vector database (for semantic similarity) and a *knowledge graph* (for structured relationships) to build a richer context for the *LLM*.

I

Ingestion pipeline: An asynchronous data pipeline that cleans, chunks, embeds, and stores documents into a vector database to prepare them for *RAG* retrieval.

K

Knowledge graph (KG): A structured database that stores data as entities (nodes) and relationships (edges), enabling the retrieval of information based on logical connections.

L

Lambda architecture: A big data processing pattern that combines two data processing paths: a batch layer for accurate, historical analysis and a speed layer for real-time insights, merged in a serving layer to provide comprehensive, fault-tolerant, and scalable data views for complex applications like recommendation engines.

Large language model (LLM): An *AI* model trained on a huge (internet-scale) dataset designed to understand and generate human language for general-purpose tasks.

LLM gateway: A centralized microservice pattern that acts as the single entry point for all LLM calls, handling routing, authentication, rate limiting, and failover.

LLM-as-a-Judge: An evaluation pattern where a highly capable *LLM* (e.g. GPT-4) is used to score the quality of responses generated by another model against a *golden dataset.*

LPOP: An operation in Redis that removes and returns the first elements of the list stored at key.

M

Machine learning (ML): A branch of *AI*, which also intersects with data science, in which systems learn to perform tasks and recognize patterns from data without being explicitly programmed with rules.

Modality: The type or format of data an *AI* model can process, such as text, images, audio, or video.

Model router: A logic component within the *LLM gateway* that dynamically directs requests to the most appropriate model (e.g. cheap vs. powerful) based on task complexity or cost constraints.

N

Natural language processing (NLP): A branch of *AI*, connecting deeply with computational linguistics, that aims to confer on computers the ability to understand, interpret, and produce human language.

PII (personally identifiable information): Any data that can be used to identify a specific individual, either directly, like a name or social security number, or indirectly, like an IP address or date of birth when combined with other info.

Pre-training: The initial, computationally expensive phase of training an *LLM* on a massive dataset to teach it the fundamentals of language and world knowledge.

Prompt: The input instruction or question given to an *AI* model to trigger a response.

Prompt engineering: The practice of structuring and optimizing input *prompts* (using context, personas, and constraints) to improve the output quality of an *LLM*.

Prompt injection: A security vulnerability where malicious inputs trick an *LLM* into ignoring its system instructions and performing unauthorized actions.

R

Reasoning: The ability of an *LLM* to process information logically and generate a conclusion, often simulated via chain-of-thought processing.

Retrieval-augmented generation (RAG): An architectural pattern that retrieves relevant, private data from an external source and injects it into the *context window*, grounding the *LLM*'s response in fact.

S

Small language model (SLM): A compact *AI* model trained for efficiency and specific domains, capable of running on local devices with lower latency and cost than *LLMs*.

Stochastic: Involving randomness. *LLMs* are stochastic because they select the next *token* based on probability, meaning the same input can yield different outputs.

Stopword removal: A text preprocessing step in *natural language processing* (*NLP*) where common, grammatically essential words (such as 'the', 'a', 'in', 'is') that carry little semantic meaning are filtered out.

T

Temperature: A parameter that controls the randomness of an *LLM*'s output. Low temperature (e.g. 0.1) makes it *deterministic*/focused; high temperature (e.g. 0.8) makes it creative/random.

Time to first token (TTFT): A latency metric measuring the time elapsed between the user sending a *prompt* and seeing the first character of the response.

Time per output token (TPOT): A metric measuring generation latency (time per single *token* generated). High TPOT indicates a slow model or overloaded provider.

Time to live (TTL): A feature (used in Redis etc.) that automatically deletes data after a set time (e.g. 5 minutes).

Token: The fundamental unit of text (part of a word) that an *LLM* processes. Usage and billing are calculated per token.

V

Vector search: A search technique that uses *embeddings* to find data that is semantically similar to a query, even if it shares no keywords (e.g. matching 'pay' with 'salary').

8

Unlock Your Exclusive Benefits

Your copy of this book includes the following exclusive benefits:

Follow the guide below to unlock them. The process takes only a few minutes and needs to be completed once.

Unlock this Book's Free Benefits in 3 Easy Steps

Step 1

Keep your purchase invoice ready for *Step 3*. If you have a physical copy, scan it using your phone and save it as a PDF, JPG, or PNG.

For more help on finding your invoice, visit `https://www.packtpub.com/en-us/unlock?step=1`.

> **Note**
>
> If you bought this book directly from Packt, no invoice is required. After *Step 2*, you can access your exclusive content right away.

Step 2

Scan the QR code or go to `packtpub.com/unlock`.

On the page that opens (similar to *Figure 8.1* on desktop), search for this book by name and select the correct edition.

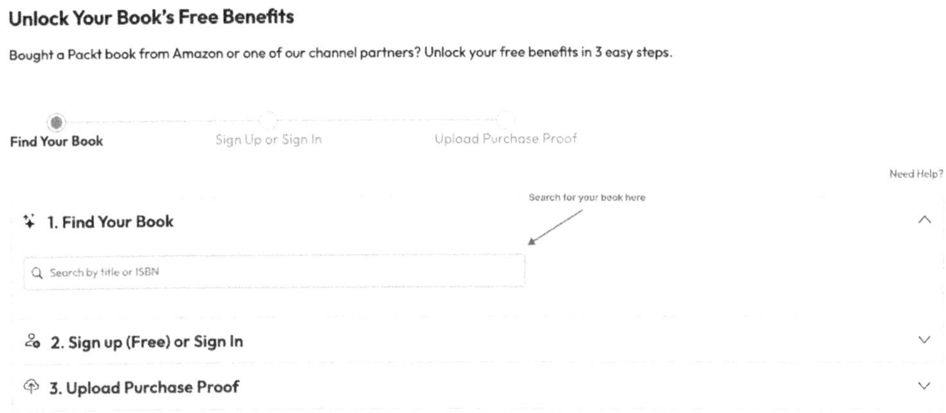

Figure 8.1: Packt unlock landing page on desktop

Step 3

After selecting your book, sign in to your Packt account or create one for free. Then upload your invoice (PDF, PNG, or JPG, up to 10 MB). Follow the on-screen instructions to finish the process.

Need Help

If you get stuck and need help, visit `https://www.packtpub.com/unlock-benefits/help` for a detailed FAQ on how to find your invoices and more. This QR code will take you to the help page.

> **Note**
>
> If you are still facing issues, reach out to `customercare@packt.com`.

packtpub.com

Subscribe to our online digital library for full access to over 7,000 books and videos, as well as industry leading tools to help you plan your personal development and advance your career. For more information, please visit our website.

Why subscribe?

- Spend less time learning and more time coding with practical eBooks and Videos from over 4,000 industry professionals
- Improve your learning with Skill Plans built especially for you
- Get a free eBook or video every month
- Fully searchable for easy access to vital information
- Copy and paste, print, and bookmark content

At www.packtpub.com, you can also read a collection of free technical articles, sign up for a range of free newsletters, and receive exclusive discounts and offers on Packt books and eBooks.

Other Books You May Enjoy

If you enjoyed this book, you may be interested in these other books by Packt:

Architecting AI Software Systems

Richard D Avila, Imran Ahmad

ISBN: 9781804615973

- Understand the challenges of building AI-enabled systems and managing risks like underperformance and cost overruns
- Learn architectural tools to design and integrate AI into traditional systems
- Master AI/ML concepts like inference and decision-making and their impact on architecture
- Use architectural models to ensure system cohesion and functionality
- Simulate and optimize AI performance through prototyping and iteration
- Design scalable AI systems using patterns and heuristics
- Integrate AI into large systems with a focus on user experience and performance

Agentic Architectural Patterns for Building Multi-Agent Systems

Dr. Ali Arsanjani, Juan Pablo Bustos

ISBN: 9781806029570

- Apply design patterns to handle instruction drift, improve coordination, and build fault-tolerant AI systems
- Design systems with the three layers of the agentic stack: function calling, tool protocols (MCP), and A2A collaboration
- Develop responsible, ethical, and governable GenAI applications
- Use frameworks such as ADK, LangGraph, and CrewAI with code examples
- Master prompt engineering, LLMOps, and AgentOps best practices
- Build agentic systems using RAG, fine-tuning, and in-context learning

Packt is searching for authors like you

If you're interested in becoming an author for Packt, please visit `authors.packt.com` and apply today. We have worked with thousands of developers and tech professionals, just like you, to help them share their insight with the global tech community. You can make a general application, apply for a specific hot topic that we are recruiting an author for, or submit your own idea.

Share your thoughts

Now you've finished *Systems Design for the LLM Era*, we'd love to hear your thoughts! Scan the QR code below to go straight to the Amazon review page for this book and share your feedback or leave a review on the site that you purchased it from.

https://packt.link/r/1807789934

Your review is important to us and the tech community and will help us make sure we're delivering excellent quality content.

Index

A

B

C

D

E

F

G

H

I

K

L

M

N

O

Made in the USA
Monee, IL
16 September 2026

63306931R00151